1988
The Supreme Court Review

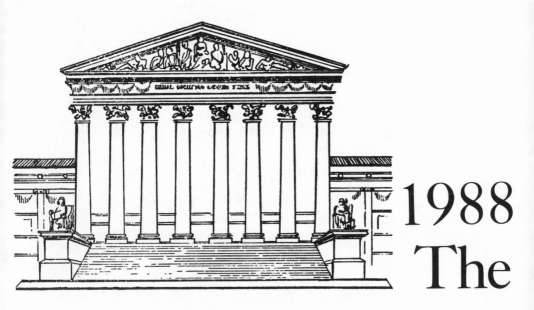

1988
The

"Judges as persons, or courts as institutions, are entitled to
no greater immunity from criticism than other persons
or institutions . . . [J]udges must be kept mindful of their limitations and
of their ultimate public responsibility by a vigorous
stream of criticism expressed with candor however blunt."
—*Felix Frankfurter*

". . . while it is proper that people should find fault when
their judges fail, it is only reasonable that they should recognize the
difficulties. . . . Let them be severely brought to book,
when they go wrong, but by those who will take the trouble
to understand them."
—*Learned Hand*

THE LAW SCHOOL

THE UNIVERSITY OF CHICAGO

upreme Court Review

EDITED BY

PHILIP B. KURLAND

GERHARD CASPER

AND DENNIS J. HUTCHINSON

 THE UNIVERSITY OF CHICAGO PRESS

CHICAGO AND LONDON

INTERNATIONAL STANDARD BOOK NUMBER: 0-226-46441-5

LIBRARY OF CONGRESS CATALOG CARD NUMBER: 60-14353

THE UNIVERSITY OF CHICAGO PRESS, CHICAGO 60637

THE UNIVERSITY OF CHICAGO PRESS, LTD., LONDON

© 1989 BY THE UNIVERSITY OF CHICAGO, ALL RIGHTS RESERVED, PUBLISHED 1989

PRINTED IN THE UNITED STATES OF AMERICA

The paper used in this publication meets the minimum requirements of American National Standard for Information Sciences—Permanence of Paper for Printed Library Materials, ANSI Z39.48-1984. ∞

TO

PAUL M. BATOR
In Memoriam

The fulfillment, satisfaction, and happiness
lawyers count as salvation comes, we think,
from the life of energetic and beneficent action.
But don't forget Shelley's words, that
poets are the unacknowledged legislators of the world.

—From a speech
by Paul Bator to the 1979 graduating class
at The University of Chicago Law School

CONTENTS

MORRISON v. OLSEN, SEPARATION OF POWERS,
AND THE STRUCTURE OF GOVERNMENT   1
Richard J. Pierce, Jr.

PATTERSON AND THE POLITICS OF THE JUDICIAL
PROCESS   43
Mark Tushnet

CONTINUING THE CONVERSATION:
CREATIONISM, THE RELIGION CLAUSES, AND
THE POLITICS OF CULTURE   61
Lawrence Rosen

CONDITIONAL SPENDING: FEDERALISM'S
TROJAN HORSE   85
Thomas R. McCoy and Barry Friedman

VALUE PLURALISM AND THE CONSTITUTION:
IN DEFENSE OF THE STATE ACTION DOCTRINE   129
Maimon Schwarzschild

THE CONSTITUTION AND CENTRAL PLANNING:
THE THIRD NEW DEAL REVISITED   163
Barry D. Karl

THE BLACK-JACKSON FEUD   203
Dennis J. Hutchinson

CHIEF JUSTICE REHNQUIST, JUSTICE JACKSON,
AND THE BROWN CASE   245
Bernard Schwartz

RICHARD J. PIERCE, JR.

MORRISON v. OLSON, SEPARATION OF POWERS, AND THE STRUCTURE OF GOVERNMENT

Over the last dozen years the Court has relied upon the constitutional law doctrine of separation of powers to resolve seven major controversies concerning the permissible structure of government.[1] Its decisions have had significant direct effects—invalidation of the agency Congress created to regulate financial contributions in federal elections, invalidation of the institution Congress created to administer the nation's bankruptcy laws, invalidation of legislative veto provisions contained in nearly 200 statutes, and invalidation of the complicated system Congress devised to reduce the budget deficit. The potential implications of the Court's invocation of separation of powers to determine the permissible structure of government extend far beyond the direct effects of its recent decisions. Lower court judges, emboldened by the Court's apparent enthusiasm for separation of powers as a decisional rule, have relied upon the doctrine as a basis for reducing significantly the classes of parties that can obtain judicial review of government

Richard J. Pierce, Jr., is Visiting Professor of Law, Columbia University, and George W. Hutchison Professor of Law, Southern Methodist University.

AUTHOR'S NOTE: I greatly appreciate helpful comments from Kenneth C. Davis and Peter Strauss.

[1] Morrison v. Olson, 108 S.Ct. 2597 (1988); Commodities Futures Trading Commission v. Schor, 106 S.Ct. 3245 (1986); Bowsher v. Synar, 106 S.Ct. 3181 (1986); Thomas v. Union Carbide Agricultural Products Co., 473 U.S. 568 (1985); INS v. Chadha, 462 U.S. 919 (1983); Northern Pipeline Co. v. Marathon Pipe Line Co., 458 U.S. 50 (1982); Buckley v. Valeo, 424 U.S. 1 (1976).

actions,[2] holding unconstitutional the independent counsel provisions of the Ethics in Government Act,[3] and suggesting in dicta that all "independent" agencies are unconstitutional.[4] Scholars have embraced the doctrine and suggested that it requires many additional changes in the relationships among the institutions of government.[5] My goal in this article is to determine where we are in this process of constitutional restructuring and to suggest where we should be when the process is complete.

I start by comparing Justice Scalia's vision of where we should be with the reality of where we are and with the best evidence available concerning the structure of government intended by the Framers. I then turn to an analysis of the Court's recent holdings and opinions to determine where we are in terms of the constraints the Court has imposed on the structure of government and the sources of those constraints. I complete the picture of where I think we should be by suggesting a "justiciable standard" for limiting Congress' power to limit the President's power to control the executive branch. I then illustrate that standard by applying it to the now-pending dispute concerning the constitutionality of the Sentencing Commission.[6]

I. JUSTICE SCALIA'S VISION OF WHERE WE SHOULD BE

In *Morrison v. Olson*,[7] a seven Justice majority reversed the D.C. Circuit and upheld the independent counsel provisions of the Ethics in Government Act. I begin the search for answers to

---

[2]See Center for Auto Safety v. Thomas, 847 F.2d 843 (D.C. Cir. 1988); Barnes v. Kline, 759 F.2d 21, 55 (D.C. Cir. 1985) (dissenting opinion of Bork, J.), vacated as moot, 107 S.Ct. 734 (1987).

[3]In re Sealed Case, 838, F.2d 476 (D.C. Cir.), rev'd *sub nom.*, Morrison v. Olson, 108 S.Ct. 2597 (1988).

[4]See Synar v. United States, 626 F. Supp. 1374 (D.D.C.), aff'd *sub nom.*, Bowsher v. Synar, 106 S.Ct. 3181.

[5]See *e.g.*, Fallon, On Legislative Courts, Administrative Agencies and Article III, 101 Harv. L. Rev. 915 (1988); Shapiro & Levy, Heightened Scrutiny of the Fourth Branch: Separation of Powers and the Requirement of Adequate Reasons for Agency Decisions, 1987 Duke L. J. 387 (1987); Lowi, Two Roads to Serfdom, Liberalism, Conservatism and Administrative Power, 36 Am. U.L. Rev. 295 (1987); Currie, The Distribution of Powers after Bowsher, 1986 Supreme Court Review 19; Miller, Independent Agencies, 1986 Supreme Court Review 41.

[6]See United States v. Johnson, 682 F. Supp. 1033 (W.D. Mo.) (1988). The Court decided the case while this paper was in press. Mistretta v. United States, 109 S.Ct. 647 (1989).

[7]108 S.Ct. 2597.

the question of where we are and where we should be by analyzing
selected passages from Justice Scalia's dissenting opinion in *Morrison*. I have chosen this unusual starting point because Justice Scalia
provides a clear picture of one type of governmental structure that
the Court could create by applying a strong doctrine of separation
of powers.

Justice Scalia concludes that the functions performed by the
independent counsel are inherently "executive" because law enforcement has been performed by the executive "always and
everywhere."[8] This ends the case for Justice Scalia. Article II
provides: "The executive power shall be vested in a President of the
United States." Article II "does not mean *some of* the executive
power, but *all of* the executive power."[9] Since the Ethics in
Government Act limits the extent of the President's control over
independent counsel, and since independent counsel exercise executive powers, the Act violates Article II. This provides part of
Justice Scalia's picture of a constitutionally permissible governmental structure: all powers characterized as "executive" must be
subject to total and exclusive control by the President. He com-
pletes the picture later in his opinion by asking and answering two
rhetorical questions.

Justice Scalia asks whether the Court would tolerate "a statute
depriving [Congress] of less than full and entire control over some
insignificant area of legislation. . .?" He responds: "Of course we
would have none of that. Once we determined that a purely
legislative power was at issue we would require it to be exercised,
wholly and entirely, by Congress."[10]

Finally, Justice Scalia asks: would we tolerate "a statute giving to
non-Article III judges just a tiny bit of purely judicial power in a
relatively insignificant field, with substantial control, though not
total control, in the courts . . . ?" Again, he answers the question
with an unequivocal no: "We would say that our 'constitutionally
assigned duties' include complete control over all exercises of the
judicial power. . . ."[11]

If the Court takes seriously the proposition that separation of
powers constitutes a free-standing, self-defining doctrine of consti-

---

[8]*Id.* at 2626.
[9]*Ibid.*
[10]*Id.* at 2628.
[11]*Id.*

tutional law, as many of the Court's opinions imply, Justice Scalia's depiction of the constitutionally compelled structure of government logically follows. The Court must undertake responsibility to characterize each function performed by any federal institution as executive, legislative, or judicial. The process of characterization then dictates which institution must perform the function exclusively. If the function is executive, as Justice Scalia characterizes all investigation and prosecution, it can only be undertaken by an executive branch official subject to "at will" removal by the President. If the function is judicial, it can be performed only by an Article III judge, appointed for life and subject to removal only by impeachment. If it is legislative, it can be performed only by Congress through the process of statutory enactment. It follows that executive, legislative, and judicial functions cannot be combined in a single governmental institution, and that no executive branch official can exercise any degree of control over a function that is characterized as legislative or judicial.

II. WHERE WE ARE IN THE REAL WORLD

If a majority of the Court were to accept Justice Scalia's strong version of separation of powers, the Court would confront a daunting task in restructuring the federal government. Most federal agencies routinely exercise a range of functions that fit most comfortably in all three of the categories referred to in Articles I, II, and III.

If legislative power means the power to make rules of conduct that bind everyone based on resolution of major policy issues, scores of agencies exercise legislative power routinely by promulgating what are candidly called "legislative rules." The agency action affirmed in *American Textile Manufacturers Institute, Inc. v. Donovan*[12] (*Cotton Dust*) provides one of thousands of illustrations of agency exercises of "legislative" power delegated by Congress. Congress required that workers be protected from hazards like cotton dust "to the extent feasible." Neither the statute nor its legislative history provided guidance as to the meaning of "feasible." Congress delegated to an officer of the executive branch, subject to "at will" removal by the President, the task of issuing legislative rules governing the conduct of all employers. The

[12]452 U.S. 490 (1981).

estimated cost of the legislative rule promulgated by the executive branch in *Cotton Dust* was 2.7 billion dollars.[13] That rule and the basic policy decision it reflected did not come from Congress but from an Executive Branch agency, with nothing more than the ambiguous and undefined word "feasible" as congressional guidance.[14]

Agencies, both executive branch and independent, make legislative rules based on agency policy decisions virtually every day. Agencies of both types also execute the laws in every conceivable sense of the word, specifically including the functions of investigation and prosecution that Justice Scalia characterizes as uniquely "executive" in *Morrison*. Agencies also adjudicate far more disputes involving individual rights than all of the federal courts combined—a function that would seem to bear most comfortably the label "judicial." These powers routinely are combined in a single agency, and the same individuals—Cabinet Secretaries, Administrators, or Commissioners—are responsible for the agency's many functions.

Two examples illustrate the reality of today's structure of government. The Department of Health and Human Services (HHS) is an executive agency, headed by a Secretary who is a member of the President's Cabinet and who can be removed by the President "at will." HHS exercises enormous executive functions. Yet, under authority delegated by Congress, HHS also has huge "legislative" and "judicial" functions. Its output of legislative rules fills more than 3,000 pages in Titles 42 and 45 of the Code of Federal Regulations, and its 600 administrative law judges (about equal to the number of federal district judges) adjudicate about 320,000 contested cases a year (more than the number of civil cases resolved annually in all federal district courts). All three functions are the responsibility of a single person, the Secretary of HHS.

The Federal Energy Regulatory Commission (FERC) is an "independent" agency, headed by five Commissioners who can be removed by the President only "for cause." Like HHS, FERC performs myriad "executive" functions, including investigation and prosecution. Its legislative rules fill 1,300 pages of Title 18 of the Code of Federal Regulations. A single legislative rule promulgated by FERC in 1987, with virtually no guidance from Congress,

---

[13]*Id*. at 532.

[14]See Pierce, The Role of Constitutional and Political Theory in Administrative Law, 64 Tex. L. Rev. 469, 475–78.

changed the entire structure of the natural gas industry and
redistributed an estimated 51 billion dollars among the participants
in that industry.[15] FERC also resolves thousands of adjudicatory
disputes between individuals annually, disposing of hundreds of
millions of dollars in contested claims. All three functions are the
responsibility of the Commissioners, each of whom serves a
specified term of years, subject only to potential Presidential
removal "for cause." No President has exercised this removal power
in FERC's fifty-four-year history.[16]

Three observations about separation of powers are clearly warranted based on the examples of HHS and FERC: (1) agencies are
saturated with mixtures of legislative, executive, and judicial
powers; (2) decisions about combining or separating the three kinds
of power long have been made primarily on the basis of convenience
and efficiency, not on the basis that the powers must be separated;
and (3) if the combination of the three kinds of power in a single
institution of government is unconstitutional, the entire structure of
government must be changed radically. The new structure of
government would be far less efficient than the present structure.
This is not necessarily an impediment to a constitutionally compelled restructuring of government, of course. The Court has often
stated that the purpose of separation of powers is "not to promote
efficiency."[17] To the contrary, "the fact that a law or procedure is
efficient, convenient, and useful in facilitating functions of government, standing alone, will not save it if it is contrary to the
constitution."[18]

III. THE ORIGINAL INTENT OF THE FRAMERS

Given the increasing importance of separation of powers in
the Court's decisions and the potential massive governmental
restructuring that could be compelled through uniform invocation
of the growing separation of powers doctrine, it seems appropriate
to examine the language and history of the Constitution to determine the source and scope of the doctrine. Gerhard Casper's

---

[15]FERC Order No. 500, 52 Fed. Reg. 30,334 (1987). See generally Pierce, Reconstituting
the Natural Gas Industry from Wellhead to Burnertip, 9 En. L. J. 1 (1987).

[16]I am including FERC's predecessor, FPC.

[17]Myers v. United States, 272 U.S. 52 (1926).

[18]Bowsher v. Synar, 106 S.Ct. 3181, 3194.

careful study of the history of separation of powers provides exceptionally valuable insights.[19] If the Framers decided to incorporate a requirement of separation of powers in the Constitution, that decision was implicit rather than explicit. Articles I, II, and III establish three branches of government, but they say little about the powers of each. There is no definition of "executive" or "legislative" powers, and the only definition of "judicial" power is ambiguous and negative; judicial power extends only to the resolution of cases or controversies. Conspicuously absent from the text of the Constitution is any language requiring separation of powers.

Justice Scalia refers to the explicit and strong separation of powers provision contained in the Massachusetts Constitution of 1780 as partial support for his contention that "the framers of the Federal Constitution viewed the principle of separation of powers as the absolutely central guarantee of a just government."[20] This reasoning is questionable, since the Framers twice rejected language virtually identical to that contained in the Massachusetts Constitution.[21] If the treatment of separation of powers in pre-1787 state constitutions is relevant evidence of the intent of the Framers of the Constitution, why not rely instead on the separation of powers provision of the New Hampshire Constitution of 1784? That provision contains the vague and hortatory admonition that "the legislative, executive, and judicial ought to be kept as separate from and independent of each other, as the nature of a free government will admit, or as is consistent with the claim of connection that binds the whole fabric of the Constitution in one indissoluble bond of union and amity."[22] Professor Casper observes that most of the pre-1787 state constitutions had provisions concerning separation of powers, but "as one reviews the state constitutions . . . for the ways in which they implemented separation of power notions, one cannot help but be impressed by the fact that the particulars display an exceedingly weak version of separation of powers."[23]

---

[19]Casper, An Essay in Separation of Powers: Some Early Versions and Practices, 30 Wm. & Mary L. Rev. 211 (1989).

[20]108 S.Ct. at 2622.

[21]Casper, note 19 *supra*, at 221–21.

[22]Thorpe, 3 The Federal and State Constitutions, Colonial Charters, and Other Organic Laws of the States, Territories and Colonies Now or Heretofore Forming the United States of America, 2457 (1909).

[23]Casper, note 19 *supra*, at 216. See also Madison's description in Federalist 47.

Professor Casper's meticulous study of the debates leading to enactment and ratification of the Constitution disclosed repeated references to governmental structure, the need for independence of the three branches, and the need for checks and balances. "However, what is strikingly absent is anything which might be viewed as a coherent and generally shared view of separation of powers."[24] This lack of shared meaning is not surprising, given the historical context in which the debate took place. William Gwynn's study of the use of the term separation of powers by the philosophers whose works influenced the Framers disclosed five versions of the concept, each designed to further different and often inconsistent goals.[25]

This lack of shared understanding of the concept helps to explain why the Framers chose not to address separation of powers in any way in the text of the Constitution. Based on his study of the origins of the Constitution, Forrest McDonald concludes that the "doctrine of the separation of powers had clearly been abandoned in the framing of the Constitution."[26] Professor Casper goes a step further and questions whether there ever was a doctrine that could be abandoned: "Given the state of the discussions in the last quarter of the eighteenth century, and the constitutions enacted after 1776, a 'pure' doctrine of separation of powers can be no more a political science or legal construct."[27]

Professor Casper's study of the first actions of the Framers implementing the new Constitution demonstrates further the absence of any consensus in favor of a particular version of separation of powers. Rather, the Framers evidenced a dedication to careful

---

[24]*Id.* at 220.

[25]Gwyn, The Meaning of Separation of Powers 127–28 (1965).

[26]McDonald, Novos Ordo Seclorum: The Intellectual Origins of the Constitution, 258 (1985).

[27]Casper, note 19 *supra*, at 224. In Federalist 37, Madison acknowledges that "no skill in the science of government has yet been able to define, with sufficient certainty, its three great provinces—the legislative, executive and judiciary; . . ." In Federalist 48, Madison defines the requirement of separation of powers in a manner that permits considerable flexibility: "It is agreed on all sides, that the powers properly belonging to one department ought not be *directly and completely* administered by the other departments" (emphasis added). In Federalist 65, Hamilton addresses the many complexities and ambiguities of separation of powers, as well as the need for intelligent mixtures of powers. In Federalist 75, Hamilton recognizes that the treaty power seems to fit comfortably neither in the executive nor in the legislative branch. In Federalist 81, Hamilton goes so far as to suggest that vesting the ultimate power of judging in a part of the legislative branch would not violate separation of powers.

blending of powers to achieve coordination in the exercise of a wide variety of functions that defied easy categorization.[28] This dedication is particularly apparent in the debates that took place throughout 1789 concerning the nature of the powers of the newly created Department of Treasury and the means through which each of the three branches could retain some measure of control over the diverse functions that were combined in that Department. All of the major participants in the debate, including Madison, recognized that Congress had created a Department that defied easy categorization. Some of its functions seemed executive, others partook "of a judiciary quality," while still others were to be undertaken in support of the legislative function.[29] Congress considered a wide variety of ways of allowing each branch to maintain a measure of control over the initial hybrid, finally settling on an ambiguous control structure which authorized both the President and the Congress to give binding instructions to Treasury officials with respect to some matters.[30] Madison affirmatively acknowledged the need to limit the President's power to remove the Comptroller within the Department of Treasury because his diverse responsibilities suggested the desirability of less-than-plenary control by the President.[31] The Comptroller's duties included investigation and resolution of claims against the government, as well as authorization of disbursements from the Treasury.[32] Madison characterized these duties during the debate as executive, judicial, both, and neither.[33]

IV. WHERE WE ARE IN THE SUPREME COURT

It is impossible to reconcile Professor Casper's findings concerning the original meaning of separation of powers (or lack thereof) with Justice Scalia's apparent insistence that each power be characterized and placed within the exclusive and total control of the President, Congress, or the Judiciary. It is also difficult to reconcile Professor Casper's findings with many of the majority

---

[28]*Id.* at 238–42.

[29]*Id.* at 238–41.

[30]*Id.* at 238–42.

[31]*Id.* at 238.

[32]*Ibid.*

[33]*Id.* at 238–39.

opinions of the Court, however. Even before the recent flurry of opinions invoking separation of powers as a basis for resolving major disputes concerning the structure of government, many of the Court's opinions referred to separation of powers as if it were a strong, free-standing doctrine of constitutional law.[34] Some of the recent opinions seem far more formalistic than the opinions of the past, suggesting that the Court sees both a textual justification and a functional need for a strong, self-defining doctrine of separation of powers.[35]

Paul Verkuil's analysis of the most celebrated old decisions involving separation of powers helps considerably to reconcile the seeming inconsistency between some of the Court's opinions and Professor Casper's well-supported conclusion that the Framers never intended to adopt separation of powers as an independent principle of constitutional law.[36] Verkuil argues that formal analysis of disputes under separation of powers is meaningless and open-ended, since separation of powers is no more than a maxim.[37] The doctrine can be given content and boundaries only be reference to other constitutional law doctrines that are more specific and more firmly rooted in the text and history of the Constitution.[38] Verkuil shows that many of the Court's early opinions invoking separation of powers are better explained as applications of the Due Process Clause.[39] Peter Strauss joins Verkuil in arguing that, while some of the Court's opinions employ rhetoric that suggests the existence of an independent, highly formalistic doctrine of separation of powers, the Court's pattern of decisions can be explained only by analyzing the disputes functionally with reference to other principles that are supported by the text and history of the Constitution.[40] Viewed in this manner, the holdings of six of the seven major separation of powers cases of the past dozen years are explicable on grounds independent of separation of powers.

---

[34]See, *e.g.*, Myers v. United States, 272 U.S. 52 (1926).

[35]See, *e.g.*, Buckley v. Valeo, 424 U.S. 1, 119–20 (1976).

[36]Verkuil, Separation of Powers, The Rule of Law, and the Idea of Independence, 30 Wm. & Mary L. Rev. 301 (1988).

[37] *Id.* at 301–2.

[38]*Id.* at 307–8.

[39]*Id.* at 320–22.

[40]Strauss, Formal and Functional Approaches to Separation of Powers Questions—A Foolish Inconsistency? 72 Corn. L. Rev. 488 (1987).

In *Buckley v. Valeo* the Court unanimously held unconstitutional the congressional decision to confer significant regulatory power upon a Federal Election Commission consisting of two appointees each of the President, the House, and the Senate.[41] The Court characterized "the doctrine of separation of powers" as "the heart of our constitution,"[42] and then waxed eloquent on Montesquieu's theory of separation of powers.[43] It continued, however, by recognizing that "the constitution by no means contemplates total separation of each of these three essential branches of government."[44] The Court then determined the content of the principle of separation of powers by reference to specific provisions of the Constitution, focusing in *Buckley* on the explicit and dispositive language of the Appointments Clause.[45]

In *INS v. Chadha*, the Court held unconstitutional the system of legislative veto of agency action that Congress previously had incorporated in nearly 200 statutes delegating power to agencies.[46] Some of the language in the majority opinion suggests recognition of a strong, self-defining doctrine of separation of powers.[47] As in *Buckley*, however, the majority found meaning in the doctrine only through reference to other specific constitutional law doctrines firmly rooted in the text. The constitutional defect in the one House veto lay in its attempt to permit one House of Congress to take an action that purports to have the same binding effect as a statute while circumventing the structural safeguards on the process of statutory enactment created by the requirements of bicameral action and presentment to the President for potential veto.[48] These provisions are part of the system of checks and balances the Framers explicitly incorporated as means through which any one politically accountable institution—the House, the Senate, or the President—can protect the public from the risk that a single

---

[41]424 U.S. 1.

[42]*Id.* at 119.

[43]*Id.* at 120.

[44]*Id.* at 121.

[45]*Id.* at 124–25.

[46]462 U.S. 919 (1983).

[47]*Id.* at 946 ("the principle of separation of powers was not simply an abstract generalization in the minds of the Framers").

[48]See Breyer, The Legislative Veto After Chadha, 72 Geo. L. J. 785 (1984). But see Elliot, INS v. Chadha: The Administrative Constitution, the Constitution and the Legislative Veto, 1983 Supreme Court Review 125.

institution might act impulsively or to further the interests of a narrow faction of the public.[49]

In *Bowsher v. Synar*, seven Justices held unconstitutional Congress's conferral of power on the Comptroller General to make estimates of the annual budget deficit that would require the President to reduce federal spending in accordance with a predetermined statutory formula.[50] The five Justice majority opinion held this mechanism unconstitutional because: (1) the Comptroller General's duties under the statute are part of the "executive" power; (2) since Congress could remove the Comptroller General "for cause," it could control his conduct; thus, (3) the statute impermissibly conferred "executive" power on a member of the "legislative" branch.[51]

The reasoning of the majority opinion in *Bowsher* is troubling in two respects. First, as Justice White developed in his dissenting opinion, Congress' ability to control the Comptroller General through threat of exercise of its removal power is not readily apparent. Since this power can be exercised only through passage of a Joint Resolution, removal can take place only through a sequence of actions that satisfies the requirements of bicameralism and presentment.[52] Yet, both Congress and the Comptroller General consistently have considered the Comptroller General an agent of Congress, as the impressive series of statements collected in the majority opinion demonstrate.[53] Peter Strauss reconciles the apparent conflict between the existence of the formal power of the President to veto a resolution of removal of the Comptroller General and the long-standing belief of Congress and the Comptroller General that the Comptroller General is an agent of Congress.[54] He restates the relevant question as whether Congress has aggrandized itself at the expense of the other branches of government, thus "imperiling the balance of American

---

[49] Sunstein, Constitutionalism After the New Deal, 101 Harv. L. Rev. 421, 496 (1987); Pierce, note 14 *supra*, at 481–84; Bruff & Gellhorn, Congressional Control of Administrative Regulation: A Study of Legislative Vetoes, 90 Harv. L. Rev. 1369, 1413–14, 1425–26, 1438–39 (1977). See Federalist 62, 73.

[50] 106 S.Ct. 3181.

[51] *Id.* at 3190–92.

[52] *Id.* at 3209–11 (White, J., dissenting).

[53] *Id.* at 3190–91.

[54] Strauss, note 40 *supra*.

government."[55] His affirmative answer is based not on the limited congressional removal power alone but on the entire set of relationships among the Comptroller General, Congress, and the President.[56]

The Comptroller General serves for a term of fifteen years and cannot be removed by the President for any reason. This combination of extraordinarily long tenure and absence of any Presidential removal power creates a relationship between the President and the Comptroller General much weaker than the relationship between the President and any member of an "independent agency."[57] Members of "independent agencies" serve more limited terms and can be removed by the President "for cause." Within a matter of months, a newly elected President is able to exercise a high degree of control over many functions performed by "independent agencies."[58] By contrast, Congress granted the Comptroller General an extraordinary fifteen-year term and reserved solely to itself the power to initiate the process of removal of the Comptroller General. In these circumstances, it is unrealistic to expect that the Comptroller General would attempt to resist an action by Congress to remove him by relying on potential presidential veto of a resolution of removal. His one certain route to job security for fifteen years lies in following the wishes of the leaders of the Legislative Branch.

The second problem with the reasoning in the majority opinion in *Bowsher* is more fundamental. The majority purports to resolve the dispute over allocation of power definitionally: the function performed by the Comptroller General is part of the "executive power" that cannot be exercised by the legislative branch. The Constitution does not define "executive" and "legislative" powers substantively, however. Most functions of government defy easy categorization. With the exception of the few powers conferred explicitly and exclusively on the President, *e.g.*, appointment of "officers" and negotiation of treaties, it is difficult to conceive of any

---

[55]*Id.* at 520. In Federalist 49, 71, and 73, Hamilton and Madison recognize the propensity of the legislative branch to usurp the powers of the other two branches and describe ways in which the structure of the Constitution provides defenses against this constant danger.

[56]*Id.* at 520–21.

[57]*Id.* at 520.

[58]Strauss, The Place of Agencies in Government: Separation of Powers and the Fourth Branch, 84 Colum. L. Rev. 573, 641- 63 (1984).

power exercised by the executive that cannot also be exercised by the legislative. *Bowsher* illustrates well the almost total substantive overlap between the powers of the legislative and executive branches. Congress unquestionably has the power to make an estimate of the budget deficit that binds the President and requires specific reductions in spending. Thus, the constitutional flaw in *Bowsher* cannot be the assignment of an "executive" function to a legislative branch officer.

The concurring opinion of Justices Stevens and Marshall resolves the dispute through reasoning that avoids the impossible task of labeling the power at issue as "executive" or "legislative." Instead, they focus on the constitutionally mandated procedure for taking legislative action: "when Congress . . . seeks to make policy that binds the Nation, it must follow the procedures mandated by Article I of the Constitution—through passage by both Houses and presentment to the President."[59] Under this reasoning, any binding action undertaken by Congress or an agent of Congress is "legislative action," valid if but only if Congress followed the procedure explicitly mandated by the Constitution for legislative action. Stripped of some of the unfortunate language in the majority opinion, the holding of *Bowsher* does not depend on judicial creation of some version of a doctrine of separation of powers. *Bowsher* represents a logical extension of *Chadha* based solely on the explicit commands of Article I.

The Court's decision in *Northern Pipeline Co. v. Marathon Pipe Line Co.*[60] went further than any other in the dangerous and insupportable direction of recognizing and enforcing a free-standing doctrine of separation of powers. In enacting a complicated new bankruptcy statute, Congress modified the substantive law of contracts in circumstances in which a bankrupt entity is a party to a contract. The process of administering the new statute required some institution to take two steps related to contracts involving bankrupt entities: (1) interpret the contracts under state law and, (2) modify the rights of the parties to reflect Congress's method of restructuring debtor-creditor relations in the bankruptcy context. Not surprisingly, Congress assigned these closely related tasks to the same institution—the newly created, specialized Article I bankruptcy

---

[59]106 S.Ct. at 3194.

[60]458 U.S. 50.

courts in which all disputes involving a bankrupt entity were to be centralized.

The Court held the bankruptcy statute unconstitutional because it empowered non-Article III judges to resolve contract disputes. The reasoning of the four-Justice plurality was formalistic and definitional: (1) only Article III tribunals can exercise "judicial power"; (2) while non-Article III tribunals, including agencies, can adjudicate "public rights," "private rights" disputes are "inherently . . . judicial"; and, (3) all contract disputes involve "private rights" because contract rights have an independent antecedent source in the judicially enforced common law.[61] Two Justices concurred in the judgment, but expressed reservations about the breadth of the plurality opinion.[62] Three Justices dissented, arguing that the reasoning of the plurality "does violence to" the many prior decisions in which the Court upheld congressional grants of power to adjudicate disputes between individuals to non-Article III tribunals.[63]

The concerns expressed by the concurring and dissenting Justices in *Northern Pipeline* were well-founded. The plurality's test had the potential to support holdings that most, perhaps even all, agency adjudicative powers are unconstitutional. Such a result would force massive restructuring of present government institutions and could not be supported based on the delphic language of Article III or the historical origins of separation of powers.[64]

Virtually all powers to resolve disputes now exercised by administrative agencies have independent antecedents previously enforced by courts. The most commonly cited illustration is the near universal replacement in the workplace of judicially enforced tort law with agency-administered workers compensation schemes.[65] Other examples abound, however. Doctors' judicially cognizable claims for reimbursement for services rendered have been replaced in many contexts by Medicare's agency-administered scheme of reimbursement. Rate disputes between railroads and

---

[61]*Id.* at 68–72.

[62]*Id.* at 90.

[63]*Id.* at 94.

[64]See Fallon, note 5 *supra.*

[65]See Crowell v. Benson, 285 U.S. 22 (1932). Crowell initiated a lively debate that continues today concerning the allocation of fact-finding and lawmaking authority among agencies, trial courts, appellate courts, and the Supreme Court. *See* Fallon, note 5 *supra;* Monaghan, Constitutional Fact Review, 85 Colum. L. Rev. 229 (1985).

shippers were adjudicated by the courts long before the Interstate Commerce Commission assumed exclusive jurisdiction over such disputes. Indeed, the common law of common carriers existed for many centuries before it was replaced completely by economic regulation administered by agencies.[66] Even environmental regulation has clear historical antecedents in the common law action for nuisance.[67]

Each of these pre-existing judicially administered private rights was replaced by an agency-administered regulatory system because the prior judicially administered system of common law rights simply did not work satisfactorily. In every case before *Northern Pipeline*, the Court welcomed Congress's decision to relieve the courts of a set of tasks they were institutionally incapable of performing. The Court acquiesced in Congress's redefinition of previously "private rights" as "public rights," to be enforced exclusively through the administrative process, as long as Congress incorporated adequate safeguards to protect the Due Process rights of the private parties affected by agency actions.[68]

In *Northern Pipeline*, for the first time, the Court attempted to define a discrete class of "private rights" that could never be redefined as "public rights" and, therefore, could never be adjudicated by an agency. The Court's definition of such "private rights" as rights with an antecedent in the common law was broad enough to encompass virtually all disputes now resolved by agencies. Fortunately, the test announced in the plurality opinion in *Northern Pipeline* was short-lived.

In *Thomas v. Union Carbide Agricultural Products Co.*, a five-Justice majority rejected an Article III challenge to a congressional requirement that a class of disputes among individuals be subjected to binding arbitration.[69] The majority opinion referred to the fact that the public right/private right distinction announced in the plurality opinion in *Northern Pipeline* "did not command a majority of the Court."[70] It also referred to several examples of the grave difficulties

---

[66]See Adler, Business Jurisprudence, 28 Harv. L. Rev. 135 (1914).

[67]See Rodgers, Handbook on Environmental Law 100–63 (1977).

[68] In this important respect, the theory espoused in Justice Brandeis's dissenting opinion in *Crowell* seems to have prevailed. 285 U.S. at 84–88. See Monaghan, note 65 *supra*, at 254–57.

[69]473 U.S. 568.

[70]*Id.* at 585–86.

that the Court would encounter if it attempted to apply that distinction to the myriad disputes now resolved by agencies, many of which involve rights asserted by one individual against another.[71] Finally, the majority redefined the term public rights: "the public rights doctrine reflects simply a pragmatic understanding that when Congress selects a quasi-judicial method of resolving matters that 'could be conclusively determined by the Executive and Legislative Branches,' the danger of encroaching on the judicial powers is reduced."[72] This functional definition of "public rights" suggests that any dispute that Congress has the power to affect substantively—a category that seems open-ended—can be adjudicated by a non-Article III tribunal.

In *Commodity Futures Trading Commission v. Schor*,[73] a seven-Justice majority again refused to apply the test announced in *Northern Pipeline*. *Schor* involved the constitutional validity of a CFTC rule that empowered the agency to adjudicate common law counterclaims when a party files an action before the agency to obtain reparations from a commodity broker based on alleged violations of CFTC rules. If the Court had applied the *Northern Pipeline* test in *Schor*, it undoubtedly would have held the CFTC rule unconstitutional, since the counterclaims CFTC sought to adjudicate arose as a result of antecedent state common law rights long recognized and enforced by courts. Two Justices reached this conclusion in *Schor*, but in a dissenting opinion.[74]

The seven-Justice majority in *Schor* took a dramatically different approach from that of the plurality in *Northern Pipeline*. It began by placing the issue in context:[75]

> [T]he constitutionality of a given congressional delegation of adjudicative functions to a non-Article III body must be assessed by reference to the purposes underlying the requirement of Article III. . . . This inquiry, in turn, is guided by the principle that "practical attention to substance rather than doctrinaire reliance on formal categories should inform application of Article III."

---

[71]*Id.* at 587–89.

[72]*Id.* at 589.

[73]106 S.Ct. 3245. For an excellent analysis of *Schor*, see Strauss, note 40 *supra*.

[74]*Id.* at 3262–66.

[75]*Id.* at 3256.

The majority then went on to uphold the constitutionality of CFTC's adjudication of "private rights" on two grounds: (1) CFTC's exercise of jurisdiction does not threaten the role of the independent judiciary within the constitutional scheme; and, (2) Schor implicitly consented to CFTC's exercise of jurisdiction over the common-law counterclaim by filing his action for reparations arising out of the same set of transactions.[76]

In deciding whether CFTC's power to adjudicate a designated class of private rights threatened the role of the independent judiciary, the majority looked at a variety of factors, including:[77]

> the extent to which the "essential attributes of judicial power" are reserved to Article III courts, and conversely, the extent to which the non-Article III forum exercises the range of jurisdiction and powers normally vested only in Article III courts, the origins and importance of the right to be adjudicated, and the concerns that drove Congress to depart from the requirements of Article III.

The Court's pragmatic approach to this inquiry is illustrated by the following passage:[78]

> [W]ere we to hold that the Legislative Branch may not permit such limited cognizance of common law counterclaims at the election of the parties, it is clear that we would "defeat the obvious purpose of the Legislation to furnish a prompt continuous, expert and inexpensive method for dealing with a class of questions of fact which are particularly suited to examination and determination by an administrative agency specially assigned to that task."

The majority distinguished *Schor* from *Bowsher* by referring to the constitutional system of checks and balances that was threatened by the delegation held unconstitutional in *Bowsher*:[79]

> Unlike Bowsher, this case raises no question of the aggrandizement of congressional power at the expense of a coordinate branch. Instead, the separation of powers question presented in this case is whether Congress impermissibly undermined, without appreciable expansion of its own power, the role of the Judicial Branch.

---

[76]*Id.* at 3256–57.

[77]*Id.* at 3258.

[78]*Id.* at 3260–61.

[79]*Id.* at 3261.

I like both the result reached by the majority in *Schor*, and its treatment of the separation of powers/checks and balances issue. Yet, the opinion seems curiously incomplete. The majority noted at the outset that Article III serves two purposes: (1) to protect "the role of the independent judiciary within the constitutional scheme"; and, (2) to safeguard litigants' "right to have claims decided before judges who are free of potential domination by other branches of government."[80]

The Court analyzed thoroughly and pragmatically the first purpose, concluding that the congressional scheme poses no danger to the role of the independent judiciary. The majority's analysis of the second purpose of Article III, however, was limited to its assertion that Schor "waived" his right by filing a claim for reparation with CFTC.[81] The dissent expressed skepticism on this point in two respects. First, the "waiver" is "more illusory than real," since litigants "would rarely, if ever" choose not to pursue the "convenient and effective" remedy of seeking reparations at CFTC. Second, the majority's reasoning suggested to the dissenting Justices that its allusion to waiver was no more than a makeweight which is likely to be abandoned in the next case.[82]

The dissent's skepticism seems well-founded, but Paul Verkuil has provided a well-reasoned alternative to the weak "waiver" theory in the majority opinion.[83] Verkuil's analysis responds completely to any concern that administrative adjudication of disputes involving "private rights" might jeopardize litigants' rights to have adjudicative claims decided by tribunals that are free of domination by the political branches. Verkuil argues persuasively that application of the Due Process Clause to administrative adjudications, and the routine reflection of Due Process principles in the Administrative Procedure Act (APA) and most agency organic Acts, furthers the important Article III goal of insuring litigants that their rights are not jeopardized by adjudication in a forum that lacks sufficient independence.[84] The many characteristics of administrative adjudication that assure fair and impartial treatment of private rights at

---

[80]*Id*. at 3256.

[81]*Id*. at 3256.

[82]*Id*. at 3265.

[83]Verkuil, note 36 *supra*, at 316–17.

[84]*Id*. at 315–17, 330–40. See also Monaghan, Marbury and the Administrative State, 83 Colum. L. Rev. 1 (1983).

CFTC and most other agencies include: the right to a hearing before an unbiased decision-maker; review of the factual and legal basis for the agency's decision in an Article III court; separation of investigative, prosecutorial, and adjudicative functions within the agency; the right to compel the agency to follow its own rules; and the right to require the agency to explain its reasons for departing from principles announced in prior cases.[85] When Verkuil's analysis from an individual rights perspective is added to the majority's institutional analysis in *Schor*, the case for permitting Congress to delegate the power to adjudicate private rights to specialized agencies in order to serve a public purpose seems compelling.

In the Court's most recent separation of powers decision, *Morrison v. Olson*,[86] a seven-Justice majority upheld the independent counsel provisions of the Ethics in Government Act. After holding that an independent counsel is an "inferior officer" who can be appointed by a court,[87] the majority rejected the argument that limiting the President's power to remove, and hence to control, an independent counsel violates separation of powers.[88] While seeming to concede that the functions of investigation and prosecution assigned the independent counsel are "executive,"[89] the majority concluded that limiting the President's ability to control the exercise of those functions in the context of an investigation of alleged wrongdoing by an Executive Branch official does not "sufficiently deprive the President of control over the independent counsel to interfere impermissibly with his constitutional obligation to ensure the faithful execution of the laws."[90] The majority opinion contains none of the sweeping language about the importance of separation of powers that found its way into many of the Court's prior opinions. The Court distinguished its decisions in *Chadha* and *Bowsher* on the basis that "this case does not involve an attempt by Congress to increase its own power at the expense of the Executive Branch."[91]

---

[85]Davis, Administrative Law Treatise, ch. 10–14, 18 (2d ed. 1978–80); Pierce, Shapiro & Verkuil, Administrative Law and Process, §§5.1, 6.3, 6.4, 9.2 (1985).

[86]108 S.Ct. 2597.

[87]*Id.* at 2608.

[88]*Id.* at 2619–20.

[89]*Id.* at 2619.

[90]*Id.* at 2620.

[91]*Id.* at 2620.

Justice Scalia wrote a passionate dissent in *Morrison*. In addition to providing his picture of a properly structured government,[92] Justice Scalia made several significant points in criticizing the majority opinion. First, he argued that the Act was part of an effort by Congress to enhance its powers vis-à-vis the executive by placing executive branch officials in a position in which they are subject to easy intimidation.[93] Second, he argued that insulating a purely executive branch official from Presidential control eliminates political accountability for the official's exercise of his or her responsibilities.[94] Finally, he criticized the majority for "sweep[ing] into the dustbin" the prior principles used to determine the permissible scope of congressional limits on Presidential power[95] without "even attempt[ing] to craft a *substitute* criterion—a 'justiciable standard.' "[96] In the remainder of this article, I will focus on Justice Scalia's final criticism and propose a justiciable standard as part of my effort to answer the question, Where should we be?

V. WHERE SHOULD WE BE?

With the recent addition of *Morrison v. Olson*, I think we are now very close to where we should be in establishing a legal framework to govern disputes concerning separation of powers. So I will begin to describe where we should be by summarizing where I think we are.[97] First, the Court has resisted repeated calls to create a free-standing doctrine of separation of powers. The Court seems increasingly to recognize, as Madison recognized in 1789,[98] that it is impossible to characterize most important powers of government as executive, legislative, or judicial, and that effective government requires many government officials to perform a combination of functions that fit most comfortably in all three categories.

Second, the Court is granting the politically accountable branches considerable deference when they choose a particular

---

[92]See text at notes 8–11 *supra*.

[93]108 S.Ct. at 2623–24, 2626, 2630–31.

[94]*Id.* at 2638.

[95]*Id.* at 2636.

[96]*Id.* at 2629.

[97]We are remarkably close to where Peter Strauss argued that we should be in his comprehensive 1984 analysis of separation of powers. See Strauss, note 58 *supra*.

[98]See Casper, note 19 *supra*, at 238. See also note 27 *supra*.

institutional structure to perform a function or a combination of related functions. In particular, the Court seems to have recognized two important principles that Congress is free to consider in devising institutional structures. Due process considerations frequently make it desirable to limit the extent of Presidential control over an "executive branch" officer who exercises control over adjudication of disputes involving individuals.[99] This consideration explains in large measure the Court's recent decision in *Morrison v. Olson*,[100] as well as many older separation of powers decisions, including *Wiener*,[101] *Humphrey's Executor*,[102] *Carter v. Carter Coal*,[103] and *Schechter*.[104] The Court also has recognized that reallocating to a specialized agency primary responsibility to enforce a right previously enforced by common law courts frequently can render the right more effective. This recognition explains in major part the Court's recent decisions in *Schor*[105] and *Thomas*,[106] as well as older decisions like *Crowell v. Benson*.[107]

Third, the Court has defined the doctrine of separation of powers—and hence has limited the discretion of the political branches to choose particular institutional structures, allocations of power, and combinations of powers—only by enforcing other principles that are firmly rooted in the text and history of the Constitution. Thus, for instance, judicially-enforced limits on congressional power to reallocate to non-Article III institutions' responsibility to adjudicate cases involving individual rights are derived from the Due Process Clause,[108] and the limits on congressional power to make policy decisions that bind the President and the nation have their source in the Appointments Clause, the requirement of Bicameralism, and the Presentment Clause.[109]

---

[99]See Verkuil, note 36 *supra*.

[100]108 S.Ct. 2597. See Bonham's Case, 8 Co. Rep. 1136, 77 Eng. Rep. 646 (C.P. 1610). See also Federalist 80 (Hamilton).

[101]357 U.S. 349 (1958).

[102]295 U.S. 602 (1935).

[103]298 U.S. 238, 311 (1936).

[104]295 U.S. 495, 533 (1935).

[105]106 S.Ct. 3245.

[106]473 U.S. 568.

[107] 285 U.S. 22. See also cases discussed in Fallon, note 5 *supra*.

[108]See Monaghan, note 84 *supra*.

[109]See text at notes 41–59 *supra*.

I agree with Justice Scalia, however, that this is an incomplete picture of where we should be. It lacks a justiciable standard for determining the limits on Congress's power to limit Presidential control of executive branch officers. In particular, the Court has not yet indicated the type of executive branch officers that must be subject to Presidential power to remove "at will" or what constitutes adequate "cause" for removal of officers who can be removed only "for cause." Without some judicially enforced limit on Congress's power to limit the President's power to control executive branch officers, Justice Scalia's concern that Congress will emasculate the Presidency[110] seems far too plausible. While there is little textual or historical support for the proposition that the Framers adopted a rule of separation of powers, there is ample support for the more modest proposition that the Framers intended to create a strong "unitary executive."[111] Congress could frustrate that intent if the Court does not limit its power in some way.

Justice Scalia's attempt to create a justiciable standard through characterization of some powers as "purely executive" does not offer much promise. His assertion that investigation and prosecution are functions that have been performed "always and everywhere" by officers subject to plenary control by the President is factually inaccurate. "Independent" agencies headed by officers subject only to "for cause" removal long have performed both functions.[112] More broadly, Justice Scalia's historical test for defining "purely executive" functions is unlikely to identify more than a handful of functions that have been performed "always and everywhere" exclusively by the President, as Gerhard Casper's description of the original structure and functions of the Department of Treasury illustrates.[113] Even in the area of greatest Presidential authority—foreign relations—the President shares power

---

[110]108 S.Ct. at 2630, 2637.

[111]See Sunstein, note 49 *supra*, at 460; Strauss & Sunstein, The Role of the President and OMB in Informal Rulemaking, 38 Ad. L. Rev. 181 (1986); Strauss, note 58 *supra*, at 587–91, 597, 615, 642–48. Hamilton developed this theme at length in Federalist 69-73.

[112]The Federal Trade Commission, for instance, engaged in investigation and prosecution at the time the Court held that Congress could limit the President's power to remove an FTC Commissioner. See Humphrey's Executor v. U.S., 295 U.S. 602 (1935). Thus, the Court would have had to overrule the holding in *Humphrey's Executor* in order to hold the independent counsel provisions of the Ethics in Government Act unconstitutional. While much of the dicta in *Humphrey's Executor* is questionable, the holding has withstood the test of time rather well.

[113]Casper, note 19 *supra*, at 238–42.

with Congress to some degree. Jefferson recognized in 1790 that the President's undisputed power to negotiate treaties was limited in effect by the Senate's ratification power and the appropriations power of the House.[114]

My search for a justiciable standard begins with first principles. The Framers were attempting to create a constitutional democracy. The independent judiciary was assigned the task of keeping the two politically accountable branches within the boundaries established by the Constitution, but policy decisions were to be made by politically accountable officers and institutions. The concepts of politics and policy are inextricable. Indeed, the two share a common linguistic origin. The Oxford English Dictionary tells us that policy and politics evolved from the same Graeco-Latin root and often have been used synonymously.[115] It seems near certain that the Framers intended the politically accountable branches to make all policy decisions except those incident to the process of adjudicating cases under the Constitution, statutes, and the common law.[116]

The Framers did not attempt to allocate policymaking power between the two politically accountable branches substantively, however. They seem to have recognized that as an impossible task. Rather, the division between the two politically accountable branches is procedural.[117] To paraphrase Justice Jackson's explanation of this relationship,[118] when Congress makes policy through bicameral action and presentment subject to potential veto, its policy preferences bind the President and the nation. When Congress explicitly defers to the President in some context by delegating its policymaking power to the President or his agent, the President's power to make policy is limited only by the judicially enforced boundaries of the Constitution.

---

[114]*Id.* at 243–49, 256–57.

[115]VII A New English Dictionary on Historical Principles 1070-74 (Murray ed. 1909).

[116]See Verkuil, note 36 *supra*, at 334–37; Pierce, Separation of Powers and the Limits of Independence, 30 Wm. & Mary L. Rev. 365 (1988); Sunstein, note 49 *supra*, at 500; Strauss, Regulatory Reform in a Time of Transition, 15 Suffolk U.L. Rev. 903, 914–15 (1981).

[117]See text at notes 50–60 *supra*.

[118]Youngstown Sheet & Tube Co. v. Sawyer, 343 U.S. 579, 635–38 (1952) (Jackson, J., concurring). I have added to Justice Jackson's famous concurrence my interpretation of the holdings in *Chadha* and *Bowsher*.

Once it is accepted that policymaking is to be shared by the two politically accountable branches and that the division of policy making power between the two is procedural rather than substantive, the justiciable standard sought by Justice Scalia becomes apparent. Policy decisions can be made only by politically accountable individuals. If Congress delegates the power to make policy to someone other than the President, that individual must be subject to the President's control. Two corollaries follow from this principle.

First, officers whose responsibilities include both policymaking and some significant role in adjudicatory proceedings can be the subject of "for cause" limits on the President's removal power, but "cause" must include failure to comply with any valid policy decision made by the President or his agent. This corollary responds to two concerns Justice Scalia expressed about the power of independent counsels. They may produce (indeed have produced) tension in U.S. relations with foreign powers by subpoenaing officials of other countries,[119] and they may decide to risk disclosure of national security data in order to obtain a conviction.[120] Under the standard I propose, the President or the Attorney General could avoid either of these potential results by establishing policies concerning subpoenaing of officials of foreign powers and access to national security data. Those policies would be enforceable against all officers, including independent counsels.

The "for cause" limitation on the President's power to remove an independent counsel would be judicially enforced if the President attempted to remove an independent counsel because she was hot on the trail of official misconduct in the executive branch—the obvious justification for the "for cause" limitation—but not if the President removed an independent counsel for violating a generally applicable policy established by the President or one of his agents.[121] This corollary also answers the much-debated question

---

[119]108 S.Ct. at 2627.

[120]*Id.* at 226–28.

[121]I recognize the difficulty both of stating generally applicable policies in the two areas and of distinguishing between a legitimate "for cause" removal and a pretextual "for cause" removal actually motivated by concern that an independent counsel is hot on the trail of criminal conduct in the executive branch. The generally applicable policy might have to consist of conferral of discretion on another executive branch officer, e.g., the Secretary of State or the Secretary of Defense, to determine whether a foreign official should be subpoenaed or national security data jeopardized in a particular case. If that official refuses

whether the Office of Management and Budget can issue policy directives that bind "independent agencies."[122] It can, as long as Congress has not given an agency inconsistent policy directives through the legislative process. Thus, for instance, an FTC Commissioner could be removed for failure to consider the costs and benefits of a rule, but could not be removed because of his or her decision in an adjudicatory proceeding.[123]

The second corollary addresses the related issue of what officers must be removable by the President "at will." The most obvious answer is officials whose functions consist exclusively of policy-making. This presents a paradox, however, because there would then seem to be no functional distinction between a purely policymaking official who can be removed "for cause" and a purely policymaking official who can be removed "at will." Both would be subject to potential plenary control by the President, since either could be removed on the basis of any action she takes. There is an important difference between the two categories, however, in the requirement that the President specify a "cause" for removal. In many contexts, this requirement presents no problem. Indeed, it can be viewed as an aid to assuring political accountability for executive branch actions by forcing the President—the only exec-

---

to authorize an independent counsel to take either action, and the independent counsel proceeds in the face of such refusal, she would be subject to removal. Because of obvious concerns about disclosure of sensitive foreign relations or national security data, the courts might have to decline to hear any ensuing case in which the independent counsel alleged that the putative "for cause" removal was motivated instead by a desire to frustrate the independent counsel's investigation and prosecution. See Webster v. Doe, 108 S.Ct. 2047, 2054 (1988) (even in a constitutional case, a court must consider the "extraordinary needs of the CIA for confidentiality and the protection of its methods and mission"); Department of Navy v. Egan, 108 S.Ct. 818, 824 (1987) ("authority to classify and control access to information bearing on national security . . . flows primarily from this constitutional investment of power in the President . . ."); United States v. Curtiss-Wright Export Corp., 299 U.S. 304, 320 (1936) (recognized "the very delicate plenary and exclusive power of the President as the sole organ of the federal government in the field of international relations . . ."). If a confrontation of this type occurs, it may have to be "adjudicated" by the electorate or by Congress in an impeachment proceeding. With luck, it will never happen.

[122]See Strauss & Sunstein, note 111 *supra*; Mashaw, Prodelegation: Why Administrators Should Make Political Decisions, 1 J. L., Econ. & Org. 81 (1985).

[123]At the time the Court decided *Humphrey's Executor*, FTC had no policymaking role. It did not begin to exercise that function until the 1970s. See National Petroleum Refiners Ass'n v. Federal Trade Commission, 482 F.2d 672 (D.C. Cir. 1973), cert. denied, 415 U.S. 951 (1974). Moreover, the President did not state any putative "cause" for removing Humphrey. Thus, the Court did not have occasion to address the issue of whether refusal to comply with Presidential policy directives constitutes sufficient "cause" to support removal.

utive branch officer directly accountable to the electorate—to take personal responsibility for overruling a policy decision of another officer on those rare occasions when stark differences in policy preferences within the executive branch yield a visible confrontation.

In some contexts, however, requiring the President to state a "cause" for removal could have serious adverse consequences. Officials with responsibility for policymaking in foreign relations or national defense provide the most obvious illustrations. Requiring the President to state publicly the basis for his displeasure with an officer whose policymaking responsibilities lie in these areas could jeopardize the nation's relations with foreign powers and its national security. The President should not be forced to choose between jeopardizing national security and removing an officer who insists on advancing policies with which the President disagrees. The Framers recognized the need for secrecy in these contexts in their earliest attempts to govern under the new Constitution.[124] The Court has displayed similar recognition in its many decisions deferring to the executive branch when the President determines that the need for secrecy outweighs the values of public accountability in some foreign relations or national security context.[125]

The distinction between policymaking officials who must be removable "at will" and policymaking officials whose removal can be conditioned on Presidential specification of cause should turn then on the context in which the official makes policy and the need for secrecy in that context. This would distinguish, for instance, the Secretary of Defense from the Secretary of Health and Human Services.

This second corollary responds to another of the hypothetical questions Justice Scalia asked in *Morrison:* "What about a special Assistant Secretary of State, with responsibility for one very narrow area of foreign policy . . . ?"[126] Since the official exercises policymaking authority, and since requiring the President to specify "cause" for removal would raise serious foreign relations and

---

[124]See Casper, note 19 *supra*, at 245–60. Jay and Hamilton also emphasized the need for secrecy in foreign relations in Federalist 64, 70, and 75.

[125] See *e.g.*, Webster v. Doe, 108 S.Ct. 2047, 2054 (1988); Department of Navy v. Egan, 108 S.Ct. 818, 824 (1987); United States v. Curtiss-Wright Export Co., 299 U.S. 304, 320 (1936).

[126]108 S.Ct. at 2637.

national security concerns, the hypothetical Assistant Secretary must be removable "at will."

The Court has never held that policymaking is the "justiciable standard" that limits Congress's powers to limit the President's control over executive branch officers. The Court has never rejected such a standard, however, and many of its opinions contain reasoning that seems to foreshadow such a holding.

In attempting to trace the Court's treatment of policymaking, my starting point is the distinction the Court drew in *Londoner v. Denver*[127] and *Bi-Metallic Investment Co. v. State Board of Equalization.*[128] In *Londoner* the Court held that a small number of property owners were denied due process when the city refused to grant a hearing to permit each to challenge the valuation of her property for purposes of a special tax assessment. When the same city subsequently refused to grant a hearing to permit challenges to an across-the-board upward valuation of taxable real property, property owners returned to court to challenge that refusal under the Due Process Clause as well. Justice Holmes held that the Due Process Clause did not apply to situations like that presented in *Bi-Metallic:*[129]

> Where a rule of conduct applies to more than a few people it is impracticable that every one should have a direct voice in its adoption. The Constitution does not require all public acts to be done in town meeting or an assembly of the whole. General statutes within the state power are passed that affect the person or property of individuals, sometimes to the point of ruin without giving them a chance to be heard. . . .

John Ely refers to the distinction drawn in *Londoner* and *Bi-Metallic* as the difference between "process writ small" and "process writ large."[130] The former, illustrated by *Londoner*, is the judicial-type process constitutionally compelled when government singles out a few individuals for adverse action based on a unique set of contested factual characteristics. The latter, illustrated by *Bi-Metallic*, concerns the constitutionally appropriate process for making decisions that affect a large number of people—the democratically accountable political process. The Court continues to cite

---

[127]210 U.S. 373 (1908).

[128]239 U.S. 441 (1915).

[129]*Id.* at 445.

[130]Ely, Democracy and Distrust 87 (1980).

this distinction, frequently referring to it as the difference between adjudication and policymaking.[131] When policymaking is at issue, the Court does not look for "process writ small" but for "process writ large"—a decision made in accordance with principles of representative democracy.

The Court returned to policymaking as the basis for an important constitutional distinction in *Elrod v. Burns*.[132] The issue was the constitutionality of patronage dismissals of public employees based solely on their political beliefs and affiliations. A three-Justice plurality held wholesale patronage dismissals unconstitutional. The plurality excluded from its holding, however, all employees in policymaking positions. The plurality reasoned that the desire to ensure implementation of policies preferred by elected officials, and presumably by the electorate, was so important to fundamental principles of democracy that it overcame the First Amendment concerns raised by patronage-based dismissals.[133]

The plurality acknowledged that the line it created would be difficult to draw in some cases, but suggested four factors to consider in drawing that line: (1) breadth of responsibility; (2) breadth of discretion; (3) whether the employee formulates plans; and (4) whether the employee provides advice to elected officials.[134] Two concurring Justices emphasized the distinction drawn by the plurality in their restatement of the principles with which they concurred: a "nonpolicymaking, nonconfidential governmental employee" cannot be fired based solely on her political beliefs.[135] This principle, and the four factors suggested by the plurality to guide its application, seems equally appropriate as the "justiciable standard" by which to determine the limits on Congress's power to limit the President's control over executive branch officials. If their duties consist entirely of policymaking, and the nature of their duties suggests the need for confidentiality, they must be removable "at will." If their duties do not include any policymaking role, they can be insulated from all control by the President, except the

---

[131]See, *e.g.*, Minnesota Board of Community Colleges v. Knight, 465 U.S. 231, 285 (1984); Vermont Yankee Nuclear Power Corp. v. NRDC, 435 U.S. 519, 542 (1978); United States v. Florida East Coast Railway Co., 410 U.S. 224, 246 (1973). See also Pierce, Shapiro & Verkuil, note 85 *supra*, at 248–55 (1985).

[132]427 U.S. 347 (1976).

[133]*Id.* at 367, 372.

[134]*Id.* at 368.

[135]*Id.* at 375.

routine managerial power to remove or otherwise discipline any employee for poor performance. If their responsibilities encompass both a policy-making role and an adjudicatory role in which "process writ small" suggests the desirability of "independence" from outside influence, Congress can limit the President's removal power by a "for cause" requirement, but "cause" must be interpreted to include failure to follow valid policy directives from the President or his agents.

The multiple opinions in the Occupational Safety and Health Administration (OSHA) cases of 1980 and 1981 provide additional suggestions of an emerging "justiciable standard" based on policy-making. The statutory standard for regulating exposure to toxic substances in the workplace is a masterpiece of ambiguity and misdirection.[136] OSHA relied upon that standard as its basis for promulgating two controversial and expensive rules concerning benzene and cotton dust. Judicial review of the rules elicited multiple opinions from the Justices in *Industrial Union Department v. American Petroleum Institute*[137] ("*Benzene*") and *American Textile Manufacturers Institute Inc. v. Donovan*[138] ("*Cotton Dust*"). For present purposes, it is necessary to look only at the portions of those opinions that discuss the issue of standardless delegation of congressional power. Justice Rehnquist relied on the previously moribund constitutional prohibition on standardless delegation of legislative power as the basis for his concurring opinion in *Benzene*.[139] The four Justices who joined in the plurality opinion in *Benzene* apparently were influenced by Justice Rehnquist's reasoning, since they stated that their otherwise questionable interpretation of the ambiguous statutory standard was based in part on their belief that a contrary interpretation might violate the delegation doctrine.[140] In *Cotton Dust*, Chief Justice Burger joined Justice Rehnquist in dissenting based on the delegation doctrine.[141]

The interesting point for present purposes is the reasoning in the two delegation doctrine opinions. In Justice Rehnquist's words, "This Court should once more take up its burden of ensuring that

---

[136]29 U.S.C. §§652(8), 655(b)(5) (1982). See Pierce, note 14 *supra*, at 475–78.

[137]448 U.S. 607 (1980).

[138]452 U.S. 490 (1981).

[139]448 U.S. at 687.

[140]*Id.* at 646.

[141]452 U.S. at 543.

Congress does not unnecessarily delegate important choices of social policy to politically unresponsive bureaucrats."[142] I have previously criticized Justice Rehnquist's opinion on the basis that he made the inaccurate assumption that the Administrator of OSHA is a "politically unresponsive bureaucrat."[143] To the contrary, he or she is responsible to the President, and there is every reason to believe that the policy decision attacked in *Benzene* was consistent with the President's policy preferences. The principle announced by Justice Rehnquist seems unassailable, however. In our democratic form of government, important policy decisions cannot be delegated to politically unresponsive individuals. It follows that officials with policymaking responsibility must be subject to Presidential control when they act in that capacity.

The Court seems to have adopted this reasoning in its unanimous opinion in *Chevron v. Natural Resources Defense Council.*[144] The Court reversed a court of appeals interpretation of an ambiguous statutory term and affirmed instead an agency's interpretation of the term. Though the decision did not formally resolve any issue of constitutional law, the Court's reasoning seems to reflect broad principles concerning the proper structure of government and the permissible roles of the institutions of government:[145]

> Judges . . . are not part of either political branch of government. . . . In contrast, an agency to which Congress has delegated policy-making responsibility may, within the limits of that delegation, properly rely upon the incumbent administration's views of wise policy to inform its judgments. While agencies are not directly accountable to the people, the Chief Executive is, and it is entirely appropriate for this political branch of Government to make such policy choices. . . .

It seems a relatively short step from this reasoning to a holding that Congress cannot delegate policymaking power to an individual who is not subject to Presidential control.

The D.C. Circuit wrote a thoughtful opinion with analogous reasoning several years before the Court's opinion in *Chevron*. In

---

[142]448 U.S. at 686.

[143]Pierce, note 14 *supra*, at 506.

[144]467 U.S. 837 (1984).

[145]*Id.* at 865–66.

Sierra Club v. Costle,[146] the issue was whether the court should extend to rulemakings its previously announced prohibition on ex parte communications in adjudicatory proceedings. Many of the ex parte communications complained of in *Sierra Club* consisted of alleged heavy-handed arm-twisting by the White House. The D.C. Circuit's opinion is noteworthy for its careful analysis of the different types of actions agencies take.

The court began by noting that, since the challenged agency action dealt with a broad issue of policy affecting a large number of people, the Due Process Clause was inapplicable as a potential source of procedural constraints.[147] The court then turned to a discussion of why ex parte communications in proceedings that focus on policy issues are entirely consistent with democratic government:[148]

> Under our system of government, the very legitimacy of general policymaking by unelected administrators depends in no small part upon the openness, accessibility and amenability of these officials to the needs and ideas of the public from which their ultimate authority derives, and upon whom their commands must fall.

The Court emphasized the particular importance of encouraging widespread sharing of views within the executive branch in order to rationalize and legitimize agency policymaking in a democracy:[149]

> The authority of the President to control and supervise executive policymaking is derived from the Constitution; the desirability of such control is demonstrable from the practical realities of administrative rulemaking. Regulations such as those involved here demand a careful weighing of cost, environmental and energy considerations. They also have broad implications for national economic policy. Our form of government simply could not function effectively or rationally if key executive policymakers were isolated from each other or from the Chief Executive.

Like the Supreme Court's reasoning in *Elrod* and *Chevron*, the D.C. Circuit's reasoning in *Sierra Club* supports a holding that the basic concept of democracy requires that all government policymaking

---

[146]657 F.2d 298 (D.C. Cir. 1981). See also Verkuil, Jawboning Administrative Agencies: Ex Parte Contacts by the White House, 80 Colum. L. Rev. 943 (1980).

[147]657 F.2d at 400.

[148]*Id.* at 400–01.

[149]*Id.* at 406.

that does not take place through the legislative process must be subject to Presidential control.

The Court's most recent separation of power decisions also contain dicta that foreshadow adoption of policymaking as the "justiciable standard" Justice Scalia seeks. The majority opinion in *Bowsher* refers with apparent approval to the District Court's conclusion that empowering Congress to remove the Comptroller General "for cause" creates a "here and now subservience" to Congress.[150] This suggests that an officer subject to "for cause" removal by the President would be subservient to the President in important respects. Policymaking would seem to be the most logical context in which subservience to the political entity with removal power would manifest itself.

The dictum in *Bowsher* that most strongly foreshadows policymaking as a future "justiciable standard" is in Justice White's dissenting opinion. After arguing that the duties conferred on the Comptroller General were largely mechanical, Justice White distinguished officers with responsibility for policymaking:[151]

> To be sure, if the budget-cutting mechanism required the responsible officer to exercise a great deal of policymaking discretion, one might argue that having created such discretion Congress had some obligation based upon Art. II to vest it in the Chief Executive or his agent.

Chief Justice Rehnquist's opinion for the majority in *Morrison* is laced with similar dicta that foreshadow a holding based on the policymaking role of officers. Four separate sections of the opinion point in this direction. At the beginning of the opinion, the majority refers to the independent counsel's duty to comply with the policies of the Department of Justice (DOJ) "except where not possible."[152] It follows that reference with quotation of the statutory provision authorizing Presidential removal "for cause."[153] Several pages later, the majority emphasizes that the special prosecutor has no authority "to formulate policy for the Government or the Executive Branch. . . ."[154] Rather, "[t]he Act specifically provides

---

[150]106 S.Ct. 3181, 3186.

[151]*Id.* at 3208.

[152]108 S.Ct. 2597, 2604.

[153]*Id.* at 2604.

[154]*Id.* at 2608–09.

that in policy matters appellant is to comply to the extent possible with the policies of the Department [of Justice]."[155]

In a subsequent lengthy passage, the majority characterizes the Court's prior holdings in *Humphrey's Executor* and *Wiener* in a revealing manner.[156] The majority emphasizes the functional linkage between officers with adjudicative powers and a congressional finding "that a degree of independence from the Executive, such as that afforded by a 'good cause' removal standard, is necessary to the proper functioning of the . . . official."[157] It then notes again that the independent counsel is "lacking any policy-making . . . authority."[158] Finally, in its conclusory discussion, the majority links for a fourth time the "good cause" removal power and the President's power to make policy decisions that bind the independent counsel:[159]

> Nonetheless, the Act does give the Attorney General several means of supervising or controlling the prosecutorial powers that may be wielded by an independent counsel. Most importantly, the Attorney General retains the power to remove the counsel for "good cause," a power that we have already concluded provides the Executive with substantial ability to ensure that the laws are "faithfully executed" by an independent counsel. . . . [T]he Act requires that the counsel abide by Justice Department policy unless it is not "possible" to do so. . . . [T]hese features give the Executive Branch sufficient control over the independent counsel to ensure that the President is able to perform his constitutionally assigned duties.

While I share Justice Scalia's concern that the Court has not established a "justiciable standard" for determining the limits of Congress's power to limit the President's power, that absence of a standard seems to be attributable only to the fact that the Court has not yet been presented with a case that requires it to announce such a standard. When the Court is faced with the necessity to do so, the presently available evidence suggests that it will establish a standard based on policymaking. With that critical part of the picture of the constitutionally permissible structure of government filled in, we will be exactly where we should be on separation of powers. The

---

[155]*Id.* at 2609.

[156]*Id.* at 2616–19.

[157]*Id.* at 2619 n. 30.

[158]*Id.* at 2619.

[159]*Id.* at 2621–22.

scope of the limits imposed on each branch will conform simultaneously to three criteria: (1) in a democracy, policy decisions must
be made by politically accountable institutions; (2) the procedures
for exercising power must remain consistent with the intent of the
Framers—process writ small in adjudications and process writ large
in policymaking; and (3) consistent with the intent of the Framers,
the political branches must have discretion to structure government
and allocate power in ways that will permit government to function
in an efficient and effective manner.

To illustrate further the nature of the proposed standard, I will
apply it to a major separation of powers dispute now on the Court's
docket—the constitutionality of the Sentencing Commission.[160] In
the Comprehensive Crime Control Act of 1984,[161] Congress authorized the creation of a Sentencing Commission. Congress believed
that sentencing of individuals convicted of federal crimes was
characterized by an unacceptably wide variation in the length of
sentences given, the factors considered in determining length of
sentence, and the proportionality of the sentence given to the
gravity of the offense committed. The Sentencing Commission was
created as a vehicle to reduce this perceived wide variation. It was
instructed to establish guidelines for sentencing all individuals
convicted of federal crimes. The guidelines are binding on federal
district judges in two important respects: they establish percentage
based limits on judicial sentencing discretion, and they require
judges to explain any departures from the guidelines.

Each of the seven Commissioners must be nominated by the
President subject to confirmation by the Senate. Three of the seven
must be sitting federal judges selected from a list of six candidates
provided by the Judicial Conference. Congress explicitly designated the Commission a part of the judicial branch, but each
Commissioner is subject to potential Presidential removal "for
cause." This peculiar combination of power, composition, and
placement in the structure of government has given rise to a
challenge based on separation of powers. The Commission's
placement in the judicial branch seems inconsistent with its
possession of the power to issue general rules outside the context of
a particular "case or controversy," as well as with the President's
power to remove Commissioners. If the Commission is considered

[160]United States v. Johnson, note 6 *supra*.
[161]Pub. L. No. 98–473, 98 Stat. 1837 (1984).

instead to be a part of the executive branch, the mandatory inclusion of three federal judges as executive branch officers seems suspect.

I do not believe it is possible to uphold the constitutionality of the Commission as part of the Judicial Branch. I will attempt instead to resolve the issues presented by considering the Commission part of the executive branch. The establishment of general sentencing standards is a paradigmatic policy question. No one seriously questions the power of Congress to establish sentencing standards that would bind all federal judges.

The first question that arises then is whether Congress can delegate this policymaking function to an institution subject to the President's control. This raises a run-of-the-mill nondelegation doctrine argument of the type that has been the subject of frequent debate in the literature.[162] Consistent with my previously stated views on the nondelegation doctrine, I would conclude that Congress can delegate this policy decision to the President's agent.[163] In outline form, the opinion upholding this delegation would include the following elements: (1) no due process concerns arise when the government makes a policy decision that affects a large number of people;[164] (2) Article II's command that "all legislative powers . . . shall be vested in a Congress" does not preclude the executive from making policy decisions, since policy decisions can be, and frequently are, made in forms other than legislation;[165] (3) exercise of significant policymaking power by an official subject to presidential control is entirely consistent with the concept of democracy, since the President is elected based on a presumed convergence between his or her policy preferences and those of the electorate;[166] (4) the system of checks and balances is not threatened by congressional grant of policymaking power to the President, since Congress conferred the powers and Congress can revoke, limit, or modify its grant of power at any

[162]For a representative sample of that debate, see Symposium, 36 Am. U. L. Rev. 295 (1987).

[163]Pierce, Political Accountability and Delegated Power: A Response to Professor Lowi, 36 Am. U. L. Rev. 391 (1987); Pierce, note 14 *supra*, at 489–504, 506–07.

[164]Bi-Metallic Investment Co. v. State Board of Equalization, 239 U.S. 441.

[165]See Youngstown Sheet & Tube Co. v. Sawyer, 343 U.S. 579, 635–38 (Jackson, J., concurring).

[166]See Chevron v. Natural Resources Defense Council, Inc., 467 U.S. 837, 865–66.

time;[167] and (5) there is no self-defining doctrine of separation of powers.[168]

The next question is whether the Commission is subject to presidential control. Does the congressional "for cause" limit on the President's removal power impermissibly place policymaking power in the hands of politically unaccountable individuals? Since I would interpret "cause" to encompass refusal to comply with the President's policy directives, I would conclude that the Commissioners are sufficiently politically accountable to exercise policymaking power. I would be somewhat troubled by the fact that the Commissioners' responsibilities seem to consist entirely of policymaking. It is difficult to see the justification for the "for cause" limitation in the context of officers that have no role in adjudicatory proceedings.[169] I would not consider this a fatal flaw, however, since the context in which these officers make policy does not suggest any foreign relations or national security concerns arising from the congressional requirement that the President specify a "cause" for removal.

The congressional characterization of the Commission as part of the judicial branch is problematic. I would draw the inference, however, that Congress chose to characterize the Commission as part of the judicial branch solely as a shorthand means of exempting the Commission from the requirements of several burdensome federal statutes that would apply if the Commission were characterized as an executive branch agency.[170] Since the Commissioners are subject to the President's appointment and removal powers, they are executive branch officers for purposes of determining the powers they can exercise.

Finally, there is the unique mandate that three Commissioners must be sitting federal judges. Federal judges, as such, cannot be assigned the task of devising general substantive rules outside the context of a specific case or controversy, and the President cannot remove a federal judge for any reason. I would not consider the

---

[167]See Pierce, note 163 *supra*, at 413–16.

[168]See Casper, note 19 *supra*.

[169]A plausible justification is to enhance political accountability for executive branch policymaking by forcing the only directly accountable member of the branch to take responsibility for overruling a policy decision made by another executive branch officer. While this justification is less compelling than the Due Process based concern that justified limits on the removal power in *Morrison*, *Weiner*, and *Humphrey's Executor*, it seems sufficient.

[170]*E.g.*, Freedom of Information Act, 5 U.S.C. §552; Government in the Sunshine Act, 5 U.S.C. §552(b).

three judge/Commissioners to be judges when they act in their separate capacities as members of the Sentencing Commission, however. No judge is, or can be, required to perform this separate
service to the public. No judge can be removed from his or her
position as a judge, or adversely affected in any other way in her
position as a judge, based on her performance as a Sentencing
Commissioner.

Congress obviously mandated the inclusion of federal judges on
the Commission because it wanted a Commission that included
individuals with expertise in sentencing. Prosecutors, criminolo-
gists, and defense counsel can provide expertise based on important
perspectives, but only federal judges have expertise born of actually
imposing sentences in federal criminal cases. Thus, Congress's
justification for mandating inclusion of federal judges on the
Commission seems compelling. I do not see any potential harm to
the judiciary that could result from the inclusion of judges as
members of the Sentencing Commission, even in the highly
unlikely event that a President might remove a judge/Commissioner
for failure to comply with a valid policy directive. In his or her
capacity as a member of the Sentencing Commission, a judge is like
any other citizen with expertise relevant to the Commission's
assigned duties. As Maeva Marcus recently reminded us,[171] federal
judges and Justices have distinguished between their institutional
and individual capacities from the earliest days of the Republic.
Surely if a sitting Chief Justice of the Supreme Court can accept a
request by the President to negotiate a treaty with a foreign power,
as did Justices Jay and Ellsworth,[172] sitting judges can accept a
Presidential request to serve a six-year term on a Commission that
can benefit greatly from their unique perspective and expertise.

In closing I want to offer three general observations about the
state of the separation of powers debate and the troublesome
concept of "independence." First, the Court seems increasingly to
recognize the reality that "independence" is a relative term. An
officer can be more or less independent of the President depending
on a wide variety of legal characteristics. Most of the debate has
focused on the scope of the President's power to remove the officer,
and that is an important characteristic. Yet, removal of any officer

---

[171]Marcus, Separation of Powers in the Early National Period, 30 Wm. & Mary L. Rev.
269 (1988).

[172]*Id*. at 273–74.

is a rarity. In the case of most "independent" officers, the President has available more subtle, and more effective, means of assuring that the officer implements policies consistent with the President's preferences.[173] As Peter Strauss has documented, a newly elected President typically gains control over each "independent" agency within months of his election by selecting "his people" to fill the vacancies that inevitably arise.[174] Once this process takes place policy differences between the President and his appointees tend to be modest, and confrontations are rare. The Comptroller General is one of the very few officers that can be considered totally "independent" of the President because of the unusual combination of fifteen-year tenure, many duties that place her in direct communication with congressional leaders on a regular basis, no Presidential power to remove for any reason, and congressional power to initiate the process of removal.[175]

Second, "independence" depends as much on political constraints as on legal constraints. The debate over "independent" agencies frequently focuses on the Federal Reserve Board.[176] With its vast power over the nation's economy, concern often is expressed that a Fed dependent on the President might increase the nation's money supply dramatically on the eve of an election, producing a short-term burst of prosperity followed by serious long-term problems.

This concern seems greatly exaggerated. I doubt that the Fed would behave much differently if its members were subject to Presidential removal "at will." There is evidence that the now "independent" Fed generally adheres to the President's policy preferences.[177] To the extent that it does not, its "independence" is based more on the personal characteristics of its members than on the legal limits on the President's power to remove its members. The present and recent past members of the Fed might have been willing to bend a bit in response to the preferences of the incumbent President, but it seems unlikely that any Fed Chairperson would

---

[173]Strauss, note 58 *supra*, at 623, 663.

[174]*Id.* at 589–96.

[175]See Strauss, note 40 *supra*, at 519–20.

[176] See Verkuil, note 36 *supra*, at 336.

[177]Greenspan's Testimony Wins Plaudits, But Doubt Persists About Fed Autonomy, Wall St. J., Feb. 29, 1988. See Beck, Elections and the Fed: Is There a Political Monetary Cycle? 31 Am. J. Pol. Sci. 194 (1987).

act in a manner inconsistent with his or her principles in response to a similarly unlikely threat of Presidential removal.

History provides many illustrations of the "independence" of Cabinet Officers who serve at the President's pleasure. Secretary of State Schultz, for example, was not about to take a lie detector test or to speak in favor of administering such tests to other government employees even in response to intense pressure from President Reagan and Attorney General Meese. This important source of "independence" is built into the political process. Every President has a powerful political incentive to appoint officers with a reputation for integrity and independence. That reputation usually is well deserved. Moreover, most appointees to high office have independent sources of political power in Congress and in the public. The President must pay a high political price if he or she decides to engage in a confrontation with a respected executive branch officer.

Finally, the Court's increased emphasis on separation of powers seems to reflect in part increased hostility between the two politically accountable branches. If, as Justice Scalia argues in *Morrison*, Congress will take advantage of every opportunity the Court provides to emasculate the Presidency,[178] our system of government is not going to function well no matter what standards the Court uses to resolve disputes between the two political branches. As Gerhard Casper has shown, the Framers intended a governmental structure with a high degree of coordination among the Branches.[179] This structure is not likely to be effective in conditions of constant interbranch warfare.

Viewed in this manner, the separation of powers controversy may require therapy more powerful than the Court can provide. The root of the problem of increased interbranch conflict lies in the reduced power of political parties.[180] Our unique form of government functioned reasonably well for the 170 years in which the existence of powerful political parties made it a de facto parliamentary system. The same political party controlled both the executive and the legislature most of the time.[181] If people perceived that "the government" was not performing well, enough switched party

[178]108 S.Ct. at 2630, 2637.

[179]Casper, note 19 *supra*, at 238–42.

[180]See Cutler, Now Is the Time for All Good Men, 30 Wm. & Mary L. Rev. 387, 388–93 (1988).

[181]*Ibid.*

loyalty in the next election to hand over the reigns of both branches to the other party.

With the decreased power of political parties over the last three decades, we have come to expect that the Republicans almost always will control the executive while the Democrats almost always will control the Congress. This expectation has three unfortunate effects. First, it is more difficult for the electorate to determine which branch, political party, or individuals are responsible for perceived problems in the functioning of government, *e.g.*, the budget deficit.[182] Second, the natural tendency for some friction to develop between the branches is magnified by the partisan political dimension of all differences in policy preferences.[183] Third, there seems to be an increasing tendency for judges to see many public law controversies as power struggles between "their" party and "the other" party. The otherwise healthy debate about competing models of government with a "strong" or "weak" Presidency has developed a powerful partisan component. It has become far too easy to predict a judicial decision addressing a major structural issue of government based solely on the political affiliation of the judges who decide the issue.[184] Judges of all political affiliations should be constrained by the realization that tipping the balance one way or the other in power struggles between the President and Congress sometimes will benefit "their party" and sometimes "the other party." That healthy constraint is not strong today.

If this situation persists, the only solution may be radical surgery. Lloyd Cutler has proposed a series of constitutional amendments that would tend to restore the influence of political parties and increase the likelihood that the executive and legislative branches are controlled by the same party.[185] I am uneasy about making such major changes in government structure, but the evidence is mounting that our present structure performs poorly when we come to expect that the executive and legislative branches will be controlled in perpetuity by different political parties.

---

[182]*Id.* at 390–91. Hamilton emphasized the need to maintain clear responsibility of elected officials in Federalist 70.

[183]Cutler, note 180 *supra*, at 390–92.

[184]See Pierce, Two Problems in Administrative Law: Political Polarity on the D.C. Circuit and Judicial Deterrence of Agency Rulemaking, 1988 Duke L. J. 300.

[185]See Cutler, note 179 *supra*, at 400–02.

MARK TUSHNET

PATTERSON AND THE POLITICS OF THE JUDICIAL PROCESS

The Supreme Court uses a number of procedural devices to control its work. Ordinarily these devices are significant primarily for their overall effects on the Court's work. Occasionally, however, a memorandum dealing with a denial of certiorari, or an opinion revising a previously published opinion, or an opinion issued when the Court was evenly divided, provides important clues about the Court's position in the legal and political system.[1] The Court's decision to hear reargument in *Patterson v. McLean Credit Union*,[2] with its request that the parties brief and argue the question of whether "the interpretation of 42 U.S.C. §1981 adopted by this Court in *Runyon v. McCrary* should be reconsidered,"[3] is such an occasion. The Court's order elicited two highly charged dissents,

Mark Tushnet is Professor of Law, Georgetown University Law Center; Visiting Professor of Law, University of Southern California Law Center, Fall 1988.

AUTHOR'S NOTE: I would like to thank Elizabeth Alexander, Erwin Chemerinsky, Ron Garet, Larry Simon, and Matthew Spitzer for their comments on a draft of this article.

[1] See, *e.g.*, McCray v. New York, 461 U.S. 961 (1983), in which a denial of certiorari was accompanied by one memorandum and one dissent from the denial, which together indicated that five Justices believed that Swain v. Alabama, 380 U.S. 202 (1965), should be reconsidered; Tushnet, Sloppiness in the Supreme Court, O.T. 1935-O.T. 1944, 3 Const. Commentary 73 (1986), examining the significance of revisions of previously published opinions; and Ohio ex rel. Eaton v. Price, 364 U.S. 263 (1960), in which Justice Brennan's opinion dissenting from an affirmance by an equally divided Court foreshadowed See v. City of Seattle, 387 U.S. 541 (1967).

[2] 108 S.Ct. 1419 (1988).

[3] *Id.* at 1420.

and drew substantial critical comment from outsiders.[4] The Court's order, the terms of the dissents, and the public response all deserve closer attention than they will get after the Court's decision on the merits of the case, because of what they reveal about what I call the politics of the judicial process.

I. The Setting

Brenda Patterson sued her employer McLean Credit Union for damages, alleging that her workplace had been pervaded by racial harassment. Although such claims are covered by Title VII of the Civil Rights Act of 1964, Patterson sought relief under 42 U.S.C. §1981, which provides that "all persons . . . shall have the same right . . . to make and enforce contracts . . . as is enjoyed by white citizens. . . ."[5] *Runyon v. McCrary* held that §1981 provided a remedy for private racial discrimination,[6] and Patterson's suit presented a relatively straightforward claim that a black employee who is the victim of racial harassment in the workplace does not enjoy the same right under her employment contract as does a white employee who does not face similar harassment. The background of *Runyon*, though, indicates why Patterson's claim is somewhat more complex than that.

The story begins with the Court's 1968 decision in *Jones v. Alfred H. Mayer.*[7] The Court there interpreted 42 U.S.C. §1982, which provides that "all citizens of the United States shall have the same right . . . as is enjoyed by white citizens . . . to inherit, purchase, lease, sell, hold, and convey real and personal property," to provide a remedy for private discrimination in the sale of housing. The Court, in an opinion by Justice Stewart, concluded that the "same right" can be impaired by those who place property on the market yet refuse to sell to blacks for racial reasons. Justice Stewart's opinion canvassed the legislative history of the Civil Rights Act of

---

[4]See, *e.g.*, Liberals Uneasy over High Court Review of Discrimination Laws, Washington Post, May 1, 1988, A4; Neuborne, The Run on Runyon: Will Stare Decisis Become Bankrupt? Legal Times, May 9, 1988, 16.

[5]Apparently Patterson invoked §1981 rather than Title VII because her claims were time-barred by the shorter statute of limitations under Title VII. In addition, relief under Title VII is more limited than that available under §1981; backpay awards cover only two years, and punitive damages are not available.

[6]427 U.S. 160 (1976).

[7]392 U.S. 409 (1968).

1866, from which §1982 derived, and concluded that the Reconstruction Congress did not intend to provide a remedy only when state courts enforced racially discriminatory rules of law, thereby making it impossible for blacks to enjoy the same rights as whites.

Justice Harlan, in a comprehensive dissent joined by Justice White, offered a different interpretation of the statute and its legislative history. Justice Harlan recognized that the fundamental issue was whether the term "right" referred to what he called "absolute" rights, which should be protected against infringements arising from whatever source, or instead referred to those rights protected only against infringements by agents of the government.[8] His examination of the legislative history convinced him that Congress had in mind the latter kind of right, that arising under positive law, rather than the former, arising under some view of natural law.

It is unfortunate that the Court in *Jones* did not fully respond to Justice Harlan's dissent. In part the difficulty with both opinions is that they confined themselves to the ordinary materials of statutory interpretation. Yet, given the context of Reconstruction, it seems reasonably clear that we can understand what Congress had in mind only by a thorough examination of the prevailing views on the nature of rights and on the proper scope of national powers. Such an examination would undoubtedly lead us into broad examinations of antislavery jurisprudence, the effects of the Civil War on thinking about federalism, and the like.[9] In addition, the debate between Justice Harlan and the majority was almost bound to be inconclusive when it was limited to reliance on excerpts from the congressional debates: Positive law rights could well be a subcategory of absolute or natural rights, in which case references in the debates, no matter how frequent, to a desire to protect positive law rights cannot dispose of the claim that Congress intended to protect absolute rights.

The language of §1981 is almost identical to that of §1982, and most lower courts followed *Jones v. Alfred H. Mayer* in interpreting §1981 to prohibit private racial discrimination in the making of

---

[8]*Id.* at 453.

[9]Justice Harlan's dissent did discuss presumptions about the scope of government, at 473–75. Unfortunately, he treated the Reconstruction era as one in which notions of laissez faire were generally prevalent, which probably telescopes developments that became more pronounced later in the century and probably overlooks distinctions that Reconstruction era members of Congress would draw between governmental action with respect to race and governmental action with respect to other aspects of the social order.

contracts. The Court endorsed these decisions, without providing an independent analysis of §1981, in *Johnson v. Railway Express Agency, Inc.*[10] When the issue was squarely presented to the Court in *Runyon v. McCrary*, it again followed *Jones v. Alfred H. Mayer*.

In *Runyon*, however, Justice White's dissent argued that the two statutes should be distinguished. He argued that, despite the similarity in language, §1981 actually derived from the Voting Rights Act of 1870 rather than the Civil Rights Act of 1866.[11] The different origin of the statute, he concluded, meant that the Court should not be bound by *stare decisis* considerations to follow *Jones v. Alfred H. Mayer*.[12] Liberated from the constraint of that precedent, Justice White argued that §1981 should be interpreted to prohibit discriminatory administration of the laws, not private discrimination. He suggested in passing that the minor differences in language between §1981 and §1982 supported his interpretation, but he acknowledged that it was not obvious why Congress would want to prohibit private discrimination in the sale of property but only public discrimination in the enforcement of contracts. Having dissented in *Jones v. Alfred H. Mayer*, Justice White clearly would have preferred to erect a doctrinal structure that resolved the tension between the Court's interpretation of §1982 and his interpretation of §1981 by finding that Congress had prohibited only public discrimination in both statutes.

Post-*Runyon* cases involving §1981 never suggested that Justice White had been correct, but *Runyon* hardly rested on bedrock. For example, in *Runyon* itself, Justices Powell and Stevens both stated that, were they free to consider the matter anew, they would accept Justice White's interpretation of §1981 and §1982. They could not accept his argument that the statutes were distinguishable. Feeling bound to interpret §1981 in the same way that §1982 had been interpreted, they relied on *stare decisis* considerations to adopt the construction of §1982 that had been adopted in *Jones v. Alfred H. Mayer*.[13]

---

[10]421 U.S. 454 (1975). See also Tillman v. Wheaton-Haven Recreation Ass'n, 410 U.S. 431 (1973) (dictum suggests that §§1981 and 1982 are to be interpreted in same way).

[11] 427 U.S. at 195–202.

[12]The Court responded to this argument in a long footnote. 427 U.S. at 168–70 n.8.

[13]Justice Powell said that the question of how to interpret §1982 had been considered "maturely" in Jones v. Alfred H. Mayer, 427 U.S. at 186. Yet, the first time the question of distinguishing §1981 from §1982 received extended consideration was in *Runyon* itself. *Stare decisis* considerations come into play only after one concludes that the present case is indistinguishable from the prior one; Justice Powell therefore should have said more about

When *Patterson* came to the Court, then, the stage was set for the possibility of reconsidering *Runyon*.

II. REQUESTING ARGUMENT

Justice Stevens, dissenting from the Court's order in *Patterson*, contended that in requesting argument on an issue that no party had raised, the Court had "decide[d] to cast itself adrift from the constraints imposed by the adversary process and to fashion its own agenda."[14] The Court responded to this claim by noting that it had merely requested argument on the *Runyon* issue and had not "decided today to overrule" *Runyon*, and that it was "no affront to settled jurisprudence to request argument on whether a particular precedent should be overruled or modified."[15] The Court appeared to divide over a question of judicial role, with the usually activist Justices chastizing the others for lack of "restrain[t]."[16] I believe that the dissenters were right, though for a reason they failed to identify clearly.

We can begin by asking why it might be inappropriate for the Court to request that the parties brief and argue an issue that they had previously failed to present to the Court. Plainly the Credit Union could have raised the *Runyon* issue on its own, even if it had not done so in the lower courts, because the plaintiff's claim could prevail only if *Runyon* was correctly decided. Seen in this light, requesting argument is apparently no different from a Justice asking Patterson's attorney at oral argument whether she could prevail only if *Runyon* was correctly decided. That is, any proposition fairly implicated in the claim made by the plaintiff is necessarily open to inquiry by the Court.

As a matter of practice the Court usually confines its attention to the issues raised by the parties. The reasons are suggested by Justice Stevens's concern about the adversary process. Courts usually

---

why he believed that Justice White's attempt to distinguish the two statutes was unpersuasive. Justice Stevens said that Jones v. Alfred H. Mayer had been wrongly decided but was now "an important part of the fabric of our law," 427 U.S. at 190, and that repudiating it, presumably by accepting Justice White's distinction between the two statutes, would send the wrong signal as "a significant step backwards." *Id.* at 191–92. For additional discussion of this latter point, see text accompanying note 43 *infra*.

[14]108 S.Ct. at 1423 (Stevens, J., dissenting). Because the Court's per curiam opinion consists of responses to the dissents, I describe the dissents' views first.

[15]*Id.* at 1420.

[16]*Id.* at 1421 (Blackmun, J., dissenting).

confine themselves to the issues raised by the parties for two reasons, which I label the "incentive" and the "litigant autonomy" reasons. Yet, in the context of litigation at the Supreme Court, both reasons are rather weak.

A. PARTY INCENTIVES

Adversarial parties have the right incentives to investigate facts and define legal arguments in the way most likely to produce the strongest case on each side. When a judge asks parties to investigate some fact they have overlooked, or to develop a legal argument they have forgone, the presentation of the case may become muddied. At the least, the parties are forced to reorder their priorities by devoting resources to questions that they had regarded as elements they could omit from their strongest case.[17]

Yet, there is something odd about the incentive argument for deferring completely to the way in which parties frame the case. The incentive argument has its greatest force with respect to facts. If we lived in a legal universe where law were essentially fact-like, the incentive argument might have some force to the extent that adversaries' incentives to discover the best legal arguments might overcome the judges' advantages derived from expertise. In our largely positivist legal universe, though, the incentive argument as to law is almost weird. When a judge who is to decide the case tells a litigant that an omitted argument is likely to lead to a decision in favor of the litigant, it is hard to see the basis on which the litigant could claim that the judge's assessment is wrong because the litigant has better incentives to discover the best arguments. The judge's request to argue an omitted issue is a rather powerful bit of evidence in favor of the proposition that the omitted issue is the strongest argument available, notwithstanding the litigant's prior evaluation.[18]

---

[17]The Court itself has recognized this. *See* Jones v. Barnes, 463 U.S. 745 (1983). Parties might respond to a request for argument on an issue they had omitted by refusing the request. There are obvious disadvantages to such a response. There is a prisoner's dilemma aspect to the request, in that both sides might present stronger cases if they both ignored the request but a party who ignores the request to which the other side has acceded may be at a severe disadvantage. In addition, the request itself should be an important signal of the Court's thinking, as I argue below.

[18]In Jones v. Barnes, 463 U.S. at 753, the Court summarized its point about litigant incentives by saying that a rule that required all arguments to be made "runs the risk of burying good arguments . . . in a verbal mound made up of strong and weak arguments."

B. LITIGANT AUTONOMY

Litigant autonomy is served by allowing the parties to define the terrain of their disagreement.[19] Parties may have a complex set of relationships, and may wish to preserve as much common ground as they can even as they attempt to resolve a particular controversy. If they are forced to expand their dispute under pressure from a court, the entire set of relationships may be disrupted. Consider in this connection a non-union employer with a substantial minority work force. The employer is willing to defend itself against specific charges of discrimination. It might, however, be unwilling to mount an attack on the basic anti-discrimination law because of the effects such an argument might have in future union organizing campaigns. The employer may believe that a leaflet saying "Join the union because the employer demoted Smith for racist reasons" would be much less effective than one saying "Join the union because the employer opposes anti-discrimination laws that the union supports." Further, the employer may decide that, all things considered, it is better to lose the lawsuit and promote Smith than to win the lawsuit by attacking the anti-discrimination law.

A more elaborate version of the autonomy argument relies on the argument that anti-discrimination legislation solves a problem of collective action.[20] Suppose that a majority of employers and employees prefers to have a workplace free of racial discrimination, and that a minority consisting of skilled white employees prefers not to work with blacks. In a competitive environment employers can profit by discriminating, thereby gaining a competitive advantage over non-discriminatory employers who are unable to employ the skilled racists. The majority can eliminate this competitive advantage by deploying the power of government to bar employers from giving in to the racists. The important point to make here is that

---

Clearly the problem is quite different when, as in *Patterson*, a judge indicates to an attorney that an omitted argument may be stronger than the ones the attorney has already made.

[19]The discussion here deals only with litigant autonomy, that is, with autonomy within the confines of a lawsuit. Plainly once we go outside those confines the autonomy arguments are quite different. Preserving autonomy within the lawsuit, for example, might lead the Court to refrain from overruling *Runyon*, which has the effect outside the lawsuit of restraining the autonomy of people who act in ways that subject themselves to liability under *Runyon*.

[20]This argument is derived from Becker, The Economics of Discrimination (2d ed. 1971), though it presents a highly simplified and fundamentally unrealistic account of the origins of discrimination. For an application to antidiscrimination law, see Donohue, Is Title VII Efficient? 134 U. Pa. L. Rev. 1411 (1986).

employers who do not want to discriminate are "forced" to do so by competition. Of course, there can be controversy over what constitutes discrimination, and employees may sue employers for acts that the latter believe to fall outside the bounds of the problem of collective action to which the basic anti-discrimination law responded. Nonetheless, the employers want to preserve the basic law, and would rightfully feel that something had gone wrong if they were asked to argue against it.

Here too the argument is rather weak. The argument rests on the view that the only interests to be considered when assessing the propriety of requesting argument on an omitted issue are the interests of the litigants before the court. This classical view of litigation has been substantially displaced by the view that the resolution of even individual disputes has a public dimension.[21] Whatever might be said about trial-level courts, the only sensible view of the Supreme Court's work is the public law one. Thus, because the autonomy argument rests on a view of litigation that is patently inappropriate in understanding the Supreme Court, Justice Stevens's criticism of the Court for disregarding the constraints of the adversary process is misplaced.[22] The only anomaly is that the dissenters to the *Patterson* order usually also dissent from Court decisions that reject the public law model of litigation in favor of the classical one.[23]

C. AGENDA CONTROL

As a general matter, it may not "affront . . . settled jurisprudence to request argument" because the adversary process arguments are not particularly powerful. Still, there may be criteria to determine when requesting argument is appropriate. Justice Stevens's state-

---

[21]See, *e.g.*, Fiss, Against Settlement, 93 Yale L. J. 1073 (1984).

[22]In addition, numerous rules already constrain the autonomy of litigants once they seek the assistance of the courts. A notable example is the rule that the federal courts must examine their subject matter jurisdiction even if the parties do not question it. The proper form of the argument from autonomy is that the incremental loss in litigant autonomy due to the Court's requesting argument on a new issue is greater than the benefit flowing from the Court's request. We can get some leverage on the cost-benefit analysis by comparing the situation in *Patterson* to the subject-matter jurisdiction rule, where the judgment is that the loss in litigant autonomy is outweighed by the benefits of the rule. As I suggest in the text, the Court's public law role almost certainly outweighs the loss in litigant autonomy in the present situation.

[23]See, *e.g.*, Pennhurst State Hospital v. Halderman, 465 U.S. 89 (1984); Rizzo v. Goode, 423 U.S. 362 (1976).

ment that the Court should not "fashion its own agenda" provides a useful starting point. Public choice theorists have shown that in many situations, roughly speaking, the person who controls the agenda controls the outcome.[24] The adversary process arguments leave control of the agenda to the parties. Once those arguments are rejected, the issue becomes who on the Court will control the agenda and, perhaps thereby, the outcome.

Patterson provides a good illustration of the consequences of agenda control. To simplify the exposition, I assume that after the original argument in *Patterson* nine Justices revealed their firmly held views on two questions: whether *Patterson* can be fairly distinguished from *Runyon*, and whether *Runyon* was correctly decided.[25] Consider first the extreme case: four Justices (the "liberals") believe that *Patterson* cannot be fairly distinguished from *Runyon* and that *Runyon* was correctly decided, while five Justices (the "conservatives") also believe that *Patterson* cannot be fairly distinguished from *Runyon* but believe that *Runyon* was wrongly decided.[26] (See table 1.) If the liberals—or their surrogates in this context, the parties—control the agenda by confining the issue to whether *Patterson* can be distinguished from *Runyon*, the result will be a unanimous decision in favor of Patterson.[27] The conservatives might find that outcome especially disturbing for two reasons. The party who they believe should have been held free of liability will be found liable, and, perhaps more important, the Court's unanimity may send a signal to lower courts and the public that the Court

---

[24]For an introduction, see Levine & Plott, Agenda Influence and Its Implications, 63 Va. L. Rev. 561 (1977).

[25]Perhaps the fact that *Patterson* was argued on the fourth argument day of Justice Kennedy's tenure has some bearing on the propriety of requesting argument on the issue of overruling *Runyon*.

[26]The discussion that follows assumes that the Justices are committed to making only "fair" distinctions between cases. If they are willing to distinguish *Patterson* from *Runyon* on grounds that cannot withstand minimal examination, it is even more difficult to understand why a request for reargument is appropriate. I would think that under these circumstances the sensible course would be to distinguish *Runyon* and then, a few years later, say that because the distinction preferred in *Patterson* was both unworkable and analytically unsatisfying the time had come to overrule *Runyon* openly. For a similar two-step, see Lloyd Corp. v. Tanner, 407 U.S. 551 (1972), and Hudgens v. NLRB, 424 U.S. 507 (1976).

[27]There is some reason to believe that this is exactly what happened in St. Francis College v. Al-Khazraji, 107 S.Ct. 2022 (1987). According to the Washington Post, a majority of the Justices who joined Justice White's unanimous opinion expressed doubt about *Runyon's* correctness. Rehnquist's Offhand Remark Triggered Unusual Reappraisal, Washington Post, May 21, A1.

TABLE 1

	Patterson Distinguishable from *Runyon*	Patterson Not Distinguishable from *Runyon*
Runyon correct	0	4 Patterson loses 5–4 on new issue
Runyon wrong.................................	0	5
Patterson wins 9–0 on first issue		

enthusiastically endorses broad liability under §1981. Retrieving control of the agenda allows the conservatives to produce the right outcome from their point of view.

Agenda control matters in this extreme case because Patterson wins if the Court considers only the first question and loses if it considers the new one as well. Are there circumstances in which it seems all right for Patterson to *lose* on the first question once the second has been injected into the case? The Court said that requesting argument on the new question was appropriate "in light of difficulties posed by [Patterson's] argument for a fundamental extension of liability" under §1981.[28] The extreme case I have sketched should be described in exactly the opposite way: Patterson's argument for imposing liability is so easy that the conservatives must add the new issue if the outcome is to be correct. I believe that the Court's description suggests that the request for argument was not a response to real problems of agenda control.

To see this we must consider two additional scenarios. Table 2 describes a "divided Court." Four Justices believe that *Runyon* was correctly decided, but they are divided on whether *Patterson* is distinguishable from *Runyon*. The other five Justices believe that *Runyon* was wrong, and three of them think that *Patterson* is distinguishable from *Runyon*. A majority of five rejects Patterson's claim on the ground that it falls outside the scope of §1981 as interpreted in *Runyon*; two others would concur in the result, believing that *Runyon* should be overruled. In the "divided Court" scenario there is no need to request argument on the second issue.

---

[28] 108 S.Ct. at 1420.

TABLE 2

	Patterson Distinguishable from *Runyon*	Patterson Not Distinguishable from *Runyon*
Runyon correct	2	2
		Patterson loses 5–4 on new issue
Runyon wrong................................	3	2
	Patterson wins 5–4 on first issue	

Finally, assume that the four "liberal" Justices would vote as in the first scenario. After reargument, could Patterson lose on the initial issue of the scope of *Runyon?* The answer, I think, is that she could not. There is no way to complete the table of votes so that there is a majority against Patterson on the initial issue—at least not a majority that was not already available before reargument was ordered. If a majority thinks that *Patterson* is fairly distinguishable from *Runyon*, it can achieve a result that is legally correct without addressing the issue of overruling, thereby serving the Court's public law role albeit perhaps not as fully as would be the case were the same majority to overrule *Runyon.* Here the loss in litigant autonomy from requesting argument on a new issue appears to contribute rather little to the Court's public law role, and so may be unjustified.[29]

Two conclusions can be drawn from these tables. First, the more accurate the Court's characterization of Patterson's claims as seeking a fundamental extension of *Runyon*, the less likely it is that it was appropriate to request argument on overruling *Runyon.* Second, given the expressions of views by the four dissenters from the Court's order, it is difficult to imagine a scenario in which Patterson loses on the initial issue once reargument has occurred.[30]

---

[29]My argument would be strengthened were I able to deploy a theory about the circumstances under which it is appropriate to overrule a precedent in a case that is fairly distinguishable from the precedent, where the parties have themselves presented the issue of overruling to the Court. As it is, I can rely only on arguments derived from concerns about implementing the adversary system.

[30]The analysis would not be substantially different were one or more Justices uncertain about their position on *Runyon's* correctness. (Presumably the initial argument in *Patterson* allowed each Justice to clarify his or her position on the question there presented. But see note 25 *supra*.) If some Justices are uncertain about *Runyon*, we cannot divide the five

In this sense, the majority was wrong in saying that the dissenters had improperly implied that the Court had decided "today" to overrule *Runyon*.[31]

The *Patterson* order might be justified, however, if a possible decision on whether to overrule *Runyon* was not independent of the decision on whether it was fairly distinguishable from *Patterson*. For example, five Justices might believe that the cases were fairly distinguishable, but might anticipate difficulties in implementing the distinction in future cases. The distinction could be advanced in support of a ruling against Patterson, yet these Justices might be concerned that, once the distinction were embedded in the law, it would become undesirably complex. At the least, they might want to consider whether they could avoid introducing that kind of complexity by overruling *Runyon*, but only if the case for overruling were strong enough.

One last point deserves mention here. As I will argue, if *Runyon* is overruled, there are reasonable prospects that Congress will respond by enacting a new version of it. Justices who believed that distinguishing *Patterson* from *Runyon*, while possible, would introduce undesirable complexity into the law, might also believe that a modern legislative solution to the problem of private discrimination not covered by existing anti-discrimination laws, arrived at after hearings and the like, could be more effective than a jerry-rigged judicial solution predicated on an 1866 (or 1870) statute.

II. The Controversy Over the Patterson Order

On the face of it, it is difficult to understand why the Court's decision to request argument on overruling *Runyon* was so controversial. There is substantial overlap between §1981 and other

---

"conservative" Justices among cells of the tables. That inability, however, does not overcome the fact that no matter how they are divided, Patterson should lose after reargument only if *Runyon* is overruled.

[31] This conclusion gains some modest support from the Court's opinion, which listed four cases in the past twenty years in which it had requested argument on a new issue. 108 S.Ct. at 1420. The reargument led twice to overrulings, in Garcia v. San Antonio Metropolitan Transit Authority, 469 U.S. 528 (1985) (opinion for the Court by Blackmun, J.), and Benton v. Maryland, 395 U.S. 784 (1969) (opinion for the Court by Marshall, J.); once to a decision confined to the initial issue, for which the Court offered its "apologies to all," Illinois v. Gates, 462 U.S. 213, 217 (1983) (opinion for the Court by Rehnquist, J.); and once to a highly fractured decision on the initial issue, Alfred Dunhill of London, Inc. v. Republic of Cuba, 425 U.S. 682 (1976).

anti-discrimination laws, as the dissenters from the *Patterson* order acknowledged.[32] Overruling *Runyon* would have some effects on plaintiffs' recourse to certain procedures and remedies, and would eliminate a remedy for discrimination in those relatively few situations not covered by other laws. Overall, however, it cannot be said that overruling *Runyon* would have any significant impact on incentives to refrain from discriminating.[33] In addition, the dissenters from the *Patterson* order have vociferously urged the Court to overrule its 1881 decision in *Hans v. Louisiana*,[34] an issue that was again presented to the Court in the 1988 term.[35] Finally, just five weeks before ordering reargument in *Patterson*, the Court unanimously overruled a statutory precedent.[36]

These last two points suggest that the controversy over the Court's order rested on disagreement over the merits. The dissenters believed that *Runyon* was correctly decided and so should not be overruled, and that *Hans* was wrongly decided and so should be. There is, however, another difference between *Hans* and *Runyon*. The Court in *Runyon* interpreted a statute, while the *Hans* Court interpreted the Constitution.[37] It is conventionally said that the Court should be more reluctant to overrule statutory precedents than constitutional ones.[38] The primary reason is that Congress can overturn erroneous statutory precedents by the same simple majority by which its predecessors enacted the statute, whereas erroneous constitutional precedents can be overturned only by the supermajorities of the amendment process. As time passes, the

---

[32] 108 S.Ct. at 1420.

[33] I do not mean by this to suggest that there are no cases in which only a remedy under §1981 is available. There are many reported and unreported cases of that sort, though I have done no search to determine what proportion of those cases involve claims that were merely procedurally barred under modern antidiscrimination statutes. For an examination of filings under §1981 and other civil rights statutes, see Eisenberg & Schwab, The Importance of Section 1981, 73 Corn. L. Rev. 596 (1988). Eisenberg and Schwab report that 30 of 321 filings claiming discrimination in employment relied on §1981 and not on Title VII of the 1964 Civil Rights Act. *Id.* at 603.

[34] 134 U.S. 1 (1881).

[35] Pennsylvania v. Union Gas Co., 832 F.2d 1343 (3d Cir.), cert. granted, 108 S.Ct. 1219 (1988).

[36] Gulfstream Aerospace Corp. v. Mayacamas Corp., 108 S.Ct. 1133 (1988).

[37] *Hans* held that notwithstanding the precise language of the Eleventh Amendment, it precluded citizens of a state from suing their own state.

[38] For a comprehensive discussion, see Eskridge, Overruling Statutory Precedents, 76 Geo. L. J. 1361 (1988).

failure to overturn the interpretation can be taken as an admittedly modest indication that the interpretation is an acceptable one, and the interpretation becomes woven into the relevant body of law in such a way that its removal by overruling would be disruptive. These last conditions indicate when overruling a statutory precedent might be appropriate: when the issue is one that is unlikely to have attracted Congress's attention, or when the interpretation does not fit well with the law as it has developed. Further, if the erroneous interpretation occurred without full consideration by the Court of relevant materials, the weight to be given the statutory interpretation may be diminished, though even here if it has become woven into the law the erroneous interpretation still should have some weight.

The Court in *Patterson* listed seven cases in which it had overruled statutory precedents,[39] most of which satisfy the conditions described. For example, *Boys Markets, Inc. v. Retail Clerks* overruled an earlier interpretation of the Norris-LaGuardia Act that could not be readily integrated with the Court's emerging jurisprudence of arbitration under collective bargaining agreements.[40] Others, however, seem to involve overruling decisions simply because the Court came to believe that its initial interpretation had been wrong.[41]

On the surface, *Patterson* appears to present a situation in which neither condition for statutory overruling is satisfied. Congress regularly has paid attention to anti-discrimination law: as Justice Stevens pointed out and indeed as the overlap between §1981 and modern anti-discrimination law shows, Congress's actions since *Runyon* have produced a body of law into which §1981 as interpreted in *Runyon* fits rather well. However, as Justice White argued in *Runyon*, perhaps the Court mistakenly assumed that §1981 derived from the Civil Rights Act of 1866 and therefore erroneously relied on the legislative history of the 1866 Act as the ground for its decision in *Runyon*.

There is something odd about the conclusion that *Runyon* should not be overruled because the conditions for statutory overruling are not satisfied. Consider the ramifications of the fact that the conditions are not satisfied: Congress does pay attention to the

---

[39]108 S.Ct. at 1420–21. Oddly, the list did not include the *Mayacamas* case.

[40]398 U.S. 235 (1970).

[41]See, *e.g.*, Monell v. New York Dept. of Social Services, 436 U.S. 658 (1978).

issue, and the prior interpretation fits well with the law as it has developed. Under the circumstances, it is not difficult to imagine Congress responding to overruling *Runyon* by enacting a civil rights restoration statute that would return the law to its pre-*Patterson* state.[42] Precisely because the Court should not overrule *Runyon*, that is, doing so might well be insignificant in the long run.

The controversy over the *Patterson* order begins to make sense, I think, when we consider the larger political context to which the foregoing analysis directs our attention. One path into that context begins by noting that Justice Stevens's dissent to the *Patterson* order reiterated his concern, earlier expressed in his concurrence in *Runyon*, that the order would send the wrong signals to the public: "The Court's spontaneous decision . . . is certain to engender widespread concern in those segments of our population that must rely on a federal rule of law as a protection against invidious private discrimination. . . . The Court's order today will, by itself, have a deleterious effect on the faith reposed by racial minorities in the continuing stability of a rule of law that guarantees them the 'same right' as 'white citizens.' "[43] The Court responded to this "intimat[ion] that the statutory question involved in *Runyon v. McCrary* should not be subject to the same principles of *stare decisis* as other decisions because it benefited civil rights plaintiffs by expanding liability under the statute" by saying that "the Court may [not] recognize any such exception to the abiding rule that it treat all litigants equally: that is, that the claim of any litigant for the application of a rule to its case should not be influenced by the Court's view of the worthiness of the litigant in terms of extralegal criteria. We think that this is what Congress meant when it required

---

[42]Although I would not draw strong inferences from the examples, something akin to the scenario I have described has occurred with some frequency since 1976 in the civil rights area. See Civil Rights Attorney's Fees Award Act of 1976, 42 U.S.C. §1988, responding to Alyeska Pipeline Service Co. v. Wilderness Society, 421 U.S. 240 (1975); Voting Rights Act Amendment of 1982, 42 U.S.C. §1973c, responding to City of Mobile v. Bolden, 446 U.S. 55 (1980); Pregnancy Discrimination Act, 42 U.S.C. §2000e, responding to General Electric Co. v. Gilbert, 429 U.S. 125 (1976); Civil Rights Restoration Act of 1987, 20 U.S.C. §1681, responding to Grove City College v. Bell, 465 U.S. 555 (1984). Note that by calling the 1987 statute a "restoration" act, Congress expressed the view that the Court in *Grove City* had misinterpreted Title IX of the Education Act Amendments of 1972. See also Rehabilitation Act Amendments of 1986, 42 U.S.C. §2000d-7, responding to Atascadero State Hospital v. Scanlon, 473 U.S. 234 (1985); Handicapped Children's Protection Act of 1986, 20 U.S.C. §1415(e) (4), responding to Smith v. Robinson, 468 U.S. 992 (1984).

[43]108 S.Ct. at 1422–23 (Stevens, J., dissenting).

each Justice . . . to swear to 'administer justice without respect to persons, and do equal right to the poor and to the rich.' "[44]

Understanding this argument requires us to distinguish between the Court's role as a legal institution and its role as a political institution. Justice Stevens's argument requires careful qualification if it is taken as a legal argument, as the majority appeared to take it. Consider two unrelated cases in which the legal arguments for the plaintiffs are equally strong, and in which one plaintiff is a corporation and the other is a union. It would indeed be outrageous if the Court ruled in favor of the plaintiff in the first case and against the plaintiff in the second solely because of the identity of the litigants.[45] Suppose, however, that the question is not whether to rule on the merits but to exercise discretion committed to the Court: for example, both plaintiffs have lost in the courts of appeals and seek certiorari. Because the decision to grant certiorari is discretionary, it would not seem quite so improper were a Justice to vote to grant review in the case brought to the Court by the corporation and to vote to deny review in the case brought to it by the union, solely because of the identity of the litigants. To the extent that Justice Stevens meant to describe the signal sent by the order in *Patterson*, he was describing the effects of a discretionary decision, as to which the identity of the litigants may not be improper. Further, the imagery of "weight" that accompanies discussions of the propriety of overruling statutory precedents suggests that the decision to overrule a statutory precedent contains some discretionary elements, among which may be the kind of concern for the identity of the litigants to which Justice Stevens referred.[46]

Justice Stevens's concern about the signals the Court sends is, I suspect, rather more political than legal. That is, he understands that the Court acts in the overall political system of the United States. Indeed, he and the other Justices could hardly have been unaware of that fact, in light of the recent defeat of the nomination

---

[44]*Id.* at 1421.

[45]The classic statement of this claim is Wechsler, Toward Neutral Principles of Constitutional Law, 73 Harv. L. Rev. 1 (1959).

[46]See also Justice Blackmun's formulation, which also refers to the decision to request argument: "I am at a loss to understand the motivation of five Members of this Court to reconsider an interpretation of a civil rights statute that so clearly reflects our society's earnest commitment to ending racial discrimination. . . ." *Id.* at 1422 (Blackmun, J., dissenting).

of Judge Bork.[47] The politics of that defeat were quite complex, but it is clear that civil rights sentiments made a major contribution, if only by inducing Southern Democrats to vote against the nomination because their black constituents opposed it.[48] In addition, an important theme in the opposition to Judge Bork's confirmation was that his appointment would increase the possibility that important civil rights precedents would be overruled. The opponents of the nomination, including civil rights forces, may have believed that the defeat of Judge Bork's nomination had done more than give us a somewhat less conservative justice in Anthony Kennedy. They may have believed that the defeat ratified their view of the Constitution and the Supreme Court as the activist defender of civil rights with a continuing commitment to the landmarks that Judge Bork's opponents revere.

In this political context, the *Patterson* order sent a signal that the defeat of Judge Bork's nomination had not permanently altered the landscape.[49] It dispelled any illusions the civil rights community might have had about its relation to the contemporary Supreme Court. Cries of outrage could be expected because the *Patterson* order, even if it had little substantive significance, had a great deal of symbolic importance.

We can see the political and symbolic significance of the *Patterson* order best by contrasting two hypothesized decisions. The first is a decision rendered at the end of last Term: instead of ordering reargument in *Patterson*, the Court rules against Patterson, holding by a 5–4 vote that §1981 does not cover her claim. I suspect that such a decision would have been received by the civil rights

---

[47]See, *e.g.*, Symposium, 101 Harv. L. Rev. 1146 (1988).

[48]The complexity of the politics is suggested by the fact that Sen. John Stennis (D-Miss.) voted against the nomination. Sen. Stennis is not known for his sympathies to civil rights, and he cast his vote after he had announced that he was not running for reelection. He may have voted against the nomination to protect his younger colleagues from criticism from some white voters, but I suspect that his vote was largely on principle.

[49]I should emphasize that, like Justice Stevens, I am here describing an effect of the *Patterson* order, and do not mean to suggest that the majority consciously intended to send such a signal or consciously were responding to the defeat of the Bork nomination. Perhaps, however, the Justices voting for reargument in *Patterson* wanted to send such a signal to dispel ambiguity about their general views. Political actors sometimes find ambiguity strategically useful, but it is also sometimes a disadvantage, for example when ambiguity is likely to generate expectations that the actor knows are likely to be defeated, with the effect of exacerbating the actor's political difficulties at a later date. The aftermath of the Bork nomination may have been an occasion on which clarity was particularly desirable to these Justices.

community without much controversy as just another decision indicating that the Supreme Court was not its friend. The second is a decision rendered this Term, reaffirming *Runyon* and upholding Patterson's claim. I suspect that such a decision would be received by the civil rights community as a narrow escape, once again demonstrating that it can win occasional victories from a Court that is basically not its friend. In this sense, the *Patterson* order is significant no matter how the Court resolves the *Patterson* case.

III. Conclusion

As time passes, the Court's decision to order reargument in *Patterson* will fade from our view, overshadowed as it properly will be by the Court's decision on the merits. I hope to have shown, however, that what has already happened provides some insights into the internal politics of the judicial process, that is, the deliberative process within the Court, and into the external politics of that process, that is, the Court's location in the political system of the United States.

LAWRENCE ROSEN

CONTINUING THE CONVERSATION: CREATIONISM, THE RELIGION CLAUSES, AND THE POLITICS OF CULTURE

Critics of the Supreme Court's jurisprudence of religion often point to the apparently inconsistent and unprincipled decisions the Court has rendered in recent years. At various times the Court has held that the posting of the Ten Commandments in a public school classroom is impermissible[1] but that the erection of a Nativity scene on municipal property is not;[2] that the delivery by a clergyman of an opening prayer to the state legislature is allowable[3] but that religious headgear may not be worn if military regulations bar such attire;[4] that the provision from public funds of books to parochial school children[5] or released time for off-campus religious instruction[6] is constitutional

Lawrence Rosen is Professor of Anthropology, Princeton University, and Adjunct Professor of Law, Columbia University School of Law.

AUTHOR'S NOTE: I am grateful to John Mitchell and the Northwestern Law School Faculty Research Fund for assistance in the research for this article, and to William Felstiner and the American Bar Foundation for their support during my residence as a Visiting Research Fellow.

[1]Stone v. Graham, 449 U.S. 39 (1980).

[2]Lynch v. Donnelly, 465 U.S. 668 (1984).

[3]Marsh v. Nebraska, 463 U.S. 783 (1983).

[4]Goldman v. Weinberger, 106 S.Ct. 1310 (1987).

[5]Board of Education v. Allen, 392 U.S. 236 (1968).

[6]Zorach v. Clauson, 343 U.S. 306 (1952).

but that providing parochial school students with remedial aid is not.[7]

At first sight the decision in *Edwards v. Aguillard*,[8] the so-called "creationism case," would appear to be one more item that raises questions about the consistency of the Court's rulings and the clarity of its guidance for the future. Confronted with a Louisiana statute requiring the teaching of "creation science" whenever evolutionary theory is also offered in public institutions, the court held that on its face the statute constitutes an impermissible establishment of religion by the state. Depending on one's point of view the decision can be seen in different ways: (1) that the Court pierced the veil of legislative obfuscation to spot the statute for what it was—an attempt to impose on society at large the religious beliefs of a particular group; (2) that the Court has for too long exaggerated the conflict between the Establishment and Free Exercise Clauses thus inhibiting the expression of religious attachment, especially when state-supported deference to the sentiments of one part of the population would do little harm to the political or religious choice of others; or (3) that the Court jeopardizes its own legitimacy when its decisions on sensitive issues appear to be based on the momentary views of its current members rather than enduring precepts that join disparate cases and times into a coherent scheme.

The presence or absence of consistency and principle in the decisions of a body that speaks with different voices to different cases is, of course, largely a question of where and how one chooses to posit order and direction. To seek coherence solely at the level of doctrine may blind us to the larger context within which the meaning of the Court's decisions is engendered and to the special kind of logic by which an institution like the Court operates as part of a cultural system. *Aguillard* and its related cases afford an opportunity to see how power and knowledge interact, how understanding the logic of a legal decision may depend on our understanding of the logic of a system of cultural meaning, and how the role of a political institution like the Court must be gauged in relation to the culture it seeks to direct.

---

[7]Grand Rapids School District v. Ball, 105 S.Ct. 3216 (1985), Aguilar v. Felton, 105 S.Ct. 3232 (1985).

[8]107 S.Ct. 2573 (1987).

I. Arguing Aguillard

Knowledge, Americans are fond of saying, is power, and competition for control of the channels of knowledge has long been a predominant aspect of American political life. Nowhere has this feature been more richly displayed than in *Aguillard* and its precursors.

In 1982 the state legislature of Louisiana passed the "Balanced Treatment for Creation-Science and Evolution-Science in Public School Instruction" Act. The Act provided that no school is required to teach creationism or evolution but that if either is taught the other must also be taught.[9] The subjects are defined as "the scientific evidences for [creation or evolution] and inferences from those scientific evidences."[10] The Act requires that curriculum guides be developed for creation science courses, although it does not provide for the preparation of comparable guides for teaching evolution.[11] Research services are to be supplied for the teaching of creationism, though none are provided in the statute for evolution.[12] Panels are to be appointed with the task of providing the necessary research services for creation science: only creation scientists may serve on these panels.[13] School boards may not discriminate against anyone who "chooses to be a creation-scientist" or to teach creationism: no comparable provision is made in the statute for evolutionists.[14]

Like other statutes that had preceded it for more than half a century, the Louisiana law was born of a combination of religious ardor and legislative acquiescence:[15] to many believers, particularly

---

[9]La. Rev. Stat. Ann. ¶17:286.4A (West 1982).

[10]*Id.* at ¶¶17:286.3(2) and (3).

[11]*Id.* at ¶17:286.7A.

[12]*Id.* at ¶17:286.7B.

[13]*Ibid.*

[14]*Id.* at ¶17:286.4C.

[15]Thus the statute at issue in the *Scopes* "Monkey Trial," the Butler Act, was enacted by the Tennessee legislature with little enthusiasm and signed by the Governor with no expectation that it should ever be enforced. Indeed, William Jennings Bryan had himself urged the legislators not to include any provision for penalties. See Ginger, Six Days or Forever? 7–24 (1958). See also de Camp, The Great Monkey Trial (1968); Gould, Ever Since Darwin (1977). On the circumstances surrounding the passage of the Arkansas balanced treatment act in 1981, see Nelkin, The Creation Controversy 138–39 (1982). The intellectual underpinnings for the current series of balanced treatment acts were developed by Wendell Bird in his student note, Freedom of Religion and Science Instruction in Public Schools, 87 Yale L. J. 515 (1978).

Christian fundamentalists, evolutionary thought constitutes a mortal challenge to the Biblical concept of creation, while to many legislators laws restricting the teaching of evolution constitute an acceptable vehicle for expressing deference to the teaching of values they believe central to our society's well-being. The Louisiana statute differed from its precursors in several key respects. Whereas the statutes in the famous *Scopes* trial and the more recent Arkansas case[16] barred the teaching of evolution outright, the Louisiana statute, like those adopted in others states,[17] called for "equal" or "balanced" treatment of evolutionary and creationist thought. This legislative strategy was a response to earlier court decisions which had struck down strictly anti-evolutionary laws, and to the criteria by which the Supreme Court had come to approach religion cases in general.

On its surface the Court's rhetoric in religion cases would appear to have turned on the ambiguities present within and between the two religion clauses of the First Amendment.[18] Acknowledging that "the language of the Religion Clauses of the First Amendment is at best opaque,"[19] and that the line of separation between Church and State, "far from being a wall, is a blurred, indistinct, and variable barrier,"[20] the Court, under Chief Justice Burger, attempted to pull together various criteria from earlier cases when, in the *Lemon* decision of 1970, it held that a statute must have a secular legal purpose whose effect neither advances nor inhibits religion and fosters no excessive entanglement between government and

---

[16]Epperson v. Arkansas, 393 U.S. 97 (1968).

[17]See, *e.g.*, Ark. Stat. Ann. ¶80-1663 *et. seq.* (1981), held unconstitutional in McLean v. Arkansas Board of Education, 529 F. Supp. 1255 (E.D. Ark. 1982). A 1973 Tennessee statute stated: "Any biology textbook used for teaching in the public schools which expresses an opinion of, or relates to a theory about origins or creation of man and his world shall be prohibited from being used as a textbook in such system unless it specifically states that it is a theory as to the origin and creation of man and his world and is not represented to be scientific fact. Any textbook so used in the public education system which expresses an opinion or relates to a theory or theories shall give in the same textbook and under the same subject commensurate attention to, and an equal amount of emphasis on, the origins and creation of man and his world as the same is recorded in other theories, including, but not limited to, the Genesis account in the Bible." Tenn. Code Ann. ¶49-2008 (1973).

[18]The First Amendment provides that "Congress shall make no law respecting an establishment of religion, or prohibiting the free exercise thereof; or abridging the freedom of speech. . . ."

[19]Lemon v. Kurtzman, 403 U.S. 602, 612 (1970).

[20]*Id.* at 614.

religion.[21] These criteria, said the Court, must be seen in terms of "all the circumstances of a particular relationship." *Lemon* itself involved state aid for parochial schools. The *Lemon* court expressed the fear that if state and religion were drawn too closely into one another's affairs both might suffer, particularly, as Justice Douglas said, "by depriving a teacher, under threats of reprisal, of the right to give sectarian construction or interpretation of, say, history and literature."[22]

The issue thus becomes one of who shall have control over the preeminent public forum for the conveying of knowledge, the system of state-supported education. But implicit in *Lemon* are also questions about the process by which that knowledge shall be conveyed—whether by a system of "indoctrination" or of "interpretation," whether by involvement of beliefs that admit of no discussion or those to which diverse parties in theory may contribute, whether by opening education to contradictory viewpoints or restricting it to those professed by the people in power. By characterizing the Religion Clauses as "indistinct" *Lemon* combines the settled rhetoric of entanglement with the emerging rhetoric of purpose to fabricate a test which, whatever its logical merits or defects, is exceedingly ambiguous.

The absence of clear criteria for predicting how the Court might move on any given issue necessarily spawned both academic criticism and varied litigation.[23] If, at least by way of dictum, "secular humanism" can be listed along with organized faiths as a religion;[24] if a panoply of public rituals from Thanksgiving celebrations to a National Prayer Day can be characterized as part of a civic religion that the courts should realize runs deep in American

---

[21]*Id.* at 612–13. The language was already prefigured in Walz v. Tax Commission, 397 U.S. 664 (1970).

[22]Lemon v. Kurtzman, 403 U.S. at 634; Douglas goes on to say "Sectarian instruction, in which, of course, a State may not indulge, can take place in a course on Shakespeare or in one on mathematics. No matter what the curriculum offers, the question is what is *taught*? We deal not with evil teachers but with zealous ones who may use any opportunity to indoctrinate a class." *Id.* at 634–355 (Douglas, J., concurring).

[23]See, *e.g.*, McConnell, Accommodation of Religion, 1985 Supreme Court Review 1 (1986); Marty, Of Darters and Schools and Clergymen: The Religion Clauses Confounded, 1978 Supreme Court Review 171 (1979); Henkin, The Wall of Separation and Legislative Purpose, Religion, Morality, and the Law 145, 148 (Pennock & Chapman, eds.) (1986); Wallace v. Jaffree, 472 U.S. 38 (1985).

[24]Torcaso v. Watkins, 367 U.S. 488, 495 n.11 (1960).

culture;[25] and if the basis for defining a religion should lie within the ambit of judicial reckoning by virtue of its inclusion in the Constitution, then clearly the Court would seem to be in need of establishing bases by which a changing society can assess the parameters of its permissible acts.

But the rhetoric of the religion cases—a rhetoric of "effect," "purpose," and "entanglement"—is not the only rhetorical element in the debate, for the rhetoric of the legal arguments and decisions is part of a larger discourse. The choice of terms by which the Court characterizes situations embodies the assumption, common to Western endeavor since at least the seventeenth century, that there is a division between reality and the way in which that reality is reflected and described, and that it is both possible and desirable to match the one to the other.[26] Positivistic science seeks to relate representation to reality by fostering a vision of objective experimental testing; common law courts seek to garner control over the world not simply through the declaration of winners and losers but by capturing the framework of discussion in such a way that even the losers appear to ratify the categories, the boundaries, and the procedures involved. Since this style of shaping facts and establishing acceptable procedures finds resonance in many other domains of life—from the dynamics of family and marriage to narrative style and sport—the law partakes of a common discourse that necessarily acquires meaning by its very embeddedness in the multiplicity of cultural forms. What *Aguillard* demonstrates is just how much, in cases affecting the public control of knowledge, one must attend to this larger discourse.

It was George Bernard Shaw who once said that "Darwin had the good luck to please anyone with an axe to grind." The most recent reaction to the widespread reception of Darwinian thought, the creation science movement, took on its present shape in the 1960s when a number of Christian fundamentalists began to recast the traditional fundamentalist opposition to the idea that living forms evolved from a single source of life and proliferated into a multiplicity of species that have themselves altered in response to the

---

[25]See generally Bellah, Civil Religion in America, 96 Daedalus 1 (1967); Mirsky, Civil Religion and the Establishment Clause, 95 Yale L. J. 1237 (1986).

[26]See generally Foucault, The Archaeology of Knowledge (1972); Reiss, The Discourse of Modernism (1982).

forces of adaptation and genetic change.[27] Several research organizations were formed, journals initiated, and training programs
begun. That these particular fundamentalists should have turned to
"science" as the vehicle for added claims of legitimacy to their beliefs
should have come as no surprise. As we have noted, the predominant
discourse in our society tends strongly to the belief that reason is the
proper means for relating concepts to experience. To many religious
people reason can be rendered compatible with faith by its provision
of external evidence for faith, by casting doubt on philosophies
committed solely to reason, and by affirming that, if reason is
"neutral," issues may not be closed off to "facts" that human intel-
ligence has yet to apprehend. Thus many groups—including Christian Science, Scientology, and holistic medicine—have attached
themselves to the idiom of science, envisioning it as a system that
may prove but can never disprove issues of faith. The creationists'
challenge to evolutionary thought, therefore, rested in no small part
on attaching themselves to a discourse whose legal and authenti-
cating implications would serve as the foundation for an assault on
the predominant biological ideas taught in public school systems.

As part of their attempt to capture the terms of science for their
own purposes the creationists also allied themselves with two other
key ideas: (1) that one can distinguish "fact" from "theory" and thus
devalue evolution as merely the latter and hence on no higher plane
than creationism, and (2) that by denominating itself a science
creationism should be accorded the same sort of "fair hearing,"
"equal time," and "balanced treatment" to which any theoretical
model is entitled. Indeed, they argue, since this particular model is
one to which a vast number of Americans are attached it is
especially worthy of legislative and judicial deference.[28] During the

---

[27]On the creationist movement and the controversies it has spawned, see generally
LaFollette (ed.), Creationism, Science, and the Law: The Arkansas Case (1983); Larson,
Trial and Error: The American Controversy over Creation and Evolution (1985); Gilkey,
Creationism on Trial: Evolution and God at Little Rock (1985); Nelkin, The Creation
Controversy (1982); McKim, Evolution vs Creation: A Selected Bibliography, 24 Anthro-
pology Newsletter 5 (October 1983); Gould, Hen's Teeth and Horse's Toes (1984).

[28]A Gallup poll of May 1985 indicated that 35 million Americans who would identify
themselves as evangelicals (i.e. believe in a literal reading of the Bible) have accepted Jesus
Christ as their personal savior, and believe themselves to have been born again. A 1981
Gallup poll found that 44 percent of American adults agreed with the statement "God
created humanity pretty much in its present form within the last 10,000 years or so," and that
76 percent favored the teaching of both evolution and creationism. New York Times,

1970s creationists had succeeded in getting several state legislatures to pass laws favorable to their position and had been particularly effective in forcing textbook publishers to water down their presentation of evolution or to accord considerable space to the creationist position.[29]

Like the Supreme Court, the lower courts hearing *Aguillard* held that it was not necessary to provide defendants a trial on the scientific standing of the ideas that teachers would now be called upon to teach. But many of these issues had already been aired in the district court case of *McLean v. Arkansas Board of Education.*[30] Tracing the development of the creationist movement in modern times, Judge Overton found that the "sponsorship and lobbying effort in behalf of the [Balanced Treatment for Creation-Science and Evolution-Science] Act were motivated solely by [the sponsor's] religious beliefs and desire to see the Biblical version of creation taught in the public schools."[31] He noted that the leading creationist organization, the Institute for Creation Research, is an affiliate of the Christian Heritage College, and that members of another creationist think-tank, the Creation Research Society, must sign membership statements affirming their belief in the "direct creative acts of God during Creation Week as described in Genesis."[32] He quoted from letters by the author of the model balanced treatment statute urging the bill's sponsor to play down the supporter's attachments to fundamentalist beliefs,[33] and noted that the bill itself was referred to no committees and was passed virtually without discussion. He discounted the argument that creation could mean "creation out of nothing" since even that phrase implies in our religious heritage a power we ascribe only to God. Judge Overton also characterized the antithesis that creation-

---

November 18, 1981. See also Harrold & Eve, Patterns of Creationist Belief among College Students, in Cult Archaeology and Creationism 75 (Harrold & Eve, eds.) 1987. One survey showed that a quarter of the high school biology teachers in Ohio supported the teaching of creationism even though only 10 percent said they had ever been subjected to any pressures to do so. The Chronicle of Higher Education, October 28, 1987, at A7. During the 1980 presidential campaign Ronald Reagan gave support to the creationists' position when he said that scientists themselves have come to doubt evolution and "the biblical story of creation should also be taught." Gurin, The Creationist Revival, 23 The Sciences 16 (April 1981).

[29]See generally Nelkin, The Creation Controversy (1982).

[30]529 F.Supp. 1255 (E.D. Ark. 1982).

[31]*Id.* at 1263.

[32]*Id.* at 1260 n.7.

[33]*Id.* at 1261–62.

ists set up between creation and evolution as "a contrived dualism which has no scientific factual basis or legitimate educational purpose."[34] On the issue of academic freedom the *McLean* court ruled that "the need to monitor classroom discussion in order to uphold the Act's prohibition against religious instruction will necessarily involve administrators in questions concerning religion."[35] Teachers "face an impossible task," he said, of answering questions without entering into a religious opinion if the only source of authority is the Bible itself.

But it is in the definition of science that the court made its most distinctive mark. Indeed, *McLean* appears to be the first case to involve a court formulated definition of science that goes beyond simple reference to dictionary entries.[36] Specifically, the court stated that "the essential characteristics of science are:

1. It is guided by natural law;

2. It has to be explanatory by reference to natural law;

3. It is testable against the empirical world;

4. Its conclusions are tentative, i.e., are not necessarily the final word; and

5. It is falsifiable."[37]

This definition is unusual in several respects. The court did not indicate exactly what it meant by "natural law," though it presumably implies that only falsifiable propositions about phenomena will be used to support a given assertion.[38] The criteria stress that ideas will have been worked on by many scholars independently and that they will have been discussed and published in reputable journals. To the criticism that alternative ideas may still be excluded, the court said: "It is, however, inconceivable that such a loose knit group of independent thinkers in all the varied fields of science could, or would, so effectively censor new scientific thought."[39] Because creationists "start with a conclusion and refuse to change it regardless of the evidence developed during the course of the

---

[34]*Id.* at 1266.

[35]*Id.* at 1272.

[36]Gordon, McLean v. Arkansas Board of Education: Finding the Science in "Creation Science," 77 Nw. L. Rev. 374, 389 (1982).

[37]McLean v. Arkansas Board of Education, 529 F. Supp. at 1267.

[38]See Gordon, McLean v. Arkansas Board of Education: Finding the Science in "Creation Science," 77 Nw. L. Rev. 374, 395 (1982).

[39]McLean v. Arkansas Board of Education, 529 F.Supp. 1255, 1268 (E.D. Ark. 1982).

investigation"[40] they have, the judge concluded, taken themselves beyond the pale of scientific discussion.

Overton's opinion was greeted by many as both a vindication of evolution and as a protection from legislative interference in the process of scholarly activity.[41] Left unresolved, however, was whether the courts should be the ones to define science at all, whether it is indeed accurate to treat science as a neutral marketplace of ideas from which the truth will always emerge untainted by ideological proclivity, and precisely where the locus of power over knowledge ought in various instances to be located. These are concerns that one might have hoped a Supreme Court decision on the Louisiana Balanced Treatment Act would have addressed. This was not, however, to be the case.

By the time *Aguillard* had made its way up to the Supreme Court the terms of the creationists' case had been at once enlarged and contracted—enlarged because the ideas of scientific neutrality and equal time had been appended to a set of religious ideas of considerable secular import, contracted because the supporters of creationism could not or would not relinquish their insistence on the proposition that the choice between creationism and evolution was of the either-or variety. These issues and the competing discourses in which they are set come out most clearly in the amicus briefs and in the oral argument.

Of the many briefs filed five are of particular note. In a brief submitted jointly by the states of New York and Illinois the Attorney General of New York argued that because twenty-two states have textbook adoption commissions and the dozen or so textbook publishers who dominate the trade claim that they can only afford to produce books for a national market, states like their own will be forced to use books that downplay evolutionary thought.[42] Aware of the intensity with which textbook disputes have been waged in other states,[43] the New York brief sought to convince the Court that balanced treatment requirements actually

---

[40]*Id.* at 1269.

[41]See, *e.g.*, Gould, The Verdict on Creationism, The New York Times Magazine, July 19, 1987, at 32–34; letters to the editor, New York Times, August 23, 1987.

[42]Amicus Curiae Brief of the State of New York, Joined by the State of Illinois, Edwards v. Aguillard, at 7.

[43]See Nelkin, The Creation Controversy 55–132 (1982), including the discussion of the pressures brought to bear on the National Science Foundation when they sought to produce model texts for the teaching of the biological sciences.

have the effect of chilling the depth of scientific discussion well beyond the boundaries of the states that have statutes favoring this approach.

Several briefs were addressed directly to the characterization of science and who should have the power to assert what science may be taught. The American Association of University Professors argued that if universities had to consider credentials to teach creation science in their appointment decisions it would amount to an ideological test, very much like a loyalty oath, and an infringement on academic freedom by a legislative body that is not competent to determine what constitutes science.[44] Science and its boundaries, they said, "must be defined by the collaborative and competitive work of minds devoted to its study."[45] On the critical issue of what powers the state should exercise over knowledge the AAUP argued that "the objective of the school and university is not to indoctrinate but to explore ideas with an open mind and an impartial and scientific approach. Requiring indoctrination in a doctrine mandated by statute, rather than by the best academic judgment, in an attempt to rebut generally accepted scientific theories is not academic freedom."[46]

The American Jewish Congress and the Synagogue Council of America urged the Court to use common sense conceptions of science: "Just as the Court knows judicially what is 'religious' . . . it knows what people in our time call science. And that does not include creation-science."[47] They implied that it is not possible to discuss issues like creation with those who possess *a priori* assumptions based on religious belief, and cited a proponent of creationism as saying: "There is not the slightest possibility that the *facts* of science can be contradicted by the Bible."[48]

In 1984 the National Academy of Sciences unequivocally proclaimed that creationism is not a science, and they followed this with a brief that asserted criteria similar to those Judge Overton had

[44]Brief Amici Curiae of the American Association of University Professors and the American Council on Education in Support of Appellees, Edwards v. Aguillard, at 15.

[45]*Id.* at 14.

[46]*Id.* at 16.

[47]Brief of the American Jewish Congress and the Synagogue Council of America as Amici Curiae in Support of Appellees, Edwards v. Aguillard, at 34.

[48]*Id.* at 7–8.

adopted in *McLean*.[49] Moreover, the Academy brief sought to place science, as they comprehend it, at the center of a conversational, give-and-take process that Americans tend to see as the fairest forum for the determination of truth: "The explanatory power of a scientific hypothesis or theory is, in effect, the medium of exchange by which the value of a scientific theory is determined in the marketplace of ideas that constitutes the scientific community. Creationists do not compete in the marketplace, and creation-science does not offer scientific value."[50]

The most intriguing arguments were perhaps those put forth by several religious groups and members of Congress in a brief filed by the Rutherford Institute.[51] The authors began with the familiar argument that both evolution and creationism are interpretive schemes rather than empirically determinable facts. To equate creationist ideas with, e.g., claims that the earth is flat undermines their status as one ideology among others that students may be mandated to study. Creationists, they said, are entitled to the recognition that in the real world "majoritarian pressure against idiosyncratic views will be greatest at the borderline between fact and ideology, or, in other words, at the point where the definition of the fact/ideology distinction matters most."[52]

The Rutherford argument is flawed by its failure to indicate why an ideology which is religious in nature does not violate the Establishment Clause when its teaching is mandated by the state,

---

[49] Besides the qualities of being "testable or falsifiable by empirical observation or experimentation . . . tentative or subject to modification or abandonment," the Academy added the feature, not present in the *McLean* definition, of science being able to "*predict* or explain phenomena in the natural world." Brief for Amicus Curiae, The National Academy of Sciences, Urging Affirmance, Edwards v. Aguillard, at 12 (emphasis added). They did not use the term "natural law" by which Judge Overton perhaps sought to link law and science under a rubric that has deep resonance throughout Western legal thought.

[50] *Id.* at 15.

[51] Brief of the Rabbinical Alliance of America, The Catholic Center, The Free Methodist Church of North America, The Honorable Robert K. Dornan, The Honorable William E. Dannemeyer, The Honorable Patrick L. Swindall, and the Committee on Openness in Science, Amici Curiae, in Support of the Appellants, Edwards v. Aguillard. The Rutherford Institute of Manassas, Virginia describes itself as a "non-profit legal defense organization that protects the freedom of religious expression." They have brought cases opposing abortion and favoring "family values," and, in a message from their founder and president, said of the film "The Last Temptation of Christ": "There is not room in the United States of America for this hateful denigration of Christianity or any religion." Action: A Monthly Publication of the Rutherford Institute 7–8 (August 1988).

[52] Brief of the Rabbinical Alliance at 11.

or whether the fact/ideology distinction really speaks to the issue of whether even a legislature has the right to require the teaching of a demonstrably false proposition simply because they choose to characterize it as an "interpretation." More troubling, however, is the argument of the Rutherford brief that any set of ideas is shot through with the meanings that those in power manage to have ascribed to them, and that those whose views are not part of the dominant discourse should be accorded the highest protection lest the possibility for articulating an alternative view be unduly burdened. They cite Thomas Kuhn for the proposition that "scientific knowledge, like language, is intrinsically the common property of a group or else nothing at all,"[53] and they thereby introduced a theme which continues to hover in the background of the Court's considerations.

When *Aguillard* was argued before the Court in December 1986 Louisiana was represented by Wendell Bird, a lawyer at the Institute for Creation Research and the same man whose 1978 Yale Law Journal student note served as the basis for the balanced treatment statutes passed by Arkansas and Louisiana.[54] Conceding at the outset that the statute did not have an exclusively secular purpose,[55] Bird insisted that creation science does not entail teaching about a personal Divinity.[56] However, on close questioning from the Court he did acknowledge that it was the State's view that one could not believe in both the Divine origination of life and its subsequent alteration through the processes described by the evolutionists.[57] He further responded, on rebuttal, to the question whether it would advance academic freedom if a legislature required that any student who studies German may not do so unless he gives equal time to the study of French by saying that the legislature would be free to do so if what they had in mind was "a basic concept of fairness; teaching all the evidence."[58]

---

[53]Kuhn, The Structure of Scientific Revolutions 210 (2d ed. 1970). On the social embeddedness of science, see text at note 90 *infra*.

[54]Note 15 *supra*. On the actual drafting of the statute see Nelkin, The Creation Controversy 99–100, 137–47 (1982).

[55]Official Transcript, Proceedings before the Supreme Court of the United States, Edwards v. Aguillard, December 10, 1986, at 4.

[56]*Id.* at 17.

[57]*Id.* at 23–29.

[58]*Id.* at 60.

It was mainly in the exchange between Justice Scalia and the lawyer for the statute's opponents, Jay Topkis, of the New York firm of Paul, Weiss, that the discussion turned to the relation between the state's purpose and its control over knowledge. Scalia posed the hypothetical of a teacher who, in order to call into question the Biblical version of the Crucifixion, instructs students that the Roman Empire did not extend to the eastern Mediterranean in the first century A.D. He asked whether the principal, responding to the concerns of religious students, could validly direct the teacher to teach the version of history that accords with those students' beliefs. Topkis acknowledged that it was indeed his client's burden to show that the motivation involved was to further religious ideas and not merely an action whose secular implications outweigh any religious impetus.[59] He continually returned for support to the plain meaning of "creation" as implying the presence of a Deity. Thus he answered the Court's question whether the legislature could rectify what they saw as a teaching imbalance by requiring equal time for creationism by reasserting that it is a particular religion which is here being given equal time.

The oral argument was noteworthy as much for what it left unsaid as for the topics that were considered. For instance, nothing was said about what would be the precise consequences of allowing the statute to stand or what, if anything, courts should declare science to be. That such issues were relevant appeared more clearly when the Court announced its decision.

Justice Brennan's majority opinion began by considering the state's argument that the predominant secular purpose of the statute was the promotion of academic freedom. Citing Mr. Bird's statement at the oral argument that the legislature had in mind a "basic concept of fairness; teaching all the evidence," the Court argued that such a goal is not furthered by forbidding one form of knowledge or by requiring the teaching of a religiously based alternative. Academic freedom, said the Court, means the freedom of teachers to teach what they deem appropriate. To the dissenters' argument that academic freedom inheres in the students rather than the teachers, Brennan said that, even if one accepted that position, the Louisiana approach actually limited the students' academic freedom because the teaching of creationism may result in "less

---

[59]*Id.* at 40–43.

effective and comprehensive science instruction."[60] While acknowledging that states ordinarily have full control over the school
curriculum, the majority clearly sought to limit this power when
the purpose of instruction is to further religious doctrine. In their
concurrence, Justices Powell and O'Connor similarly acknowledged that legislative control of educational policy is not limited
simply because that policy accords with those of various religions
and that "interference with the decisions of these authorities is
warranted only when the purpose for their decisions is clearly
religious."[61]

It was in the lengthy dissent of Justice Scalia, joined by Chief
Justice Rehnquist, that the issues raised by *Aguillard* become more
sharply delineated. Criticizing the majority for their refusal to
remand for a trial on the merits,[62] Scalia argued that the state is
entitled to judicial deference on the question whether creationism is
a science.[63] He attacked the use of the *Lemon* test by the majority—
as well as its overall validity—arguing that the purpose test should
mean the "actual" motives, the "sincerity," of the legislators not
whether any secular purpose can be found.[64] He challenged the
majority to realize that the religious activism that today gives rise to
the Balanced Treatment Act previously resulted in the abolition of
slavery.[65] He cited at length the creationists own assertions that
"creation science can and should be presented to children without
religious content," and that "evolution . . . is misrepresented as an

---

[60]Edwards v. Aguillard, 55 L.W. 4860, 4862 n.8 (1987).

[61]*Id.* at 4867.

[62]"...the question of [the statute's] constitutionality cannot rightly be disposed of on the
gallop, by impugning the motives of its supporters." *Id.* at 4868.

[63]"To begin with, the statute itself defines 'creation-science' as 'the *scientific evidences* for
creation and inferences from those *scientific evidences*.' ¶17.286.3(2) (emphasis added)." *Id.* at
4869. Scalia ignores the point made by Topkis that the choice of the word *evidences*, in the
plural, is itself derived from the rhetoric of Christian apologetics; it is never used this way
in secular statutory draftsmanship. At another point in the opinion he says "The Act defines
creation science as 'scientific evidenc[e].' ¶17:286.3(2) (emphasis added)..." thereby removing
the plural usage altogether. Moreover, by italicizing the words "scientific evidences" or
"evidenc[e]" Scalia discounts discussion of the key word "creation," and whether it
necessarily conveys the dictionary meaning of a divine act. Scalia says that creation could
involve an Aristotelian unmoved power, but then belies his own point by quoting the
statute's sponsor as having referred to "a creator *however you define a creator*" without asking
whether such a characterization could indeed include no creator at all. *Id.* at 4874 (original
italics).

[64]*Id.* at 4871.

[65]*Id.* at 4870.

absolute truth."[66] He characterized creationism as a "theory" and commented that "it surpasses understanding" how the Court can see a religious purpose in this statute.[67] He further asserted that there is "ample uncontradicted testimony that 'creation science' is a body of scientific knowledge rather than revealed belief"[68]—an apparent reference to the affidavits presented to the lower court by the creationists' experts. He closed with a renewed attack on the purpose prong of the *Lemon* test, arguing that it is time "that we sacrifice some 'flexibility' for 'clarity and predictability.' "[69]

II. COMPETING DISCOURSES

The opinions in *Aguillard* thus pose, with just that mixture of stentorial declaration and subtle indirection characteristic of many religion cases, not merely alternative results but alternative discourses. From Justice White's brief assertion that "this is not a difficult case . . . the state's primary purpose was to advance religion,"[70] to Justice Scalia's assertion that the case "cannot rightly be disposed of on the gallop,"[71] the rhetoric of the Court's members carries no terms or arguments not previously aired. Beneath the various opinions, however, there lie sets of concepts in which each places the issues and which may be insufficiently articulated precisely because they give the appearance of being insufficiently exact. Among those worth considering in this regard are the Court's idea of the relation between religion and conversation, the assessment of social harm, and the role of power over knowledge.

Although never expressed directly, a central feature of the majority's approach in *Aguillard* appears to be its concern that when strongly held religious views enter a public forum like that of the schools they put a stop to conversation rather than facilitating it: instead of engaging in the give-and-take, free play, marketplace of ideas process—all images the Court repeatedly employs— religious beliefs are often beyond discussion, beyond debate, beyond the very interchange for which these particular images are

---

[66]*Id.* at 4872.

[67]*Id.* at 4874.

[68]*Id.* at 4875.

[69]*Id.* at 4877.

[70]*Id.* at 4866.

[71]*Id.* at 4868.

supposed to stand. In the past, the issue has often been put in terms of divisiveness—the fear, as Justice Black once put it, "that state aid to religion . . . generates discord, disharmony, hatred and strife among our people."[72] At other times it has been framed in terms of tolerance, the Court itself having recently asserted that among the values "essential to a democratic society [is] tolerance of divergent political and religious views."[73]

But it might be argued that it is neither divisiveness nor tolerance as such that is at issue in *Aguillard* but to what extent, in a context like that involving the "balanced treatment" of mutually contradictory viewpoints, any position is constructed and held in such a way as to make further discussion about the issues it raises impossible.[74] It is a point that was made quite succinctly by John Dewey when he said that "democracy begins in conversation."[75] By this standard the Court could indeed allow a prayer at the commencement of legislative sessions because that prayer has nothing to do with the nature or capacity for subsequent conversation among the

---

[72]Board of Education v. Allen, 392 U.S. 236, 254 (1968) (Black, J., dissenting). Noting that even among fundamentalists the differences in sectarian prayers can be divisive, Justice Brennan, in his dissent in Marsh v. Chambers, 463 U.S. 783, 819 n.39 (1983) cited the following from a New York Times article: "Mr. [Jerry] Falwell [founder of the organization "Moral Majority"] is quoted as telling a meeting of the Religious Newswriters Association in New Orleans that because members of the Moral Majority represented a variety of denominations, 'if we ever opened a Moral Majority meeting with prayer, silent or otherwise, we would disintegrate.' "

[73]Bethel School District No. 403 v. Fraser, 106 S.Ct. 3159, 3164 (1986).

[74]The uncompromising position of many creationists is illustrated, for example, in the remarks by Paul Ellwanger, the author of the model bill from which the Louisiana and Arkansas balanced treatment acts were derived, who has said that the bill was written with "the idea of killing evolution instead of playing these debating games" and that "I view this whole battle as one between God and anti-God forces." Cited in McLean v. Arkansas Board of Education, 529 F.Supp. 1255, 1262, and 1261 (E.D. Ark. 1982). In a later suit by parents who objected to their children reading texts that would call upon the students to engage in an "occult practice" by using their imagination beyond the bounds of scriptural authority, the plaintiff-parent testified that if materials contrary to her religious views were taught her children "would have to be instructed to [the] error [of the other philosophy]." Mozert v. Hawkins County Board of Education, 827 F.2d 1058, 1064 (6th Cir. 1987), cert. den. 108 S.Ct. 1029 (1988). She further testified at trial that "We cannot be tolerant in that we accept other religious views on an equal basis with ours." Id. at 1069.

[75]Cited in White, Judicial Criticism, 20 Ga. L. Rev. 835 (1986). In a more expansive version, Dewey said: "The heart and strength of the democratic way of living are the processes of effective give-and-take communication, of conference, of consultation, of exchange and pooling of experiences—of free conversation if you will." Quoted in Flesch (ed.), The Book of Unusual Quotations 50 (1957).

legislators,[76] while refusing to require someone to affirm a belief in God when such affirmation, whatever else its defects, can do nothing to encourage further substantive discussion among those involved.[77] When the content of an instructional program is at issue this feature of conversational facilitation, arguably less controlling elsewhere, becomes preeminent and melds with the idea of democracy as a forum for exchange of ideas to yield the result that either one must be willing to engage in that give-and-take or use the nonpublic fora whose availability one is assured will be protected.

The idea of continuing the conversation is, moreover, closely connected to the Court's idea of harm.[78] For among the criteria that run through otherwise disparate results is the assessment of just how much harm is to result from allowing a given statute or practice to stand. Thus in *Marsh*, the legislative prayer case, the majority can say that there is "no real threat" posed by such a prayer. The harm to the Amish of state-mandated schooling beyond the eighth grade, by contrast, has been seen as one of potential destruction of the entire community;[79] the harm of state-mandated moments of prayer or silence is that of forcing children to do something one cannot ask them easily to refuse.[80] And requiring students to read books whose content they are not required to believe can do little harm in comparison to the benefits gained by practice in critical reading.[81] The assessment of harm turns in no

---

[76]See Marsh v. Chambers, 463 U.S. 783 (1983).

[77]See Torcaso v. Watkins, 367 U.S. 488 (1960); West Virginia Board of Education v. Barnette, 319 U.S. 624 (1943).

[78]See generally, Smith, The Special Place of Religion in the Constitution, 1983 Supreme Court Review 83, 94–100 (1984).

[79]Wisconsin v. Yoder, 406 U.S. 205 (1972).

[80]In Wallace v. Jaffree, 472 U.S. 38 (1985) the Court held unconstitutional an Alabama statute permitting a minute for meditation or voluntary prayer at the beginning of the school day. Confronted with a New Jersey statute providing only for a minute of silence at the beginning of the school day the Court held that the former presiding officers of the state legislature no longer had standing to bring the appeal, thus leaving the substantive validity of such statutes yet to be decided. Karcher v. May, 108 S.Ct. 388 (1987). Indicative of the students' ability to refuse to engage in a moment of silence may be the colloquy at the oral argument in *Karcher* between Justice Scalia and the attorney for the parents, students, and teacher, Norman L. Cantor: "Justice Scalia asked whether the students could not simply meditate during the minute of silence called for by the statute—whether they could not simply think about Ayn Rand or whatever. Third grade students are not capable of such contemplation, Cantor replied." Arguments before the Court, 56 L.W. 3282 (October 20, 1987).

[81]Mozert v. Hawkins County Board of Education, 827 F. 2d 1058 (6th Cir. 1987).

small part in these cases, then, on an assessment of whether a given practice will join people in common experiences through which a shared set of orientations can be engendered or whether it further separates people into their respective enclaves. No precise calculus of consequence can be constructed to determined when a "real threat" exists, but if the logic of the culture is one of encouraging interaction at least until, as an adult, one can assess the implications of one's difference, the concept of harm is neither empty nor unimportant.

If preservation of conversation and avoidance of real harm constitute aspects of the Court's jurisprudence of religion, how does it deal with the relationship between power and knowledge? One need not be either a legal realist or a convinced cynic to recognize that for many justices the religion clauses provide support for decisions based on other considerations, including those of public policy or the justices own "prepossessions."[82] But the Court has not made clear exactly what the limits of state control over classroom content are, short of prohibiting an outright establishment of religion. Thus Justice Black could "question whether it is absolutely certain . . . that academic freedom permits a teacher to breach his contractual agreement to teach only the subjects designated by the school authorities who hired him."[83] And the dissent in *Aguillard* would limit court oversight to demonstrations of actual religious motivation.

If the Supreme Court itself has at times avoided these issues, lower courts, working within the Court's uncertain doctrines, have occasionally confronted them more directly. Thus, in the case of *Mozert v. Hawkins County Board of Education*, the Sixth Circuit was called upon to consider the next tactical effort of the creationists, namely the claim that students should be allowed to opt out of studying the books comprising a basic reading series prescribed by the local board of education because they contain material contrary to the parents' religious beliefs. The court held that no First Amendment violation occurred inasmuch as the students were not, as Chief Judge Lively argued, required to believe what they studied

---

[82]This latter term comes from Justice Jackson's statement that in many Establishment Clause cases "we can find no law but our own prepossessions." McCollum v. Board of Education, 333 U.S. 203, 238 (Jackson, J., concurring); see also Kurland, The Irrelevance of the Constitution: The Religion Clauses of the First Amendment and the Supreme Court, 24 Vill. L. Rev. 3 (1978).

[83]Epperson v. Arkansas, 393 U.S. 97, 114 (1968).

or compelled to act in any way contrary to their beliefs.[84] Judge
Kennedy thought that, even if the students were burdened, the
state had a compelling interest in teaching the art of critical
reading.[85]

It is in the concurrence of Judge Boggs, however, that the most
forthright assessment of state power is articulated. Agreeing that
the schools cannot be asked to justify to courts every curriculum
decision they make,[86] Judge Boggs nevertheless found that the
school board was entitled to know that their control over curriculum is without limit so long as they do not seek to establish a
religion.[87] He noted that "we ultimately decide here, on the present
state of constitutional law, the school board is indeed entitled to say
'my way or the highway.' "[88] Plaintiffs *are* being compelled to an
irreligious act, he said, but as long as the issues are not taught as
religious truths the state may have complete power over the matter.

In *Mozert* the struggle for power over knowledge is openly
recognized. Are there, however, any limitations on state power
short of establishment?[89] It is naive, for example, to pretend that the
state is not always engaged in indoctrination through education, or
that the state favors or suppresses information less through overt
censorship than through the broader process by which a political
culture adopts and encourages information that supports the social
forms and institutions of those in power. Judge Boggs rightly asks
why these students may not opt out. The answer is: not so much
because of administrative costs or disruptions to schedules as
because our political system relies on its control over education as
one of its vehicles for orienting its citizenry in an acceptable
fashion, and a large part of this orientation turns on the image of the
conversation, the marketplace, the give-and-take in which all are

---

[84] Mozert v. Hawkins County Board of Education, 827 F. 2d 1058, 1064, and 1069 (6th Cir.
1987).

[85] *Id.* at 1070.

[86] *Id.* at 1080.

[87] "The school board recognizes no limitation on its power to require curriculum, no matter
how offensive or one-sided, and to expel those who will not study it, so long as it does not
violate the Establishment Clause. Our opinion today confirms that right, and I would like to
make plain my reasons for taking that position." *Id.* at 1073 (Boggs, J., concurring).

[88] *Id.* at 1074.

[89] For several views on the Court's approach to religion and the effects on state power, see
Bradley, Dogmatomachy—A "Privitization" Theory of the Religion Clause Cases, 30 St. L.
U. L. J. 275 (1986); Carter, Evolutionism, Creationism, and Treating Religion as a Hobby,
1987 Duke L. J. 977; Fish, Liberalism Doesn't Exist, 1987 Duke L. J. 997.

gathered simultaneously. It is in this context, too, that the definition of science and of academic freedom becomes relevant.

As we have seen, it was the *McLean* case that first proposed a
definition of science in the context of the Arkansas creationism case.
There, as in *Aguillard*, however, the easy assumption was made that
in the free marketplace of ideas scientific truth will emerge. Yet
clearly this is not always so: social, religious, political, and professional interests frequently have kept "scientific truths" obscured.
Science is the property of particular interest groups and like other
forms of knowledge is intimately linked to those who have power
over the channels of its legitimization.[90] The creationists may not
have made the strongest case possible for themselves,[91] yet it strains
credulity to assume that state power and free thought necessarily go
together. If *McLean* and *Aguillard* are taken as victories for free
thought, one must at least be candid enough to appreciate that there
is indeed a danger in allowing the courts to be the determiners of
what is science, or to assume that the resultant content of science is
somehow totally separable from culture and power.

In theory, of course, it is through the concept of academic
freedom that some check on state power can be fashioned. But
whose freedom is it, and at what price is it to be lodged in one
domain or another? The majority in *Aguillard* posits this freedom in
the teachers; the dissent says that academic freedom, as compre-
hended in the Louisiana statute, "meant *students'* freedom from
indoctrination."[92] Both approaches are somewhat disingenuous for
both are really contending, through teachers or students, over the

---

[90]On the view of science as deeply influenced by social and cultural forces, see generally
Kuhn, The Structure of Scientific Revolutions (2d ed. 1970); Foucault, The Archaeology of
Knowledge (1972); Hull, Science as a Process (1988). However, the vast majority of scientists
themselves believe that scientific truths exist apart from human values and that science is
structured on objective truths. Cole, Politics and the Restraint of Science 88–90 (1983). On
the history of restraints on science and scientific frauds, see Broad & Wade, Betrayers of the
Truth 193 (1982) ("history shows that, to the contrary, a community of scientists is often
ready to swallow whole dogma served up to them, as long as it is palatable and has the right
measure of scientific seasoning. . . . [O]bjectivity often fails to resist infiltration by dogma."
But see Cole & Cole, Social Stratification in Science 214–15 (1973) (although the social status
of scientists "may result in the temporary ignoring of some significant discoveries . . . [i]t is
possible that resistance to scientific discovery is not a significant problem in contemporary
science").

[91]On the issue of opting-out accommodations, see Mozert v. Hawkins County Board of
Education, 827 F.2d 1058, 1075 (6th Cir. 1987) (Boggs, J., concurring); McConnell,
Accommodation of Religion, 1985 Supreme Court Review 1 (1986).

[92]Edwards v. Aguillard, 55 L.W. at 4873 (original italics).

nature and scope of the power of the state itself. The majority thus fails to establish clear criteria for asserting the right of a teacher to violate a curriculum order from the state board of education;[93] the dissenters provide no guidance as to whether students may refuse to follow a state-mandated course of study whenever they feel that "all of the evidence"[94] on the subject addressed by that curriculum is not being provided them.[95]

Yet it is precisely because such ambiguities exist that one can profitably return to the image of the conversation for some guidance. For one could find implicit in the majority approach to *Aguillard* and other curriculum-related cases the concept that the public forum requires that ideas be part of a conversation, a process by which each agrees not merely to speak and listen but to remain open to the possibility of accepting the legitimacy of the outcome of discussion even if they "lose" in the competition for the minds and hearts of their opponents. This is not, it should be noted, an image of the conversation as requiring each group to accept the deniability of its ideas nor is it an image that implies that the resultant product is some undeniable truth. Rather, it is a *process* that is at issue here—a process of peaceful articulation of differences—and a *political* result—the mutual acceptance as legitimate of a process whose particular results may go against you. It is an image that gains support from the culture of which it is a part—a culture that has institutionalized give-and-take and fair play as a means of getting those who lose any given battle to accept the system as worthy of continued loyalty.

The Court is, in essence, setting the terms of the conversation. It does so when it supports the image of science as neutral and the exchange of ideas as necessitating a willingness to give and take. It does so, too, when it supports the idea that the centers of power in American life are multiple and dispersed. The harm the courts seek to protect against is harm to the process by which differences can be stated without the legitimacy of the state being placed at risk. It may do no harm to such a goal, however, for the courts to

---

[93]As Justice Stewart put it: "The States are most assuredly free 'to choose their own curriculum for their own schools.' A State is entirely free, for example, to decide that the only foreign language to be taught in its public school system shall be Spanish. But would a State be constitutionally free to punish a teacher for letting his students know that other languages are also spoken in the world? I think not." Epperson v. Arkansas, 393 U.S. 97, 115–16 (1968).

[94]Edwards v. Aguillard, 55 L.W. at 4873.

[95]See generally McConnell, Accommodation of Religion, 1985 Supreme Court Review 1.

acknowledge that science is a domain the courts should leave undefined or to acknowledge that while the forum is indeed one in which others must accept the courts' idea of what makes for a conversation, the nature of that conversation will itself not be subject to a fixed definition.

On its face, too, a proposition like that which finds conversation a central feature of the Court's approach may itself be challenged as no more principled than any of the other theories set forth in the Court's diverse cases involving the religions clauses. But this is true only if one equates principle with a particular sort of logical construct. If, instead, one thinks of a principle, in the context of the jurisprudence of religion, as the articulation of standards of legitimate conduct as evinced in an number of cultural domains, one can see that it is a socio-logic that is involved here—an attempt in a heterogeneous society to maintain concurrence among concepts whose very power lies in their inherent, indeed necessary, open-endedness. Wittgenstein once said that we should not try to understand a cloud through lines whose sharpness is contrary to the very form it seeks to represent. Similarly, cultural forms possess an inherent indeterminacy, a capacity for creating bonds of relationship through passing acquaintance, an ability to hold diverse groups together by means of common symbols imprecisely fixed. And just as the discursive styles of cultures vary depending on the ways in which diverse aspects of a culture are integrated, so, too, the characteristic voice of an American conversation appears lacking when the demand is made that others must be subjected to my view, that I must decide what may be uttered in my presence, or that if things do not go my way I may not acquiesce in your momentary gain. It is, in short, a jurisprudence of cultural form—not one that can be pejoratively dismissed as "flexible" when practiced by one side anymore than it will be devoid of the selfsame logic when purveyed under a contrary banner. Rather, it will always be true that knowledge is part of power just as both are part of culture, and the sense that one makes of a body of decisions will be seriously truncated if the localized form of cultural knowledge is measured against the inappropriate standard of philosophic logic alone.

III. Constructing a Common Discourse?

Many of the cases that invoke aspects of the religion clauses are quintessentially indeterminable as a matter of logic: any single logically consistent principle that can be enunciated necessarily implies a diminution or contradiction of the results implied by any other comparable precept. Yet propositions that seem to be at war in terms of one discourse may appear less irreconcilable when viewed against a cultural standard. When, therefore, the Court speaks of "the traditions of our people" or invokes constitutional precepts as symbolic unifiers, it displays what is arguably its single greatest power, the power to capture the terms of the discussion. And where the Court demonstrates that the principles lie in the overall process—in the willingness of the losers to accept contrary results yet continue to acknowledge the rules of contestability themselves—it demonstrates just how deeply the logic of its thought is bounded and suffused by the assumptions that characterize much of the larger culture.

The creationism decision becomes a special instance of this process for, as we have seen, the Court presents an implicit view of itself as the facilitator of a discourse and a conversation which it hopes will sound themes—of the marketplace of ideas, of give-and-take, of the relation of words to harm—that are consonant with the unspoken assumptions by which power has come to affect knowledge in our society. Obviously not all religion cases fit a conversational model: curriculum control cases may be assessed in terms of the debate they assist or curtail, as may a number of cases involving the extracurricular use for religious purposes of school facilities or the utterance of a pledge of allegiance; but cases involving the use of tax money for parochial education or complete opt-out programs would, whatever their other constitutional difficulties, run contrary to the effort to incorporate everyone into a common conversation. No single test may be appropriate to all cases, but cases may have to be openly considered for any impact they have on this common discussion rather than their possible inclusion under one or the other of the religion clauses. The result will not be the neat, idealized fit of the philosopher's imagination, but it will, perhaps, lead to a more honest expression of how power ought to relate to knowledge and thus itself contribute to the consensual pattern of legitimacy through which law, culture, and political form are indissolubly linked.

THOMAS R. McCOY
BARRY FRIEDMAN

CONDITIONAL SPENDING:
FEDERALISM'S TROJAN HORSE

INTRODUCTION

It is basic civics that the national government is one of delegated powers. All powers not delegated are retained by the state governments.[1] Although this theory has been strained in the last fifty years by expansive interpretation of Congress's delegated powers, the core theory itself had not been challenged until the Supreme Court's decision last term in *South Dakota v. Dole.*[2]

Dole involved a challenge to a condition attached by Congress to a federal grant;[3] the condition required states to raise their drinking

---

Thomas R. McCoy is Professor of Law and Barry Friedman is Assistant Professor of Law, Vanderbilt University.

AUTHORS' NOTE: The authors were on the brief in *Dole* filed by the National Conference of State Legislatures, U.S. Conference of Mayors, National Governors' Association, and National Association of Counties, as *amici curiae* in support of petitioners. The authors would like to thank Professor Albert Rosenthal and Benna Ruth Solomon for helpful comments on an earlier draft, and Don Mizerk and Alan Greenspan for their highly valued research assistance.

[1] The Tenth Amendment to the Constitution provides "The powers not delegated to the United States by the Constitution, nor prohibited by it to the States, are reserved to the States respectively, or to the people."

[2] 107 S.Ct. 2793 (1987).

[3] For additional literature on the subject of Congress's spending power, see Rosenthal, Conditional Federal Spending and the Constitution, 39 Stan. L. Rev. 1103 (1987); Stewart, Pyramids of Sacrifice? Problems of Federalism in Mandating State Implementation of National Environmental Policy, 86 Yale L. J. 1196 (1977); Comment, The Federal Conditional Spending Power: A Search for Limits, 70 Nw. U. L. Rev. 293 (1975); Note, 40 Vand. L. Rev. 1159 (1987).

age to a national minimum standard in order to continue to receive federal highway funds.[4] The *Dole* Court was willing to assume at the outset that Congress's delegated regulatory powers were insufficient to permit it to impose a national minimum drinking age through direct legislation.[5] But the *Dole* Court held that Congress could achieve the same end by requiring state implementation of the federal goal as a condition on the state's continued receipt of federal monies.[6]

The problem confronted by the *Dole* Court was the extent to which federally induced state reliance on federal moneys gives Congress regulatory authority over the states beyond that specifically delegated to Congress in the Constitution. The question was and is of central importance to the basic constitutional scheme of federalism. Over the course of the last several decades, the federal tax burden on individuals has increased substantially, making it increasingly difficult as a political matter for state legislatures to raise state taxes. At the same time that the federal tax burden has deterred states from raising their own revenue, national grant programs for general welfare purposes such as highways, education, and health have induced states to rely increasingly on national funds (funds obtained by the national government through taxes imposed upon the states' citizens) to fund state general welfare services.[7] Substantial state reliance on moneys raised by national taxation now is an accepted (if not acceptable) fact of political life in the federal system.

As a commonsense political matter, this financial dependence of the states on Congress's beneficence invites Congress to extract concessions from the states, to require that the states accept certain "conditions" in return for some of the revenues under Congress's control.[8] To the extent that the Court in *Dole* failed to devise and enforce workable constitutional limits on the conditions that Con-

---

[4]The National Minimum Drinking Age Act, 23 U.S.C. §158 (Supp. III 1985), directs the Secretary of Transportation to withhold federal highway funds from states with a minimum drinking age below 21. According to the Act, states with lower drinking ages will lose 5 percent in the year of enactment and 10 percent in each succeeding year.

[5]*Dole*, 107 S.Ct. at 2796.

[6]*Id*. at 2799.

[7]Garcia v. San Antonio Metro. Transit Auth., 469 U.S. 528, 552–53 (1985) ("[i]n the past quarter-century alone, federal grants to States and localities have grown from $7 billion to $96 billion" and "now account for about one-fifth of state and local government expenditures").

[8]See, *e.g.*, Highway Beautification Act, 23 U.S.C. §131 (1982); Rehabilitation Act of 1973, 29 U.S.C. §§701–94 (1982); National Health Planning and Resources Department Act of

gress can attach to federal grants, Congress is authorized and invited to regulate any matters beyond the scope of its specifically delegated powers by the simple device of extracting tax revenue from the citizens of the state, pursuant to the taxing power, and then returning that revenue to the state, under the spending power, on the condition that the state impose on itself or its citizens some regulation that Congress constitutionally could not have imposed itself. The *Dole* holding thus seriously undermines the role of state government in the federal system.

The tenor of the Court's opinion in *Dole* is that *Dole* was an easy case, quickly resolved by the simple application of settled precedent.[9] This, however, was anything but the case. *Dole* cannot be supported by prior spending-power precedent, for none of the established precedents in the spending clause area raised or resolved the question at issue in *Dole*.[10] Moreover, the *Dole* decision fails even to acknowledge precedent outside the spending clause context to the effect that where Congress constitutionally cannot impose a fine to regulate certain conduct, it cannot withhold a government benefit as a penalty for engaging in that same conduct.[11]

The lack of attention that the *Dole* decision received in the press and in scholarly circles is remarkable. The lack of notice attending *Dole* stands in sharp contrast to the hue and cry caused by *Garcia v. San Antonio Metropolitan Transit Authority*.[12] The consequences of *Dole* likely will be far greater than those of *Garcia*.

1974, 42 U.S.C. §§300k-300n (1982); Federal Urban Mass Transportation Act, 49 U.S.C. §1609(c) (1982). See Rosenthal, note 3 *supra*, at 1137–38.

[9]Justice O'Connor, in her dissenting opinion, characterizes the majority's treatment of the case as "cursory and unconvincing." *Dole*, 107 S.Ct. at 2799 (O'Connor, J., dissenting).

[10]See notes 96–151 *infra* and accompanying text.

[11]The essence of the *Dole* decision is that although Congress is without regulatory power to achieve an end under its delegated powers, the Congress can, by threatening to withhold a benefit, enforce the same regulatory policy. In the area of individual rights this legislative tactic is referred to as an "unconstitutional condition" and is impermissible. The best- known case for this proposition is Sherbert v. Verner, 374 U.S. 398 (1963).

[12]469 U.S. 528 (1985). In *Garcia* the Court overruled its decision in National League of Cities v. Usery, 426 U.S. 833 (1976), which sought to build an enclave protecting state government from undue federal interference. *National League of Cities'* demise in *Garcia* was widely and hotly debated. See, *e.g.*, Baird, State Empowerment after *Garcia*, 18 Urb. Law. 491 (1986); Field, Garcia v. San Antonio Metropolitan Transit Authority: The Demise of a Misguided Doctrine, 99 Harv. L. Rev. 84 (1985); Howard, Introduction: Garcia and the Values of Federalism, 19 Ga. L. Rev. 789 (1985); La Pierre, Political Accountability in the National Political Process—the Alternative to Judicial Review of Federalism Issues, 80 Nw. U. L. Rev. 577 (1985); Rapaczynski, From Sovereignty to Process: The Jurisprudence of

The identity of the author of the *Dole* opinion also might well have raised eyebrows. *Dole* was the product of a seven-Justice majority led by Chief Justice Rehnquist.[13] The Chief Justice generally is regarded as the staunchest "state's rights" ally on the Court. In *Garcia*, for example, the Chief Justice (who authored the *National League of Cities* decision) wrote a bitter dissent chastising the majority for disregarding state prerogatives and strongly suggesting that in time the tide would shift again.[14] Yet the Chief Justice authored the *Dole* decision, a decision that has much greater potential than *Garcia* to alter significantly the balance of power between the federal and state governments.

I. Of Federalism and Delegated Powers

Federalism—dual sovereignty—is one of the basic concepts around which American constitutional government is structured.[15] While establishing a national government of sufficient strength to bind and govern the Union, the Framers specifically accepted the continued existence of separate and independent state governments. There are two general views one can take of the Framers' decision to allow state government to exist alongside the national government that was the focus of their efforts. On the one hand, it historically is correct that the Framers simply had no choice, that a federal system was the only system likely to be ratified; and that is,

---

Federalism after Garcia, 1985 Supreme Court Review 341 (1985); Tushnet, Federalism and the Traditions of American Political Theory, 19 Ga. L. Rev. 981 (1985); Van Alstyne, The Second Death of Federalism, 83 Mich. L. Rev. 1709 (1985). Yet *National League of Cities* never played a very significant role in restricting federal power; in fact, the *National League of Cities* case represented the only instance in nearly a decade that the doctrine served to confine federal authority. See note 52 *infra*.

[13]Justices White, Marshall, Blackmun, Powell, Stevens, and Scalia joined in the opinion. Justices Brennan and O'Connor filed separate dissenting opinions.

[14]See *Garcia*, 469 U.S. at 580 (Rehnquist, J., dissenting).

[15]Justice Black, in his majority opinion in Younger v. Harris, 401 U.S. 37 (1971), wrote that the "entire country is made up of a Union of separate state governments [and] the states and their institutions are left free to perform their separate functions in their separate ways. . . . The concept [of federalism] does not mean blind deference to 'states' rights' any more than it means centralization of control over every important issue in our national government and its court. . . . What the concept does represent is a system in which there is sensitivity to the legitimate interests of both state and national governments." *Id*. at 44.

therefore, what the Framers provided.[16] On the other hand, it is clear from the debates in the state ratifying conventions and from other contemporary materials that, at the time of ratification, some opponents and proponents of the Constitution believed the federal system had much independently to commend it.[17]

Whatever the necessity of preserving state government as an accommodation to ensure ratification of the Constitution, subsequent experience has provided (and modern experience continues to provide) ample support for the proposition that the American federal system has its special virtues. Federalism has allowed for national control over problems truly national in scope, while preserving participatory democracy at the local level of governance.

Contrary to the fears of the anti-federalists, a strong national government has not yet robbed state government of its independent advantages. States continue to serve as laboratories for regulatory experimentation,[18] provide a forum for popular participation in democratic government, and permit local values to govern where appropriate.[19] Time and again it has been state government that provided innovative solutions to difficult societal problems.

It was inevitable from the start that dual sovereignty, despite its advantages, would give rise to tensions over the respective spheres of state or national governance.[20] As state and national governments pursue their own crowded agendas, disputes naturally arise as to the proper regulatory reach of each government. Sometimes the disputes concern direct congressional regulation of the states, or the question whether national activity in a regulatory sphere preempts

---

[16]See Lofgren, The Origins of the Tenth Amendment: History, Sovereignty, and the Problem of Constitutional Intention, in Constitutional Government in America 349 (Collins, ed., 1980) (pointing out that "had Americans in 1787–1788 believed the Constitution would 'reduce them [the states] to little more than geographical subdivisions of the national domain, . . . it would never have been ratified' ").

[17]See Storing & Dry, What the Anti-Federalists Were For 9–14 (1981); The Federalist No. 10 (Madison).

[18]See New State Ice Co. v. Liebmann, 285 U.S. 262, 311 (1932) (Brandeis, J., dissenting) ("It is one of the happy incidents of the federal system that a single courageous state may, if its citizens choose, serve as a laboratory; and try novel social and economic experiments without risk to the rest of the country").

[19]Kaden, Politics, Money and State Sovereignty: The Judicial Role, 79 Colum. L. Rev. 847, 854 (1979); Merritt, The Guarantee Clause and State Autonomy: Federalism for a Third Century, 88 Colum. L. Rev. 1, 8–9 (1988).

[20]Ironically, in The Federalist No. 17, Alexander Hamilton predicted that the tension would arise from states usurping federal power. The Federalist No. 17, at 98 (Hamilton) (Lodge, ed., 1908).

parallel or conflicting state programs.[21] At other times the dispute simply is about whether a particular regulatory area has been allocated by the Constitution to national or state control.[22]

Rather than decreasing over time, disputes over governance likely will become more prominent in the future. An increasingly complex society requires greater governmental intervention. Moreover, technological advances exacerbate tensions between national and state authority; these advances make the nation appear smaller, and difficulties frequently take on an appearance of being national in scope, making national solutions increasingly attractive.[23] In such an environment, pressures for national control increase, and it is all too easy to forget the values that flow from local governance.

Ultimately, the responsibility for resolving disputes between the national and state governments over respective spheres of responsibility falls to the Supreme Court. Although the Court has looked as an initial matter to the political process to attempt to resolve these disputes, the Court has had little choice but to take up the matter when the political process failed to afford satisfactory solution.[24] The disputes never have been susceptible to easy

---

[21]See, e.g., Pacific Gas & Elec. Co. v. State Energy Comm'n, 461 U.S. 190 (1983) (Atomic Energy Act of 1964 preempts all state safety regulations of the nuclear power industry); Hines v. Davidowitz, 312 U.S. 52 (1941) (federal Alien Registration Act preempted Pennsylvania's Alien Registration Act).

[22]Even when Congress has not acted affirmatively, the "dormant" or "negative" Commerce Clause may operate to restrict state regulation. See, e.g., Kassel v. Consolidated Freightways Corp., 450 U.S. 662 (1981).

[23]See Garcia, 469 U.S. at 581 (O'Connor, J., dissenting); see also Stern, The Commerce Clause Revisited—The Federalization of Intrastate Crime, 15 Ariz. L. Rev. 271, 284–85 (1983) (hereinafter Stern, Intrastate Crime).

[24]As early as Gibbons v. Ogden, 9 Wheat. 1 (1824), the Supreme Court indicated that it would allow the political process to control federalism issues. Chief Justice Marshall wrote that "[t]he wisdom and the discretion of Congress, their identity with the people, and the influence which their constituents possess at elections, are . . . the sole restraints on which they have relied, to secure them from its abuse. They are the restraints on which the people must often rely solely, in all representative governments." Id. at 197. Despite this early policy statement the Court did not rely exclusively on the political process. In a number of cases the Court struck down commerce regulation as infringing on state sovereignty. E.g., Carter v. Carter Coal Co., 298 U.S. 238 (1936); Hammer v. Dagenhart, 247 U.S. 251 (1918). See generally Stern, The Commerce Clause and the National Economy, 1933–1946 (pt. 1), 59 Harv. L. Rev. 645 (1946) (hereinafter Stern, Commerce Clause). Although other cases have announced a return to the principles of Gibbons, see, e.g., Wickard v. Filburn, 317 U.S. 111 (1942), Garcia is the only case to adopt expressly the political process as the exclusive restriction on congressional power.

solution, and the last half-century has seen wide swings in the Court's approach to the problem.[25]

The Supreme Court has made use of two very different doctrinal constructs to resolve national/state disputes. Under one construct, the concept of delegated powers, the Court reads the body of the Constitution in general, and the Tenth Amendment in particular, as an express allocation of legislative power between the states and the national government. The Tenth Amendment provides that the states retain those powers not explicitly delegated to the national government. Under the delegation construct, the Court protects the states from excessive national legislative activity, and thereby preserves a realm in which local decision-making predominates, by defining the expressly delegated powers of Congress in such a way as to deny Congress the power to adopt the challenged regulatory scheme.[26]

The Court employed the construct of delegated powers for most of the nation's history. Beginning with the first cases raising questions concerning the allocation of national-state power, the Court examined the Constitution to determine whether the legislation in question, generally a national enactment challenged as violative of state sovereignty, fell within Congress's delegated powers.[27] If so, the enactment was proper; if not, the enactment was invalidated and regulatory control over the matter thus was retained by state government.

During the course of the New Deal the delegation construct was used with widely disparate results. At the start of the New Deal the Court looked with a spare eye upon Congress's delegated authority, repeatedly holding that federal legislation enacted to address

---

[25]For example, compare Hammer v. Dagenhart, 247 U.S. 251 (1918), which invalidated federal child labor laws, with United States v. Darby, 312 U.S. 100 (1941), which overruled *Hammer* and sustained federal legislation imposing national minimum labor standards. See generally Stern, Intrastate Crime, note 23 *supra*. Of course, *National League of Cities* and *Garcia* are illustrative of this phenomenon.

[26]Prior to 1937 the Court had employed several restrictive doctrines, including: indirect-direct effects on commerce, see Carter v. Carter Coal Co., 298 U.S. 238 (1936); the stream of commerce requirement, see Stafford v. Wallace, 258 U.S. 495 (1922); the definition of commerce limitation, see Railroad Retirement Bd. v. Alton R. R., 295 U.S. 330 (1935).

[27]See, *e.g.*, McCulloch v. Maryland, 4 Wheat. 316 (1819). There, the Court began its inquiry into the constitutionality of a federal bank by noting that the power to incorporate such a bank was not expressly enumerated in the Constitution. *Id.* at 409. However, the Court went on to find that a federal bank was a legitimate means to exercise delegated powers and there was, therefore, an implied power to incorporate a federal bank. *Id.* at 411.

pressing national difficulties was invalid.[28] Then, however, the Court came to sustain most subsequent New Deal measures.[29] These later decisions adhered to the delegation construct, but adopted a sufficiently expansive view of Congress's authority under its delegated powers that even the most wide-ranging legislation could be sustained.

Once the expansion of Congress's delegated powers began, it quickly took on the appearance of being without limit. The concept of the national market was stretched, perhaps beyond recognition,[30] and then in the 1960s and 1970s Congress's commerce power was found broad enough to encompass regulation of local criminal conduct[31] and local instances of racial discrimination.[32] It became commonplace to assume Congress could do almost anything it cared to by relying on its delegated regulatory authority, the Commerce Clause in particular.[33]

---

[28]*E.g.*, Schecter Poultry Corp. v. United States, 295 U.S. 495 (1935).

[29]In five years, from 1937 to 1942, the Court completely reinterpreted the Commerce Clause to allow broad regulation of the national economy. See, *e.g.*, NLRB v. Jones & Laughlin Steel Corp., 301 U.S. 1 (1937); United States v. Darby, 312 U.S. 100 (1941); Wickard v. Filburn, 317 U.S. 111 (1942). The reversal coincided with President Roosevelt's "court-packing" plan. Not surprisingly the plan, which would have permitted the President to appoint a Supreme Court justice for every justice over the age of 70, was withdrawn as New Deal legislation was upheld by the Court. See generally, Stern, Commerce Clause, note 24 *supra*.

[30]In Wickard v. Filburn, 317 U.S. 111 (1942), the Court held that Congress could constitutionally regulate the local production and consumption of wheat. The Court sustained the Agriculture Adjustment Act on the grounds that Congress could reasonably conclude that home-produced wheat has a substantial economic effect on interstate commerce. *Id.* at 125. The Court admitted that Filburn's wheat was trivial by itself but the aggregate effect was "far from trivial." *Id.* at 127–28.

[31]See, *e.g.*, Perez v. United States, 402 U.S. 146 (1971) (sustaining congressional regulation of local loan shark activity). See generally Stern, Intrastate Crime, note 23 *supra*.

[32]See, *e.g.*, Heart of Atlanta Motel, Inc. v. United States, 374 U.S. 241 (1964); Katzenbach v. McClung, 379 U.S. 241 (1964). In the Civil Rights Cases of 1883, 109 U.S. 3 (1883), the Court had struck down the Civil Rights Act of 1875 on the grounds that neither the Thirteenth nor Fourteenth Amendment empowered Congress to reach anything but state action. In 1964, Congress was unwilling to risk a similar result. Thus, Congress, at the urging of Attorney General Robert Kennedy, based the Civil Rights Act of 1964 on the commerce power. See Hearings Before the Senate Committee on Commerce on S.1732, 88th Cong., 1st Sess., pts. 1 & 2.

[33]The civil rights cases and criminal cases show that Congress may regulate acts with no independent effect on interstate commerce, but which are part of a class that, as a whole, could be said to have such an effect. Fry v. United States, 421 U.S. 542, 547 (1975). As Justice O'Connor noted in her dissent to *Garcia*, "virtually every activity of a private individual [] arguably 'affects' commerce." *Garcia*, 469 U.S. at 584 (O'Connor, J., dissenting). See Perry, The Constitution, the Courts, and Human Rights 41 (1982) (arguing that the

The second theoretical construct found its genesis in what was perceived as the inadequacy of the original construct to limit federal authority, and thereby protect state sovereignty. Under the second construct, the Court read the delegation of legislative power to Congress essentially as unlimited (consistent with many post–New Deal decisions), while finding in the Tenth Amendment some protection of state autonomy from excessive national interference.[34]

This second construct—the enclave construct[35]—was devised by Chief Justice Rehnquist in his opinion for the Court in *National League of Cities v. Usery.*[36] The *National League of Cities* Court sought to carve out areas of "traditional governmental functions" where state freedom from national intervention would be paramount. If national regulatory requirements imposed on the states hampered state performance of essential functions within these areas of traditional governmental activity, then the national enactment would be invalidated as an interference with the state's constitutional right of autonomy.[37] Despite its apparent potential as a means

---

delegated powers are "quite indeterminate in scope"); Light, Jr., The Federal Commerce Power, 49 Va. L. Rev. 717, 728 (1963) ("In the light of Wickard v. Filburn, it is difficult to discern a meaningful limit to the [commerce] power, which now, as the Court asserted in 1946, 'is as broad as the economic needs of the nation.' "). See also Note, 41 Vand. L. Rev. 1019 (1988).

[34]The Court in *National League of Cities* seemed to be conceding the defeat of any attempt to limit Congress under the original construct and seemed to be offering the autonomy construct in place of the original construct. See Redish & Drizin, Constitutional Federalism and Judicial Review: The Role of Textual Analysis, 62 N.Y.U. L. Rev. 1, 9 (1987) ("As a practical matter, . . . it appears clear after *Garcia* that the Court will abstain from enforcing limits on the commerce power inherent in the structure of article I"). If one accepts that reading of *National League of Cities*, then *Garcia* will be seen not as a return to an earlier construct but as the abandonment of the only current attempt to restrain Congress with any construct at all. See note 32 *supra*. *Dole* then is perfectly consistent with *Garcia* as simply the continuing abandonment of any attempt to limit Congress through any doctrinal construct, new or old.

[35]Ely, The Irrepressible Myth of Erie, 87 Harv. L. Rev. 693 (1974), discusses the "enclave" approach and its effect on the Court's implementation of the *Erie* doctrine. For consideration of the dual federalism/enclave and delegation/checklist constructs, see Bator, National Supremacy or Dual Sovereignty, in Federalism: The Founders' Design 49–76 (Berger, ed., 1987).

[36]426 U.S. 833 (1976).

[37]*Id.* at 855. The Court later formalized the test in Hodel v. Virginia Surface Mining & Reclamation Ass'n., 452 U.S. 264 (1981), requiring that "in order to succeed, a claim that congressional commerce power legislation is invalid under the reasoning of *National League of Cities* must satisfy *each* of three requirements. First, there must be a showing that the challenged statute regulated the 'States as States.' Second, the federal regulation must address matters that are indisputably 'attribute[s] of state sovereignty.' And third, it must be

of limiting national authority, *National League of Cities'* impact was purely symbolic; that decision was the only instance in which the Court employed the test to invalidate national legislation.[38]

National League of Cities was destined for failure from the start. First, the *National League of Cities* construct rested upon the ability of the courts to draw distinctions that could not be drawn meaningfully. The protection from federal legislative interference with state government activities was confined to "traditional" and "essential" state functions. There was, however, no workable basis for determining those state functions that were traditional and those that were not.[39] The same verbal distinction between traditional and nontraditional functions already had been abandoned by the Court in related areas of constitutional analysis.[40] Even more important, the distinction between "traditional" activities reserved to the states and nontraditional areas over which the national congress could legislate had no basis in the constitutional scheme[41] or the set of values a federal government preserves. The essence of the federal system is that it is fluid and flexible, relegating certain problems to the national government when national solutions are needed, but leaving freedom for state regulation when state experimentation and local values are important.[42] The rigidity of the

---

apparent that the States' compliance with the federal law would directly impair their ability 'to structure integral operations in areas of traditional governmental functions.' . . . Demonstrating that these three requirements are met does not . . . guarantee [success]. There are situations in which the nature of the federal interest advanced may be such that it justifies state submission." *Id.* at 287–88.

[38]In the nine years between *National League of Cities* and *Garcia*, the Court handed down four decisions interpreting the *National League of Cities* doctrine and found the doctrine inapplicable in each one. See EEOC v. Wyoming, 460 U.S. 226 (1983) (no state government immunity from the Age Discrimination Act); FERC v. Mississippi, 456 U.S. 742 (1982) (no immunity for state public utilities from federal energy regulation); United Transp. Union v. Long Island R. R., 455 U.S. 678 (1981) (no immunity for state commuter railroads from Railway Labor Act); Hodel v. Virginia Surface Mining & Reclamation Ass'n, 452 U.S. 264 (1982) (federal surface mining regulations did not infringe state sovereignty).

[39]*Garcia*, 469 U.S. at 531.

[40]For examples, see *Garcia*, 469 U.S. at 540–44 (intergovernmental tax immunity) and *id.* at 545 (governmental tort liability).

[41]*Garcia*, 469 U.S. at 548–49.

[42]Stewart, Federalism and Rights, 19 Ga. L. Rev. 917, 917 (1985) ("Federalism seeks to maintain political decentralization and social diversity while simultaneously promoting national measures to meet national needs and prevent localized oppression"); Kaden, note 19 *supra*, at 855 ("The ultimate justification for federalism must be found in its potential to merge the advantages of localism for enhancing liberty with the necessity of a national government to cope with threats to security and prosperity"); Merritt, note 19 *supra*, at 36 ("a

"traditional governmental function" analysis was misplaced in an area where flexibility is essential.[43]

Second, there is the difficulty that the Constitution was drafted with the delegation construct in mind, not the enclave construct. The constitutional text expressly envisions a national Congress of delegated powers, with all powers not delegated being reserved to the states.[44] Indeed, the Tenth Amendment, frequently cited as the source of constitutionally based federalism principles, speaks explicitly of the delegation construct. The Tenth Amendment does not state that Congress shall make no law infringing the autonomy of the states. Rather, that Amendment states that those powers not delegated to the national government are retained by the states.[45] The *National League of Cities* decision was swimming upstream when it tried to impose a construct contrary to the one set out in the constitutional text.

Finally, and most important from the standpoint of federalism, the enclave construct as formulated by the Court lacked the capability of protecting the interests ostensibly protected by the constitutional text and the delegation construct. The *National League of Cities* test did not even come into play unless the federal enactment regulated "States qua States."[46] The concept thus was effective to invalidate national legislation only in that narrow range of cases where Congress sought to regulate directly the activity of state government. The historically more common form of federal legislative excess, direct regulation of individual conduct in areas where arguably the state retained the exclusive power to regulate that conduct, was left untouched by the enclave model as enunci-

---

workable concept of federalism . . . preserves the values of independent state governments without denying the federal government the power to address compelling natural concerns"); The Federalist No. 10, at 58 (Madison) (Lodge, ed., 1908) ("The federal Constitution forms a happy combination . . .; the great and aggregate interests being referred to the national, the local and particular to the State legislatures").

[43]The *Garcia* Court reasoned, as an additional justification for its holding, that the "traditional functions" test could stifle state experimentation. Since immunity from federal regulation hinged on judicial evaluation of state conduct, state legislatures might be reluctant to adopt new approaches for fear that the innovative program would not meet the "traditional functions" test. The Court concluded that overruling *National League of Cities* would restore states as laboratories for social and legislative experimentation. *Garcia*, 469 U.S. at 546–47. See Merritt, note 19 *supra*, at 14.

[44]See generally Redish & Drizin, note 12 *supra*.

[45]For the text, see note 1 *supra*.

[46]*National League of Cities*, 426 U.S. at 847.

ated in *National League of Cities*.[47] In other words, *National League of Cities* did little to protect the individual's interest in having regulatory decisions made by locally accountable political processes rather than by a distant national government.[48] *National League of Cities* thus failed to protect the triple virtues of local governance: incorporation of local values in regulatory schemes, local political participation, and maintenance of the states as laboratories for regulatory experimentation.

It is, therefore, unsurprising that a decade after its inception, the enclave construct was abandoned. In *Garcia v. San Antonio Metropolitan Transit*[49] the Supreme Court overruled *National League of Cities*, pronounced the "traditional governmental function" analysis an impossible one,[50] and expressed basic dissatisfaction with the view of the Court as a special protector of state sovereignty. The Court expressed the hope, as it had over 150 years before in *Gibbons v. Ogden*,[51] that the political process could resolve competing demands.[52] The *Garcia* Court referred vaguely to "affirmative limits" on congressional power, but provided no clue what those

---

[47]Field, note 12 *supra*, at 93 ("*Hodel* repudiated the idea that *National League of Cities* granted any immunity against Congressional regulation of the private sphere, even in areas traditionally left to the state").

[48]Rapaczynski, note 12 *supra*, at 362 ("[T]he decision in [*National League of Cities*] did not protect the states as governmental institutions in the sense . . . of assuring their ability to impose the ultimate rules of conduct in any given area of extragovernmental activities."); Field, note 12 *supra*, at 103 ("[N]o doctrine that protects the states only from direct regulation by the federal government . . . could go far in redressing the basic shift in power [from states to federal government]. As long as the federal government is free to regulate the states' citizens and corporations whenever it operates within its broad delegated powers, the very goals [of *National League of Cities*] cannot be achieved."

[49]469 U.S. 528 (1985).

[50]*Id*. at 546–47.

[51]9 Wheat. 1, 197 (1824). See note 24 *supra*.

[52]*Garcia*, 469 U.S. at 556 ("[T]he principal and basic limit on the federal commerce power is that inherent in all Congressional action—the built-in restraints that our system provides through state participation in federal governmental action"). The *Garcia* Court noted that "[i]n the factual setting of these cases the internal safeguards of the political process here performed as intended." *Ibid*. This caveat, in combination with other language found earlier in the opinion, *id*. at 554 ("substantive restraints . . . must be tailored to compensate for possible failings in the national political process"), has led Professor Andrzej Rapaczynski to argue that the judicial role after *Garcia* is confined to assessing the weaknesses of the political process in a manner reminiscent of the role carved out in footnote four of United States v. Carolene Products Co., 304 U.S. 144, 152–53 n.4 (1938). See generally Rapaczynski, note 12 *supra*. But see Van Alstyne, *ibid*.

limits might be or under what circumstances the Court would enforce them.[53]

If constitutional federalism is to survive, the overruling of *National League of Cities* in *Garcia* must be seen as a return to the delegation construct. If the constitutionally based federal structure is to have meaning, it must find an accommodation of interests by resolving questions with reference to Congress's delegated powers. The question whether a given enactment is within Congress's delegated regulatory power concededly is a difficult one.[54] Unlike the "traditional state function" question posed in *National League of Cities*, however, this difficult question is the one compelled by the Constitution, with support in the constitutional text. This is the inquiry that seeks to strike an appropriate balance between national and state regulatory control.

A proper analysis of Congress's delegated regulatory power to pass a given enactment would focus not upon whether the enactment infringed some core state power, but upon whether the enactment was a proper subject of federal regulation. This requires an assessment of the national interest in the object of the regulation, the extent to which the object of the regulation involves interstate independence, and the appropriateness of the object for national uniform regulation. The Court would need to weigh these factors militating in favor of national regulation against the desirability of local political control, the preservation of local values, and the "experimentation" value of permitting differing state approaches to the problem.

It is true that national regulation increasingly is important to address modern problems.[55] This is to be expected in a highly industrialized and technologically advanced society. But it is equally important to bear in mind that there are other areas— education being a particularly appealing example—where local values and experimentation remain critical. Claims of absolute

---

[53]469 U.S. at 556.

[54]See Perry, note 33 *supra*, at 41.

[55]Justice O'Connor recognized this in her dissent to *Garcia*. 469 U.S. at 583 (O'Connor, J., dissenting). For example, Congress has enacted legislation governing: labor relations, see National Labor Relations Act, 29 U.S.C. §§151–169 (1982 & Supp. III 1985); civil rights, see 42 U.S.C. §§1981–2000h (1982 & Supp. III 1985); atomic energy, see 42 U.S.C. §§2011–2296 (1982 & Supp. III 1985); and environmental policy. See 42 U.S.C. §§4321– 4370 (1982 & Supp. III 1985). For an inquiry into the limits of congressional power to regulate these activities, see Note, note 33 *supra*.

national power too quickly and easily forfeit the advantages of local control.

In a post-*Garcia* world, therefore, the Court ought properly to face up to the responsibility of defining, even on a case-by-case basis, the respective spheres of federal and state government.[56] At the least, one would expect such an attempt from those Justices on the Court who avow a firm belief in the virtues of strong state government. It was no little surprise, therefore, that in *South Dakota v. Dole*, the first post-*Garcia* case raising the issue of state-national authority, the Court not only failed to utilize the delegation construct in a meaningful manner to resolve the dispute before it, but *de facto* abandoned the delegation construct entirely.

II. SOUTH DAKOTA V. DOLE

South Dakota v. Dole[57] involved a challenge to the National Minimum Drinking Age (NMDA) amendment to the National Surface Transportation Act.[58] The Surface Transportation Act authorizes the national government to provide moneys to the states for the construction of national highways.[59] The NMDA conditions receipt of some of those funds upon state enactment of a twenty-one-year-old drinking age. The NMDA instructs the Secretary of Transportation to withhold up to 10 percent of a state's federal highway funds if that state fails to enact the twenty-one-year-old minimum drinking age within one year after enactment of the NMDA.[60] Thus, through the use of a condition attached to a spending grant, Congress sought to impose a national minimum drinking age.

Although a number of states complied with the NMDA, or enacted compliant legislation that would remain in effect until such

---

[56]But see Wechsler, The Political Safeguards of Federalism: The Role of the States in the Composition and Selection of the National Government, 54 Colum. L. Rev. 543, 559 (1954) ("[T]he Court is on weakest ground when it opposes its interpretation of the Constitution to that of Congress in the interest of the states, whose representatives control the legislative process and, by hypothesis, have broadly acquiesced in sanctioning the challenged Act of Congress"); Choper, Judicial Review and the National Political Process (1980) (expanding on Professor Wechsler's theory and advocating that the Court hold federalism issues to be nonjusticiable political questions).

[57]107 S.Ct. 2793 (1987).

[58]23 U.S.C. §158 (Supp. III 1985).

[59]See 23 U.S.C. §§101–408 (1982 & Supp. IV 1986).

[60]23 U.S.C. §158(a) (2). See note 4 *supra*.

time as the NMDA might be declared unconstitutional,[61] South Dakota challenged the act. The primary basis of South Dakota's challenge, and the ground upon which the parties presented the case to the Supreme Court, was that enactment of the NMDA violated the limitations of the Twenty-first Amendment.[62] The Twenty-first Amendment, ratified to repeal Prohibition, provides generally that alcoholic beverages shall not be imported or distributed in the states in violation of state law.[63] South Dakota took the position that, under the Twenty-first Amendment, enactment of a minimum drinking age was a matter solely within the discretion of state government, and thus outside the scope of congressional control.[64]

South Dakota argued that the Twenty-first Amendment was not, as it appeared to be on its face, a simple readjustment in the allocation of powers between the states and the federal government. The state constructed its entire argument around the contention that the Twenty-first Amendment was an "independent bar" to congressional action,[65] analogous to the prohibitions found in the First and Fifth Amendments. Because the prohibitions of the First and Fifth Amendments apply to all congressional action under any

[61]For example, section 4 of South Carolina 1985 Act No. 117 states: "[If] Public Law 98–363 [the National Minimum Drinking Age Amendment] is enjoined by a court of competent jurisdiction or declared by a court to be contrary to the United States Constitution, the provisions of sections 61–9-40, 61–9-455, and 20–7-370 of the 1976 Code shall be effective under the terms and conditions as existed prior to the amendments contained in Sections 1, 2, and 3." 1986 S.C. Acts 117, §4.

[62]See Brief for Respondent at 23–36, South Dakota v. Dole, 107 S.Ct. 2793 (1987) (No. 86–260); Brief for Petitioner at 23–63, South Dakota v. Dole, 107 S.Ct. 2793 (1987) (No. 86–260).

[63]The Twenty-first Amendment was ratified December 5, 1933. Section 1 of the Amendment expressly repeals the Eighteenth Amendment and section 3 describes a seven-year time period for ratification. Section 2 provides: "The transportation or importation into any State, Territory, or possession of the United States for delivery or use therein of intoxicating liquors in violation of the laws thereof, is hereby prohibited."

[64]Dole, 107 S.Ct. at 2795. South Dakota relied on the language in California Retail Liquor Dealers Ass'n v. Midcal Aluminum, Inc., 445 U.S. 97 (1980). There, the Court stated that the Twenty-first Amendment grants the states "virtually complete control" over the regulation of liquor importation, sale, and distribution. Id. at 110. The Secretary of Transportation responded to South Dakota's argument by acknowledging the states' broad regulatory power but asserting that Congress retained the power to prohibit sales. Dole, 107 S.Ct. at 2795. The anomolous implication of the Secretary's argument is that Congress may "prohibit" but not "regulate" the sale of liquor under the Twenty-first Amendment. But cf. Champion v. Ames (The Lottery Case), 188 U.S. 321 (1903) (holding that the power to regulate included the power to prohibit).

[65]Dole, 107 S.Ct. at 2797.

delegated power, including spending,[66] the state argued that the "prohibition" of the Twenty-first Amendment also applied to any exercises of the spending power.[67] The state's exclusive reliance on this "independent bar" argument proved unwise when the Court quickly and easily concluded that the Twenty-first Amendment was not analogous to the First and Fifth Amendments and imposed no such "independent bar" to congressional action pursuant to a clearly delegated power.[68] Rather, the Court decided, the Twenty-first Amendment simply reduced the powers originally delegated to Congress in the Commerce Clause and correspondingly enhanced the powers retained exclusively by the states.[69]

Although there was considerable debate before the Court in *Dole* about the scope of the Twenty-first Amendment, the Court assumed for purposes of the case that Congress under its post-Twenty-first Amendment delegated powers could not have enacted a regulation requiring that each state government legislate a twenty-one-year-old minimum drinking age for the state.[70] Nor, concomitantly, could Congress constitutionally have enacted a simple regulation directly prohibiting all individuals within any state from purchasing or consuming alcohol before they reached twenty-one years of age. Thus, the only issue left for the *Dole* Court to resolve was whether the NMDA was constitutional as a condition accompanying a congressional grant of federal funds to the states even though Congress could not regulate drinking ages directly under any of its delegated legislative powers.

The *Dole* Court observed that, "Congress has acted indirectly under its spending power to encourage uniformity in the States' drinking ages."[71] Thus, the legislation was "within constitutional bounds even if Congress may not regulate drinking ages directly."[72] In essence, the Court held that although Congress lacks regulatory

---

[66]"Neither Congress nor the States may act in a manner prohibited by any provision of the Constitution." Hodel v. Virginia Surface Mining & Reclamation Ass'n, 452 U.S. 264, 312–13 (1981) (Rehnquist, J., concurring).

[67]South Dakota argued that "Congress may not use the spending power to regulate that which it is prohibited from regulating directly under the Twenty-first Amendment." Brief for Petitioner at 52–53, South Dakota v. Dole, 107 S.Ct. 2793 (1987) (No. 86–260).

[68]*Dole*, 107 S.Ct. at 2798.

[69]See *id.* at 2798–99.

[70]See *id.* at 2796.

[71]*Ibid.*

[72]*Ibid.*

authority to achieve a legislative end on its own, the Congress may "purchase" state compliance through the use of conditions attached to spending grants.[73] The chief limitation upon this broad view of the spending power, according to the Court, was that Congress could "tempt" the states with federal funds, but it could not "coerce" state conduct in this manner.[74]

For the Court, the conclusion that Congress could use conditions attached to federal grants to achieve ends otherwise outside the scope of Congress's delegated regulatory powers apparently was an easy one. According to the Court, the reach of Congress' spending power was broader than that of the delegated regulatory powers.[75] Moreover, the Court frequently had upheld the use of conditions on federal grants to "further broad policy objectives."[76] Hence, Congress could impose conditions on grants to purchase compliance with regulatory objectives otherwise outside Congress's reach.[77] The very simplicity of the Court's decision suggested no new ground was being broken.

Despite the apparent simplicity of the Court's reasoning, the decision in *Dole* was unprecedented. The basis of the Court's holding is that there is a difference between coercing compliance (an exercise of regulatory power) and buying compliance (an exercise of the spending power).[78] Yet settled precedent outside the spending area makes clear that contrary to the Court's suggestion that buying compliance differs from coercing it, the two means of achieving compliance conceptually are indistinguishable.[79] Moreover, settled spending cases, rather than supporting the Court's argument as the Court's opinion suggests, make quite clear that Congress cannot attach conditions to spending grants to achieve

---

[73] The Court's holding on this point is quite explicit: "[E]ven if Congress might lack the power to impose a national minimum drinking age directly, we conclude that encouragement to state action found in [the NMDA] is a valid use of the spending power." *Id.* at 2799.

[74] See *id.* at 2798. For consideration of the coercion limitation on congressional spending power, see Rosenthal, note 3 *supra*, at 1125–42; Note, note 3 *supra*, at 1179–85.

[75] *Dole*, 107 S.Ct. at 2796 (quoting United States v. Butler, 297 U.S. 1 (1936)).

[76] *Ibid.*

[77] *Ibid.*

[78] "[I]n some circumstances the financial inducement offered by Congress might be so coercive as to pass the point at which 'pressure turns into compulsion.' . . . Here Congress has offered relatively mild encouragement to the States to enact higher minimum drinking ages." *Dole*, 107 S.Ct. at 2798 (citation omitted).

[79] See notes 88–95 *infra* and accompanying text.

regulatory goals outside Congress's power, precisely because this would eviscerate the concept of a national government of limited powers. In ignoring sound and settled principles, the *Dole* Court invited the complete abrogation of any limits on the delegated powers of Congress.

The essence of federalism and the scheme of delegated powers is that Congress may legislate or regulate only pursuant to specific powers expressly delegated in the Constitution. Congress may not impose regulatory requirements, even though admittedly in the interest of the common good and general welfare, unless the area regulated is one over which regulatory control is delegated specifically to Congress.[80] Congress may, however, spend federal funds for any purpose that can be thought to contribute to the general welfare,[81] even though none of Congress' delegated legislative powers encompasses the subject of the expenditure.[82] In other words, the delegated power to spend money for the general welfare is a power separate from and in addition to all of Congress's specific delegated legislative or regulatory powers. In its simplest form, the issue in *Dole* was whether Congress could use its spending power to offer a financial inducement, a reward, for conduct that it could not directly require or regulate under any of its delegated legislative powers. Stated another way, does Congress's grant of spending power empower Congress to purchase compliance with a legislative objective when Congress could not under any of its delegated powers require compliance with that objective?

It is true that by its terms the spending power is "broader" than the delegated regulatory powers.[83] On their face the regulatory powers are granted for specific purposes, such as raising armies,[84]

---

[80]See Hodel v. Virginia Surface Mining & Reclamation Ass'n, 452 U.S. 264, 311 (1981) (Rehnquist, J., concurring) ("the connection with interstate commerce is itself a jurisdictional prerequisite for any substantive legislation by Congress under the Commerce Clause"). Cushman, The National Police Power under the Commerce Clause of the Constitution, (pt. 1), 3 Minn. L. Rev. 289, 291 (1919). ("The enumeration of congressional powers in the Constitution does not include any general grant of authority to pass laws for the protection of the health, morals, or general welfare of the nation.")

[81]U.S. Const., Art. I, §8. See Rosenthal, note 3 *supra*, at 1111–13; Note, note 3 *supra*, at 1163–68.

[82]United States v. Butler, 297 U.S. 1, 66 (1936) ("[T]he power of Congress to authorize expenditure of public moneys for public purposes is not limited by the direct grants of legislative power found in the Constitution").

[83]*Ibid.*

[84]U.S. Const., Art. I, §8, cl. 12.

minting coin,[85] or governing interstate commerce.[86] In contrast, Congress has the power to spend (and tax) limited only by the qualification that the expenditure be for the "general welfare."[87] In this sense Congress's spending power is indeed "broader" than the delegated regulatory powers. This does not necessarily mean, however, that because Congress may spend for the general welfare, it may use the spending power to circumvent all limitations on its regulatory powers.

It is axiomatic that the power to spend carries with it the power to attach certain conditions to the expenditure. Those conditions in effect would be specifications as to how Congress intends that the grant be used. For example, if Congress grants the states funds to build highways, Congress must have the concomitant power to specify where the highways should run, or how they should be built. This power to impose conditions permits Congress to ensure that its money is spent as Congress wished. And, if Congress wishes to spend to achieve "broad policy objectives," it may use the power to attach conditions to achieve those objectives. But this does not mean that Congress may attach conditions to achieve policy objectives that are independent of the object of the expenditure.

The *Dole* problem arises when Congress seeks to purchase not goods and services, but compliance with legislative objectives that normally would be pursued by simple regulations backed by the usual regulatory penalties such as a fine for violation. In individual liberties cases, First Amendment cases in particular, the Court has recognized that offering a governmental benefit on the condition that the individual refrain from engaging in protected activities is the constitutional equivalent of imposing a fine for the violation of a regulation prohibiting the activity.[88] Either presents the same governmental interference with the individual's constitutionally protected liberty to engage in the conduct.

---

[85]*Id.* at cl. 5.

[86]*Id.* at cl. 3.

[87]*Id.* at cl. 1. See Helvering v. Davis, 301 U.S. 619, 640 (1937); United States v. Butler, 297 U.S. 1, 65–66 (1936).

[88]See, *e.g.*, FCC v. League of Women Voters, 468 U.S. 364 (1984) (invalidating conditional grant to television and radio stations because it abridged freedom of the press); Thomas v. Review Bd. of the Ind. Employment Sec. Div., 450 U.S. 707 (1981) (invalidating state unemployment benefits conditioned on religious practices); Sherbert v. Verner, 374 U.S. 398 (1963) (same). See McCoy & Mirra, Plea Bargaining as Due Process in Determining Guilt, 32 Stan. L. Rev. 887, 889–93 (1980).

Sherbert v. Verner[89] is the best known of these cases. In *Sherbert* the Court struck down a South Carolina unemployment compensation plan that conditioned the award of benefits upon the beneficiary being "available to work" on Saturdays.[90] Plaintiff, a Saturday Sabbatarian, challenged the scheme as violative of her right to free exercise of her religion. The state's defense was that the condition in question did not inhibit free exercise in a regulatory fashion—by coercing or penalizing constitutionally permitted conduct—but only withheld a grant of benefits.[91] Rejecting the defendant's argument, the Court held that "disqualification for benefits" can penalize constitutionally permitted conduct in the same way that a regulatory fine would penalize the conduct.[92] In the words of the Court, it was impermissible to use a benefit scheme to " 'produce a result which the State could not command directly.' "[93]

Sherbert v. Verner, and the line of cases that follow it, recognize what the *Dole* Court refused to acknowledge. Withholding of a state-created benefit to obtain compliance, is, in effect, identical to regulatory coercion to obtain the same end.[94] Thus, if achievement of an end is beyond Congress's means regulatorily, it also is invalid as part of a benefit scheme. In *Dole* the Court was willing to assume that Congress could not impose a minimum drinking age through the exercise of its regulatory powers, but permitted Congress to withhold benefits (highway funds) to obtain the same end. Yet the *Dole* Court did not acknowledge, let alone explain, the fundamental inconsistency between its position and the established doctrinal basis of *Sherbert v. Verner*.[95]

Cases arising under the spending clause prior to *Dole* already had recognized that there is no conceptual difference between withhold-

---

[89]374 U.S. 398 (1963).

[90]*Id*. at 400 n.3.

[91]*Id*. at 403.

[92]*Ibid*.

[93]*Id*. at 405 (quoting Speiser v. Randall, 357 U.S. 513, 526 (1958)).

[94]*Sherbert*, 374 U.S. at 404 ("[Conditional benefits exert] the same kind of burden . . . as would a fine").

[95]Another interpretation of the majority opinion might be that the Court considered, yet implicitly rejected, the Sherbert v. Verner argument in the context of the *Dole* case, which involves "state's rights" rather than individual rights. It is hard to believe that is what occurred in *Dole*, however. It would be quite curious for the Court to resolve this novel and important question without any discussion, *sub silentio*. The most likely explanation for *Dole* is that the majority never considered the Sherbert v. Verner problem.

ing a benefit and imposing a fine to achieve a regulatory end and had applied this principle in the federalism context. The two seminal spending cases, *United States v. Butler*,[96] and *Steward Machine Co. v. Davis*[97] not only are consistent with *Sherbert v. Verner* in this regard, but they also specifically repudiate the Court's claim in *Dole* that Congress could, through spending conditions, achieve ends outside Congress's delegated regulatory powers. Justice Rehnquist's opinion in *Dole* purported to rely heavily upon *Butler* and *Steward*, but that reliance demonstrably was misplaced.

The starting point for analysis is *Butler*. *Butler* involved a challenge to portions of the Agricultural Adjustment Act of 1933, pursuant to which processors of certain agricultural goods were taxed, the proceeds from the tax being earmarked to make payments to producers to allow their land to lie fallow.[98] The purpose of the scheme was to stabilize farm prices by controlling the supply of farm goods in the market.[99] Respondents challenged the scheme as beyond the scope of Congress's delegated powers, primarily the interstate commerce power, because the act sought to regulate purely local activities. The United States did not attempt to defend the scheme as a valid commerce regulation, but argued that the appropriations for fallow land payments were valid under the spending clause.[100] In essence, the United States argued that, assuming the program was outside Congress's regulatory powers, it still could be sustained as a valid exercise of Congress's authority to spend "for the general welfare."[101]

The *Butler* Court disagreed, holding that the scheme was invalid precisely because Congress used its spending power to achieve a regulatory effect otherwise outside the scope of Congress's delegated powers.[102] In reaching that conclusion the Court conceded that the taxing and spending powers, limited only by the requirement that they be exercised for the general welfare, necessarily were broader than the other delegated powers.[103] In fact, this is the

---

[96] 297 U.S. 1 (1936).

[97] 301 U.S. 548 (1937).

[98] *Butler*, 297 U.S. at 58–59.

[99] *Id.* at 63–64.

[100] *Id.* at 64.

[101] *Id.* at 62.

[102] *Butler*, 297 U.S. at 77.

[103] *Id.* at 66.

very language relied upon by Justice Rehnquist in *Dole* for the same proposition,[104] but the proposition carried different implications for the *Butler* Court. The *Butler* Court invalidated the scheme because it was not a simple exercise of Congress's power to spend, but was "[a]t best . . . a scheme for purchasing with federal funds submission to federal regulation of a subject reserved to the states."[105] Thus, in a holding directly pertinent to *Dole*, the *Butler* Court distinguished between an expenditure valid because it was an exercise of spending for the general welfare, and one invalid because it was instead an attempt at regulation by buying compliance. The Court distinguished between conditional appropriations where the condition specifies how money is to be spent, which is valid, and conditional appropriations where the goal of the condition is regulation:[106]

> There is an obvious difference between a statute stating the conditions upon which moneys shall be expended and one effective only upon assumption of a contractual obligation to submit to a regulation which otherwise could not be enforced.

Butler did not involve a condition that specified how money was to be spent; rather, the Agricultural Adjustment Act involved an expenditure only if the recipients agreed to be bound by federal regulation. Justice O'Connor dissented in *Dole*, relying precisely on this distinction made in *Butler*.[107] Justice O'Connor's dissent makes clear that she would uphold conditions that specify how federal money is to be spent, and would strike conditions that go beyond this, to the extent the condition could not otherwise be supported by one of Congress's delegated regulatory powers. Quoting directly from the brief of *amici*, she states:[108]

---

[104]*Cf. Dole*, 107 S.Ct. at 2797.

[105]*Butler*, 297 U.S. at 72.

[106]*Id.* at 73. What was obvious to the *Butler* Court evidently eluded Chief Justice Rehnquist completely in *Dole*. Not only is *Dole* squarely contrary to this aspect of *Butler*, but the Chief Justice explicitly rejects the distinction set out above. *Dole*, 107 S.Ct. at 2799. Justice O'Connor's dissent, however, heeded the distinction. *Id.* at 2802 (O'Connor dissenting) ("Rather than a condition determining how federal highway money shall be expended, [the NMDA] is a regulation determining who shall be able to drink liquor. As such it is not justified by the Spending Power").

[107]*Dole*, 107 S.Ct. at 2801 (O'Connor, J., dissenting).

[108]*Id.* (quoting from Brief of the Nat'l Conference of State Legislatures et al. as Amici Curiae, South Dakota v. Dole, 107 S.Ct. 2793 (1987) (No. 86–260)).

Congress has the power to *spend* for the general welfare, it has the power to *legislate* only for delegated purposes. . . .

The appropriate inquiry, then, is whether the spending requirement or prohibition is a condition on a grant or whether it is a regulation. The difference turns on whether the requirement specifies in some way how the money should be spent, so that Congress' intent in making the grant will be effectuated. Congress has no power under the Spending Clause to impose requirements on a grant that go beyond specifying how the money should be spent. A requirement that is not such a specification is not a condition, but a regulation, which is valid only if it falls within one of Congress' delegated regulatory powers.

Butler, therefore, rather than supporting the Court's decision in *Dole*, is precisely to the contrary. *Butler* holds that Congress cannot use an expenditure, or a condition attached to a grant, to achieve a regulatory purpose outside the scope of Congress's delegated regulatory authority.[109] Because regulation of local agriculture was deemed by the *Butler* Court to be outside of Congress's commerce power, the scheme was invalid, even though it was accomplished not by coercive regulation but by taxing and spending.[110]

It is fair to caution against undue reliance upon *Butler*. By modern standards *Butler* was decided wrongly, and widely is seen as discredited.[111] But it is important to focus precisely upon why this is so. *Butler's* error was not in holding that spending legislation could not be used to accomplish regulatory ends outside Congress's delegated powers, but in defining the scope of Congress's delegated regulatory powers too narrowly. After recognizing the Agricultural Adjustment Act for what it was—not an exercise of the spending power, but a regulatory scheme—the Court turned to the question whether the regulatory scheme nonetheless was valid under Congress's commerce power.[112] *Butler's* error, by modern standards, was in adopting a narrow interpretation of Congress's commerce power that disallowed price-support legislation. Such a result

---

[109]*Butler*, 297 U.S. at 74.

[110]*Ibid.*

[111]See, *e.g.*, Rosenthal, note 3 *supra*, at 1126–28.

[112]The government preemptively disclaimed reliance on the Commerce Clause as a means to justify the Agricultural Adjustment Act and, therefore, the Court did not analyze the issue in detail. *Butler*, 297 U.S. at 64. The Court in prior cases and in *Butler* itself gave every indication that the Act would be invalid under the Commerce Clause. *Id.* at 63–64; *id.* at 68.

would not obtain today.[113] But the *Butler* Court's perception that the AAA was regulation, not spending, is unassailable.

Despite relying heavily on *Butler* for propositions about the breadth of the spending power, Chief Justice Rehnquist directly assaulted *Butler's* holding that conditional spending is the conceptual and economic equivalent of direct regulation.[114] The Chief Justice reverted to the thoroughly discredited notion that compliance with a condition attached to a benefit is "voluntary" as long as the potential recipient can choose to forgo the benefit in order to avoid compliance with the condition.[115] As authority for this proposition, he cited *Steward Machine Co. v. Davis*,[116] which many casual observers, apparently including Chief Justice Rehnquist, feel effectively overruled the essential analytical elements in the *Butler* holding.

Justice Rehnquist's reliance on *Steward* in rejecting *Butler* is at best misleading. Unfortunately, a good bit of loose or imprecise language in *Steward* lends itself to the interpretation assigned by Chief Justice Rehnquist that the basic analytical premises of *Butler* were being rejected. A close reading of *Steward*, however, belies that interpretation. In fact, on close reading *Steward* undermines the *Dole* rationale.

Steward involved a federal unemployment compensation program.[117] The program was funded by a tax imposed upon

---

[113]See Wickard v. Filburn, 217 U.S. 111 (1942). In *Wickard*, the Court upheld the Agricultural Adjustment Act of 1938 as a legitimate exercise of the commerce power. The 1938 Act was substantially identical to the 1933 Act struck down in *Butler*.

[114]*E.g.*, *Dole*, 107 S.Ct. at 2796 ("Congress has acted indirectly under its spending power to *encourage* uniformity in the States' drinking ages. . . . [W]e find this legislative effort within constitutional bounds even if Congress may not *regulate* drinking ages directly" (emphasis added)).

[115]*Dole*, 107 S.Ct. at 2798 ("Congress has directed only that a State desiring to establish a minimum drinking age lower than 21 lose a relatively small percentage of certain federal highway funds").

[116]301 U.S. 548 (1937).

[117]Titles IX and III of the Social Security Act of 1935 were challenged. Title IX provided for a tax on employers of eight or more to be imposed as a percentage of wages and paid into the U.S. Treasury. *Id.* at 574. Title III authorized future appropriations from the federal treasury to the states for the purpose of assisting in the administration of state unemployment benefits programs. *Id.* at 577.

employers under the Social Security Act (SSA).[118] The SSA provided that if a state established an unemployment compensation scheme that met federal standards, that state's taxpayers could credit payments into the state program against their federal tax liability under the SSA.[119] In *Steward* a state taxpayer paid the federal tax under protest and sued for refund on the grounds that the federal tax was unconstitutional,[120] citing *Butler*.[121] The plaintiff argued that the effect of the tax exemption or offset was to coerce the state into establishing its own unemployment compensation program and providing support for the program,[122] a legislative objective that was beyond federal power under the then restrictive view of Congress's commerce power.

Stated thus, the issue in *Steward* would seem to be the same as that in *Butler* and *Dole*, *i.e.*, whether Congress may, through use of the taxing and spending powers, achieve a regulatory objective otherwise outside the scope of Congress's delegated regulatory powers. If this were a correct statement of the issue, the fact that the *Steward* Court upheld the scheme might support Chief Justice Rehnquist's citation of *Steward*. In fact, however, the two cases are very different. First, unlike *Butler*, the *Steward* plaintiff was not challenging the tax *exemption*, which was the conditional government benefit that allegedly was coercive. The plaintiff's challenge was directed at the tax *liability* to the federal government that supported the federal unemployment compensation scheme.[123] The plaintiff was not arguing that the federal government should not

[118]Although the tax revenues were not earmarked specifically for federal unemployment compensation, the Court asserted that "[e]very dollar of the new taxes will continue in all likelihood to be used and needed by the nation [for unemployment relief]." *Id*. at 588–89.

[119]*Id*. at 574. The Act required certification of the state program by the Social Security Board to the Secretary of the Treasury before tax credits could be claimed. *Ibid*.

[120]*Id*. at 573.

[121]*Steward*, 301 U.S. at 592. The *Steward* Court distinguished *Butler* on four grounds: (1) the Social Security tax was not for the benefit of a special group (as opposed to the farmers benefited by the Agricultural Adjustment tax); (2) the unemployment compensation law on which tax credit was conditioned is a state law; (3) the state is not bound to continue its compensation program (the farmers entered a binding contract with the federal government); and (4) the relief of unemployment is not an end which Congress may not seek. *Id*. at 592–93.

[122]*Id*. at 578.

[123]All of the plaintiff's challenges to the SSA implicated the taxing power. Plaintiff argued that the tax was not an excise; was not uniform; was so arbitrary as to violate the Fifth Amendment; was not designed to raise revenue; and finally, that the states were coerced by the tax into adopting unemployment compensation plans. *Steward*, 301 U.S. at 578.

have made available to the states the option of funding their own unemployment compensation scheme.[124] Thus, from the plaintiff's perspective, *Steward* was a taxing power challenge, and not a condition on spending case. The plaintiff was forced to argue, in effect, that the federal government could not tax for and fund a national unemployment relief scheme. The challenged federal tax, however, clearly was within the power of the federal government under the taxing clause, and funding an unemployment relief scheme equally clearly was within Congress's power to spend for the general welfare.[125]

Second, to the extent *Steward* could be read as a conditional spending case, the claim was that the *state* was being coerced by a conditional benefit scheme contrary to the state's retained powers.[126] This aspect of the plaintiff's claim lacked credibility, however, because it was being made by an individual, not the state that supposedly was the victim of coercion under the conditional benefit scheme. When the state fails to challenge an allegedly coercive federal program, there is reason to doubt the coercive nature of the program, despite the claim being advanced by the individual.[127]

---

[124]The federal tax was to be imposed whether or not the states adopted unemployment compensation programs. The SSA merely provided that if a state had such a program, that state's citizens would receive federal tax credits and avoid double taxation. The SSA created the possibility that a taxpayer support either the federal program or his state's program—but not both.

[125]The Court recounted the unemployment statistics describing the need for federal legislation. The Court thereupon concluded that "[i]t is too late today for the argument to be heard with tolerance that in a crisis so extreme the use of the moneys of the nation to relieve the unemployed and their dependents is a use for any purpose narrower than the promotion of the general welfare." *Steward*, 301 U.S. at 586- 87.

[126]The petitioner argued that the SSA was "an unlawful invasion of the reserved powers of the states . . . and that the states in submitting to it have yielded to coercion." *Id.* at 578.

[127]One could argue that an individual citizen should not have standing to challenge federal action directed at his state government, claiming that the federal regulation exceeds the delegated regulatory powers of Congress, even where the federal action clearly is coercive. This argument would distinguish third-party standing cases, in which one person asserts the constitutional rights of another because the interests of both parties coincide. In this case, the individual would be attempting to assert the constitutional position of a collective unit of which he is a member when the unit through its internal political processes has determined not to assert its own constitutional protection. Where the state government is the object of the federal regulation, the individual citizen's interest should be considered to have been subsumed in the decision by the state either to resist or acquiesce. For example, if the state in *National League of Cities* or *Garcia* had chosen to comply with the arguably unconstitutional federal regulation by paying employees the federally specified minimum wage, it would have been most unwise to allow an individual citizen to attack the federal regulation. If, however,

It should come as no surprise that there was no state challenge to the unemployment compensation scheme and the option of a state-run program in *Steward* because in fact there was no coercion or regulation of the state in the *Sherbert* sense.[128] The federal legislature had determined that it would require state taxpayers to support an unemployment compensation scheme for the workers of the state that met certain requirements of permanence and fiscal responsibility. As noted earlier, it clearly was within the taxing and spending power of Congress to enact such a scheme.[129] It then was perfectly sensible for Congress to exempt state taxpayers from the obligation to support a federal scheme to the extent that the state taxpayers already supported a satisfactory program at the state level. Because it was within the power of Congress to establish such a taxing and spending scheme, the taxpayers would be forced to support such a scheme in any event. The state simply was offered the option to administer a substitute scheme at the state level if the state preferred. Thus, there was no benefit to the state whose availability was conditioned on the state's acquiescence in a regulatory objective that was beyond the scope of Congress's regulatory powers. There only were specifications for the state unemployment compensation scheme that Congress would consider an acceptable alternative to a federally funded scheme. Certainly, if Congress had the power under the taxing and spending clause to establish a federal unemployment compensation program, Congress had the authority to accept from the state a substitute scheme that was the fiscal equivalent of a federal scheme.[130]

---

the federal regulation required that the state do something that itself would violate an individual's constitutional rights, the individual should have standing to challenge that federal action. Similarly, if a spending condition "induce[d] the States to engage in activities that would themselves be unconstitutional," the "independent constitutional bar" limitation on congressional spending power would operate to invalidate the condition, *Dole*, 107 S.Ct. at 2798, and an individual citizen should have standing to challenge the conditional spending on that ground.

[128]The Court asked: "Who then is coerced through the operation of this statute? . . . Not the state. Even now she does not offer a suggestion that in passing the unemployment law she was affected by duress." *Steward*, 301 U.S. at 589. See note 130 *infra*.

[129]See note 125 *supra* and accompanying text.

[130]In fact, there is good reason to believe that the *Steward* program not only was not coercive in the *Sherbert* sense, but in fact was welcomed by the states. *E.g.*, *Steward*, 301 U.S. at 589; see Kaden, note 19 *supra*, at 884 (noting that federal action relieved states desiring to institute unemployment compensation from fears of economically disadvantaging local businesses); Rosenthal, note 3 *supra*, at 1127 (same). Alabama's choice gave the state more control. As the Court pointed out, by adopting its own unemployment compensation plan, Alabama "chose

In this context, the *Steward* Court's loose language relied on by Chief Justice Rehnquist in *Dole* about the difference between motive or temptation and coercion or compulsion[131] simply bears no relation to the situation in *Dole*. In context, that language must be read as a simple observation by the Court that the facts of *Steward* simply did not present the kind of conditional benefit that gives rise to the coercion problem. In fact, the *Steward* Court specifically distinguished *Steward* from cases like *Butler* with the statement that:[132]

> It is quite another thing to say that a tax will be abated upon the doing of an act that will satisfy the fiscal need, the tax and the alternative being approximate equivalents.

Moreover, *Steward* specifically rejects the anticipated argument that *Steward* would produce the *Dole* result:[133]

> We do not say that a tax is valid, when imposed by act of Congress, if it is laid upon the condition that a state may escape its operation through the adoption of a statute unrelated in subject matter to activities fairly within the scope of national policy and power. No such question is before us. In the tender of this credit Congress does not intrude upon fields foreign to its function.

Yet that is precisely what the Court in *Dole* assumed Congress was doing—intruding upon a field clearly foreign to its function as a result of the Twenty-first Amendment.[134]

Steward, therefore, does not stand for the proposition for which Chief Justice Rehnquist cites it. *Steward* does not hold that Congress may, through the "temptation" of withholding spending grants, achieve ends otherwise outside Congress's delegated powers, so long as the "temptation" does not become "coercion." *Steward* does teach that the Court will not strike down congressional statutes at the behest of affected individuals when no state conduct is in fact required, and when Congress is acting *within* the scope of its delegated authority. But *Steward* provides no clue what the

---

to have relief administered under laws of her own making, by agents of her own selection, instead of under federal laws, administered by federal officers, with all the ensuing evils . . . of federal patronage and power. *Steward*, 301 U.S. at 590.

[131]See *Dole*, 107 S.Ct. at 2798.

[132]*Steward*, 301 U.S. at 591.

[133]*Id*. at 590.

[134]See note 5 *supra*.

Court would do if Congress required the state—either through imposition of a penalty or the equivalent withholding of a benefit—to advance a regulatory goal *otherwise outside* Congress's delegated powers.

Thus, *Dole* simply was not an unremarkable application of well-settled principles. In fact, *Dole* was the decision that Chief Justice Rehnquist would have us believe *Steward* was. *Dole* was the first case of a state challenging the withholding of a federal benefit because of the state's refusal to conform to a federal legislative objective that Congress had no constitutional authority to impose. The Court said that it was constitutional for Congress to compel such compliance by withholding the reward, though the Court assumed that it would not have been constitutional for Congress to fine the state for a refusal to comply. This is contrary to *Sherbert v. Verner* and inconsistent with both *Butler* and *Steward*.

In issuing this remarkable holding packaged as an unremarkable application of well-established doctrine, the Chief Justice relied on a string cite of cases involving federal spending: *Fullilove v. Klutznick*,[135] *Lau v. Nichols*,[136] *Ivanhoe Irrigation Dist. v. McCracken*,[137] and *Oklahoma v. United States Civil Service Commission*.[138] None of those cases, however, held what Chief Justice Rehnquist would have us believe *Steward* held, and none of them lends significant support to his reading of *Steward*. Upon close inspection, each of the cases cited by Chief Justice Rehnquist turns out to involve federal specifications defining the object of the expenditure or assuring that the expenditure will be made in pursuance of that object.

The Court in *Fullilove* rejected an equal protection challenge to the minority business enterprise (MBE) provision of the Public Works Employment Act of 1977. The MBE conditioned receipt of federal public works grants upon agreement by the state or local government recipient that at least 10 percent of the grant money would fund contracts with minority businesses.[139] Before reaching the equal protection problem, the Court observed that the MBE was within Congress's spending power because the spending power

---

[135]448 U.S. 448 (1980).

[136]414 U.S. 563 (1974).

[137]357 U.S. 275 (1958).

[138]330 U.S. 127 (1946).

[139]*Fullilove*, 448 U.S. at 475.

is at least as broad as Congress's regulatory powers and the MBE was within Congress's regulatory powers under the Commerce Clause and the Fourteenth Amendment.[140] That fact alone distinguishes *Fullilove* from *Dole* where the condition was assumed not to be within Congress's regulatory power because of the Twenty-first Amendment.

But more fundamentally, the MBE did not present a problem of conditional spending that could be sustained only by reference to a delegated regulatory power. In fact, the MBE simply set forth specifications for the federal expenditure defining one of the several purposes of the expenditure. That purpose was enhancement of opportunities for minority businesses. In other words, one of the things that Congress sought to purchase with its expenditures was the services of minority businesses. Attaching a "condition" that the recipients of the federal grant money spend a certain portion on minority business contracts is simply assuring that the federal money is spent for the purpose intended. The MBE presented no problem of federal money being expended to purchase compliance with a regulatory objective. Thus, the MBE would not have presented the unconstitutional condition problem of *Dole* even if the MBE had not been within any of Congress's delegated regulatory powers.

In *Lau*, the Court interpreted and applied §601 of the Civil Rights Act of 1964 which conditioned federal grants to public schools on the elimination of discrimination based on race, color, or national origin in the recipient schools.[141] Congress was willing to support or "purchase" only nondiscriminatory education and specified that purpose for the expenditure. The *Lau* holding simply assumed that Congress could impose specifications on how federal grants are to be expended. As in *Fullilove*, no question of unconstitutional conditions was presented by the case or decided by the Court. Moreover, even if the conditions in *Lau* had been regulations they would have been sustainable as independent exercises of congressional regulatory power under section five of the Fourteenth Amendment.[142]

The *Ivanhoe* case does not even appear to present a problem of conditional spending in any normal sense of the term. *Ivanhoe*

---

[140]*Ibid.*

[141]*Lau*, 414 U.S. at 566.

[142]See United States v. Price, 383 U.S. 787 (1966).

involved numerous statutory and constitutional challenges by large
landowners to contracts between the United States and several state
irrigation agencies. According to those contracts, the federal government agreed to provide water to the state agency for distribution
and the state agency agreed that the water would be distributed to
each landowner for a maximum of 160 acres per landowner. An
owner with acreage in excess of 160 acres could continue to use
existing sources of irrigation water for the excess acreage or could
sell the excess acreage to a purchaser who owned less than 160 acres
and who could thus qualify for federal water on the purchased
tract.[143] In essence, the federal scheme was intended to distribute up
to 160 acres worth of irrigation water (procured at enormous
expense to the federal taxpayer) to each California Central Valley
landowner on an equal basis. In fact, that is nothing more than a
classic case of federal specifications defining how a federal expenditure is to be made and for what purpose it is to be made. No
individual or state was confronted with the choice of engaging in
some course of conduct and forgoing a federal benefit on one hand
or refraining from the conduct and receiving the federal benefit on
the other hand.

The decision in *Oklahoma v. United States Civil Service Commission*
is the only one of the cited cases that even arguably lends any
support to Chief Justice Rehnquist's opinion in *Dole*. In the face of
a challenge based on the *Butler* holding, the Court in *Oklahoma*
refused to invalidate a condition on receipt of federal funds that
required state administrators of the federal funds to abstain from
political partisanship.[144] In holding that Congress has power "to fix
the terms upon which its money allotments to states shall be
disbursed,"[145] the Court implied that the condition was valid as a
specification and not a regulation. The congressional purpose
behind the condition was not to regulate conduct as such but to
ensure responsible administration of federal funds by avoiding
opportunities for conflicts of interest or political partisanship by the
state administrators of the federal funds.

Even more important than *Dole's* being "wrong" in the preceden-
tial sense is the fact that the *Dole* holding in effect eviscerates the
doctrine that the national government is one of limited delegated

---

[143]*Ivanhoe*, 357 U.S. at 285–86.

[144]*Oklahoma*, 330 U.S. at 142.

[145]*Id*. at 143.

powers. No one would argue that Congress can impose direct regulation beyond the scope of its delegated powers. But any time that Congress finds itself limited by those delegated regulatory powers, as it did with regard to a minimum national drinking age, Congress need only attach a condition on a federal spending grant that achieves the same (otherwise invalid) regulatory objective.

Butler and *Steward* reject the *Dole* holding precisely because this result raises serious federalism concerns. In *Butler*, for example, after the Court concluded that the ends of the AAA were outside the scope of Congress's commerce authority, the Court returned to the question of whether the AAA nonetheless was valid under the spending power:[146]

> Congress has no power to enforce its commands on the farmer to the ends sought by the Agricultural Adjustment Act. It must follow that it may not indirectly accomplish those ends by taxing and spending to purchase compliance. . . . If, in lieu of compulsory regulation of subjects within the states' reserved jurisdiction, which is prohibited, the Congress could invoke the taxing and spending power as a means to accomplish the same end, clause 1 of Section 8 of article I would become the instrument for total subversion of the governmental powers reserved to the individual states.

By modern standards, again, the *Butler* Court erred in its holding that the AAA was beyond Congress's commerce power.[147] But the *Butler* Court correctly recognized that permitting Congress to achieve through the spending power what it could not achieve otherwise would "totally subdue" the notion of delegated powers.[148] In *Dole* the Court assumed that the NMDA was beyond Congress's regulatory authority.[149] Thus, the imposition of a national minimum drinking age also should be outside the spending authority.[150]

---

[146]*Butler*, 297 U.S. at 75.

[147]See notes 111–13 *supra* and accompanying text.

[148]*Butler*, 297 U.S. at 75.

[149]See note 5 *supra*.

[150]*Steward's* rejection of the *Dole* result is less explicit than *Butler's*. The *Steward* Court simply holds that *Butler* is distinguishable because unlike the situation in *Butler*, in *Steward* "[t]he condition is not directed to the attainment of an unlawful end, but to an end, the relief of unemployment, for which nation and state may lawfully cooperate." *Steward*, 301 U.S. at 593. In other words, the Court is saying that in *Steward* the spending power is not used to evade a limitation imposed by Congress's delegated regulatory powers. Any question as to the Court's meaning is eliminated by the Court's gratuitous assurance that "[w]e do not say that a tax is valid, when imposed by act of Congress, if it is laid upon the condition that a

In contrast to the cases cited by Chief Justice Rehnquist, the *Dole* decision invites the complete abrogation of any limits on the delegated legislative powers of Congress. Congress is invited to use the taxing and spending powers to accomplish any legislative objective not delegated to Congress, but rather retained exclusively to the states. The decision in *Dole*, neatly framed by the Court's own assumptions about the limits on Congress's delegated powers, invites the complete elimination of all limits on federal legislative power through the simple device of burdensome taxes accompanied by "financial incentives" to comply with any federal legislative objective that is outside the range of concerns constitutionally delegated to Congress.[151] *Garcia* having rejected the *National League of Cities* construct, *Dole* apparently rejects the only construct left to curb federal power vis-à-vis the states.

III. DOCTRINAL LIMITS ON DOLE?

Chief Justice Rehnquist takes pains in *Dole* to suggest that ample limitations exist on the breadth of the Court's holding. First he relies on the proposition that Congress's power to use the taxing and spending scheme to purchase state conduct in conformity with a regulatory objective is limited because Congress only may "induce" or "tempt" voluntary compliance, but may not "coerce" compliance.[152] Second, he concedes in a footnote that in the future the Court might require that the "condition" attached to a spending

---

state may escape its operation through the adoption of a statute unrelated in subject-matter to activities fairly within the scope of national policy and power." *Id.* at 590.

[151]In this connection, it might be more difficult to defend the constitutionality of the new federal maximum 65 mph speed limit than to defend the constitutionality of the old 55 mph speed limit. Because both are regulations in the guise of conditional spending, both are invalid unless within one of Congress's delegated legislative powers. The Commerce Clause is the only likely prospect as a source of congressional power for such a regulation. While the old 55 mph limit could easily be defended as an oil conservation measure designed to decrease national dependence on foreign oil supplies and prices and to facilitate interstate transportation in related ways, the current vestigal speed limits of 65 mph on interstate highways and 55 mph on state highways are retained solely for reasons of highway safety, an area traditionally left to state regulation under the Commerce Clause absent any discriminatory effect. Thus, absent an expansive reading of the Commerce Clause, the old 55 mph speed limit condition on federal highway funds would be constitutional as a regulation pursuant to Congress's commerce power while the new 65 mph/55 mph condition on federal highway funds would not be constitutional, at least insofar as the speed limit applies to non-federal highways.

[152]See *Dole*, 107 S.Ct. at 2798.

scheme be in some vague way related to or germane to the object of the expenditure.[153] A close look at these two doctrinal limits suggests, however, that they are verbal constructs devoid of content. This is unsurprising; as the majority sees no difficulty with Congress's using spending conditions to obtain compliance, there is no evil for the Court to limit or danger to cabin.

A. COERCION/INDUCEMENT

Chief Justice Rehnquist's primary limitation on *Dole* arises from the coercion/inducement distinction. Citing *Steward*, Chief Justice Rehnquist states: "Our decisions have recognized that in some circumstances financial inducement offered by Congress might be so coercive as to pass the point at which 'pressure turns into compulsion.' "[154] Rejecting South Dakota's argument that the very success of the *Dole* scheme demonstrates its coercive effect, the Court relied upon the fact that only 5 percent of federal highway funds are at stake to reach the conclusion that this was but a "mild encouragement" to the states to change their drinking ages.[155]

The difficulty with the coercion/inducement test as a limit on congressional action is that it simply restates the already-discredited distinction between Congress achieving an end regulatorily and achieving an end by withholding a benefit. The question of "how much benefit" simply is beside the point, for as *Sherbert v. Verner* makes clear, any benefit withheld is tantamount to a fine in that amount.[156] There simply is no conceptual difference between withholding a benefit, no matter how small, and coercing an end regulatorily by the imposition of a fine, however small. One who is subject to a threat of regulatory fine may choose to violate the regulation and pay the fine because the amount of the particular fine is modest. But that "freedom" of choice does not eliminate constitutional objections to the substance of the regulation.

This is, again, where Chief Justice Rehnquist misreads *Steward*. *Steward* does not hold that so long as the spending condition induces, but does not coerce, state conduct, the condition is valid even if the condition otherwise is outside Congress regulatory

---

[153]See *id.* at 2797 n.3.

[154]*Id.* at 2798 (citing Steward, 301 U.S. at 590).

[155]*Ibid.* In actuality, South Dakota would forfeit 5 percent for the first year of noncompliance and 10 percent each year thereafter. See 23 U.S.C. §158(a)(2) (Supp. III 1985).

[156]See notes 88–95 *supra* and accompanying text.

authority. *Steward* simply dismissed the plaintiff's claim because there was no coercion, i.e., no federal inducement of state conduct. The federal relief program at issue in *Steward* was within Congress's delegated powers and would be imposed on the state's citizens with or without action by the state.[157]

In fact, *Butler* had explicitly rejected Chief Justice Rehnquist's formulation, and as discussed, *Steward* did not undercut *Butler* on this point. The *Butler* Court flatly rejected the government's contention that the plan was constitutional because its end was accomplished by "voluntary co-operation,"[158] and not regulatory coercion:

> The regulation is not in fact voluntary. The farmer, of course, may refuse to comply, but the price of such refusal is the loss of benefits. The amount offered is intended to be sufficient to exert pressure on him to agree to the proposed regulation. The power to confer or withhold unlimited benefits is the power to coerce. . . . The coercive purpose and intent of the statute is not obscured by the fact that it has not been perfectly successful. . . . .[159] [T]he plan . . . [is] one to keep a nonco-operating minority in line. This is coercion by economic pressure.[160]

Dole itself demonstrates the illusory nature of the coercion/inducement limitation. Chief Justice Rehnquist felt the amount of the federal encouragement relatively trivial. Yet, as of this writing all states have complied, many of them under protest.[161]

The facts of the *Dole* case themselves suggest that Chief Justice Rehnquist was relying upon a distinction Congress would not even credit when he sanctioned the result because the "blandishments" were sufficiently small that the states had "a choice."[162] Congress, after all, had no intention of providing a choice. First, the building

---

[157]See note 124 *supra*.

[158]*Butler*, 297 U.S. at 70.

[159]In *Dole*, Chief Justice Rehnquist rejected South Dakota's argument that the coercive nature of the NMDA was proved by the fact that all 50 states had raised their drinking ages to 21. *Dole*, 107 S.Ct. at 2798. Apparently, while 100 percent compliance with a condition is not proof of coercion, *ibid.*, less than 100 percent compliance does not negative coercion. See *Butler*, 297 U.S. at 71. In other words, both the success of the "temptation" and the lack thereof, are irrelevant to assessing whether compliance has been coerced.

[160]*Butler*, 297 U.S. at 71.

[161]For an accounting of states aligned with South Dakota, see Note, note 3 *supra*, at 1160 n.3.

[162]*Dole*, 107 S.Ct. at 2798.

of national roads is an important end from Congress's perspective, and the end is achieved only if the roads are uninterrupted and in good repair.[163] It is unlikely Congress really was willing to have any state refuse the federal assistance. In other words, Congress would have been unwilling to risk noncompliance, and did not expect it. Second, from the perspective of the end Congress had in mind in enacting the NMDA—a national uniform drinking age—it also is inconceivable that Congress really meant to present a choice. The NMDA ostensibly was enacted to prevent blood borders— underage teens driving from one jurisdiction where the drinking age was high, to another where the drinking age was lower, then returning home drunk on the highways and causing accidents and traffic fatalities.[164] Congress's very purpose in enacting the NMDA would have been undercut seriously if not every state complied.

Given these circumstances, it is clear Congress had no intention of offering a choice. It was using the threatened withholding of a benefit to obtain regulatory compliance. In other words, Congress understood the *Sherbert* principle quite well, and made use of the fact that coercive regulation can be imposed just as well through the withholding of a benefit. By ignoring *Sherbert* and focusing on the coercion/inducement test, which is inherently useless as a limitation, the Court permitted Congress to step outside its delegated regulatory powers.

B. CONDITION RELATED TO SPENDING

In a footnote Chief Justice Rehnquist suggests that one other limitation on Congress's power to regulate through use of the spending clause might be a requirement that any condition attached

---

[163] According to Congress, "the prompt and early completion of the National System of Interstate and Defense Highways, so named because of its primary importance to the national defense . . . , is essential to the national interest." 23 U.S.C. §101(b) (1982).

[164] The sponsors of the NMDA amendment argued that a uniform minimum drinking age of 21 would "significantly reduce the drunk driving problem." 130 Cong. Rec. S8207 (daily ed. June 26, 1984) (statement of Sen. Danforth). During the debate, a variety of statistics were cited to show that teenagers disproportionately contributed to alcohol-related highway fatalities and accidents. *Id.* at S8209 (statement of Sen. Lautenberg). The lack of uniformity in drinking ages exacerbated the problem because teenagers were induced to drive to neighboring states in order to drink. "The result is that we end up with blood borders where young people drive over the State line to get alcohol," *id.* at S8212 (statement of Sen. Heinz), and return drunk, thus posing a risk to themselves and other drivers. See generally Presidential Commission on Drunk Driving, Final Report (1983).

to a federal grant bear some relationship to that grant.[165] In formulation, this appears to be the limitation relied upon by Justice O'Connor in her dissent to distinguish legitimate specifications on spending from regulations in the guise of conditions on grants.[166] It is clear from the Rehnquist use of the concept, however, that it is not intended to provide the fundamental limitation suggested in Justice O'Connor's dissent.

In setting out his test for what constitutes a valid condition, Chief Justice Rehnquist appeared to give lip service to the core of the O'Connor dissent, stating: "our cases have suggested (without significant elaboration) that conditions on federal grants might be illegitimate if they are unrelated to the 'federal interest in particular national projects or programs.' "[167] Chief Justice Rehnquist found that the standard did not require elaboration in this case either, both because of a supposed concession by South Dakota on the issue,[168] and because "in any event" "any such limitation on conditional federal grants [is] satisfied in this case."[169]

According to Chief Justice Rehnquist, the national problem to which the condition related was the problem of teenage drunk driving. This may well be a nationwide problem, but the condition does not in any way specify the characteristics of the highways which the conditioned funds were intended to purchase. Requiring that the condition simply relate to a national problem rather than specify characteristics of the particular goods and services to be purchased by the grant is tantamount to a statement that Congress can regulate perceived national problems through the spending power. Where Congress has been delegated regulatory power to legislate on the question, such a regulatory use of the spending

---

[165]See *Dole*, 107 S.Ct. at 2797 n.3.

[166]See notes 171–72 *infra* and accompanying text.

[167]*Dole*, 107 S.Ct. at 2796 (quoting Massachusetts v. United States, 435 U.S. 444, 461 (1978)).

[168]*Id.* at 2797. The Chief Justice declined to address "whether conditions less directly related to the particular purpose of the expenditure might be outside the bounds of the spending power," both because "any such limitation" was "satisfied in this case" and "[b]ecause the petitioner has not sought such a restriction," *see* Tr. of Oral Arg. 19–21. (emphasis added). Justice O'Connor chastised the Court for relying on "a supposed concession by counsel" stating "[c]ounsel's statements there are at best ambiguous. Counsel essentially said no more than that he was not prepared to argue the reasonable relationship question discussed at length in the [amicus brief]." *Dole*, 107 S.Ct. at 2800 (O'Connor, J., dissenting).

[169]*Id.* at 2797 n.3.

power is unobjectionable. But in *Dole* the Twenty-first Amendment was assumed to have deprived Congress of the power to regulate the problem through the imposition of a uniform national drinking age.[170] Permitting use of a spending condition to regulate an issue otherwise outside Congress's regulatory powers is a perversion of the notion of specific delegated powers.

In contrast to Chief Justice Rehnquist's all-inclusive notion of "related conditions," Justice O'Connor applied her distinction between legitimate specifications on how federal grants should be spent and illegitimate regulations in the guise of spending conditions. She argued that the NMDA was an invalid condition because not sufficiently related to the purpose of the grant:[171]

> When Congress appropriates money to build a highway, it is entitled to insist that the highway be a safe one. But it is not entitled to insist as a condition of the use of highway funds that the State impose or change regulations in other areas of the State's social and economic life because of an attenuated or tangential relationship to highway use or safety. Indeed, if the rule were otherwise, the Congress could effectively regulate almost any area of a State's social, political, or economic life on the theory that use of the interstate transportation system is somehow enhanced.

Only if conditions are limited to specifying how federal grants are to be spent can Congress's powers be limited.[172] The power to attach conditions exists not to give Congress sway beyond the delegated regulatory powers, but to ensure that Congress can see that national money actually is spent as Congress wishes.

---

[170]See note 5 *supra*.

[171]*Dole*, 107 S.Ct. at 2800 (O'Connor, J., dissenting).

[172]Chief Justice Rehnquist makes one argument that would be consistent with Justice O'Connor's position. He says that the purpose of the grant was to provide *safe* federal highways, and the NMDA is a specification of how to do this: it eliminates the incentive for teenage drunk driving on national highways by eliminating the "blood borders" that threatened the safety of those highways. *Dole*, 107 S.Ct. at 2797. The Chief Justice's argument is problematic, as Justice O'Connor points out in dissent. If the NMDA is a condition specifying how to provide *safe* federal highways, the condition is under- and over-inclusive. It is under- inclusive because as a factual matter most of the drunk-driving fatalities are a function of adult, and not teenage, drunk driving. It is over-inclusive because the law affects teenage conduct on a wide basis, with no regard for whether those teenagers would ever drive on a national highway (or any other highway for that matter) after drinking. *Id.* at 2800 (O'Connor, J., dissenting). A court sensitive to the federalism issues we raise here nevertheless might have saved the NMDA by emphasizing Chief Justice Rehnquist's safety argument. But to hold as the Court did that any "reasonable relation" test is met in this case underscores the fact that the Court is at best not very serious about the test.

It should not be surprising that Chief Justice Rehnquist's relatedness or germaneness requirement is a contentless restriction, because there is no independent theoretical basis for the requirement in Chief Justice Rehnquist's analysis in the first place. If the Chief Justice is willing to find that spending conditions are not regulations in disguise as long as compliance is "voluntary" in his sense of the word, there is no purpose to be served by the nexus requirement. If the direct purchase of voluntary conduct is spending—something separate and apart from regulation—there is no constitutional problem of Congress exceeding its delegated regulatory powers. Indeed, if Congress can purchase conduct, why go to the trouble of purchasing some goods and services and then attaching the purchase of conduct to the purchase of the goods and services as in *Dole?* Congress simply could pay states a flat fee to enact laws Congress desires, but which are outside the scope of Congress' regulatory power. Thus, Chief Justice Rehnquist's suggested nexus requirement is merely some ironic perversion of Justice O'Connor's dissenting position that Congress can, under the spending power, purchase only goods and services with accompanying specifications to define the goods and services to be purchased. Because Chief Justice Rehnquist rejected the essence of Justice O'Connor's definition of appropriate limitation upon the spending power, his repackaging of that definition into a "germaneness" requirement turns out to be contentless and unadministrable.

C. THE POLITICAL PROCESS AS A LIMIT

Because the suggested doctrinal limitations on *Dole* are ineffectual, *Dole* in effect relegates disputes over relative spheres of authority to the political process.[173] Relegating conditional spending to the control of the political process is, however, not without its irony. As noted at the outset, Chief Justice Rehnquist was the primary architect of the *National League of Cities* construct,[174] erected

---

[173]This may not be accidental. Chief Justice Rehnquist's treatment of the "general welfare" limitation suggests deference to Congress in the spending area. In a footnote, Rehnquist suggests that the level of deference as to what constitutes "general welfare" is such that perhaps it provides no "judicially enforceable restriction[s]" at all. *Dole*, 107 S.Ct. at 2796 n.2. If this is true, and it further is correct that once a condition is appropriate to further this general welfare the condition is valid, the only limitation left may be the political process.

[174]The *National League of Cities* opinion was delivered by then-Associate Justice Rehnquist and was joined by Chief Justice Burger and Justices Stewart and Powell. Justice Blackmun concurred separately.

when the Court sensed the delegation construct was doing little to limit Congress's power vis-á-vis the states. Chief Justice Rehnquist, therefore, was a vocal critic when the Court abandoned the construct a decade later in *Garcia* in favor of limits imposed only by the political process.[175] Yet, in *Dole* Chief Justice Rehnquist appears to have done precisely what he and the other dissenters condemned in *Garcia:* he seems to have deferred to the political branches on federalism issues because of an inability to spell out judicially enforceable limits. The irony is that in *Dole* such limits are readily accessible; in *Garcia* they were not.

A further irony is that if reliance on the political process is justified in either situation, it is more justified in the *Garcia* context than in the *Dole* context. The political process is more apt to work as a limit on excessive federal action in the *Garcia* context than in the *Dole* context. In the kind of case where Congress is buying conduct in excess of its legislative powers rather than overtly regulating in excess of its legislative powers, one cannot count on the political process to serve as an effective restraint, as an effective guardian of the state's role in the constitutional scheme. First, the national electorate simply is not as likely to recognize an abuse of federal power in schemes involving grants of federal money to the states as it is in cases of direct regulation. The average voter, even assuming he or she is well informed on the particular matter, likely will overlook the basic *Sherbert* problem. After all, it took even the Supreme Court many years to recognize the problem in other contexts and it effectively continued to refuse to recognize the problem in the *Dole* context. Second, the average voter has come to view federal tax, along with death, as one of life's eventualities. Thus, for most states' voters the only real question is how much they can get back in federal financial handouts. There is no immediate sense that it is their own money being returned to them with strings attached and that the net effect of the money's round trip to Washington is simply to carry the regulatory strings with it back to the state. Because state voters and state governments tend to view federal grants as generosity to which they are not really entitled, there is far less inclination to question federal regulatory requirements that arrive in the form of conditions on the receipt of a gift from the federal government. Thus, one generally might be

---

[175]Then-Associate Justice Rehnquist filed his own dissent to *Garcia* and also concurred in dissents written by Justices O'Connor and Powell. 469 U.S. at 580, 589.

inclined to rely on the political process to confine Congress to its constitutionally delegated powers in the usual Commerce Clause case when Congress had directly regulated matters arguably reserved exclusively to the states. Nevertheless, there is good reason to ask the Court to scrutinize closely when Congress appears to be regulating outside the scope of its delegated authority by employing the seductive device of simply contracting for the conduct that it cannot constitutionally regulate.

Even if the average voter were astute enough to recognize a *Sherbert v. Verner* problem, and were likely to complain about it, an overarching problem with relying on the political process in the *Dole* situation is that the actual workings of the process are not evident to the body politic. Consider, for example, how the average voter, regulated by the minimum drinking age law would perceive the regulation. To the voters, adult and teenage alike, the minimum drinking age appeared to be imposed by state government. Few of these voters, if any, even understood that the minimum drinking age in their state was a result of federal legislation, let alone a federal threat to cut state benefits.

When Congress is permitted to "encourage" state regulation, the regulating body is in a sense insulated from the electorate.[176] The electorate is, on the face of it, being coerced by state authority. The fact of the matter is that the state government itself was the subject of regulatory authority with which it did not agree. It is true that in a perfectly efficient political system this will be understood, and pressure ultimately will be brought to bear on the federal legislature. In practice, however, this is a thin reed on which to stake American federalism.

CONCLUSION

In *Dole* the Court effectively abrogated the notion that Congress is a government of delegated powers. Although Congress

---

[176]Justice O'Connor addressed this problem in her dissent to FERC v. Mississippi, 456 U.S. 742 (1982). In *FERC*, the majority upheld federal regulation of state utility regulatory agencies. Justice O'Connor argued that "[c]ongressional compulsion of state agencies . . . blurs the lines of political accountability and leaves citizens feeling that their representatives are no longer responsive to local needs." *Id.* at 787 (O'Connor, J., dissenting). In a similar vein, Professor Kaden pointed out that with conditional federal grants "the people are necessarily unsure which of their representatives may be called to account: the federal officials who issued the directive, or the state officials who responded to it." Kaden, note 19 *supra*, at 890.

may be constrained theoretically to its delegated powers in order to accomplish regulatory objectives, the constraint is illusory. After *Dole*, it is fair to say that no regulatory objective realistically is outside Congress's ken through the use of taxation and spending, and conditions attached to federal grants. The supposed limitations suggested by the *Dole* majority do not offer much promise to limit the scope of Congress's authority. Why did the Court accept a test that left Congress unbound by its delegated powers? It is, at best, a surprising position from the *Garcia* dissenters. It seems particularly surprising that the majority opinion in *Dole* was written by Chief Justice Rehnquist, whose inclinations appear to lean in quite the other direction.

Although it is difficult to explain the position taken by the six Justices that concurred in Chief Justice Rehnquist's opinion, particularly Justice Powell who dissented in *Garcia*, Chief Justice Rehnquist's own position actually is fairly easy to explain. In order to do so it is necessary only to identify the difference between the congressional action in *Dole* and the congressional action in *Garcia*. *Garcia*, which aroused the Chief Justice's wrath, was an exercise by Congress of its delegated regulatory authority; *Dole* was an exercise of spending authority.

Chief Justice Rehnquist does believe, in spite of the arguments in this article and the precedent on which those arguments rest, that there is a difference between obtaining an end through regulation, and obtaining the same end by a grant or withholding of benefits. This article, relying heavily on *Sherbert v. Verner*, has taken the position that the distinction is illusory. In the individual rights area, most or all of the Court agree with that position, with one exception. In every *Sherbert* "penalty" case that has come to the Court since his tenure began, Chief Justice Rehnquist has dissented from the Court's judgment, consistently asserting that legislative bodies are free to achieve with their power to dispense benefits that which they could not achieve regulatorily.

It is not surprising, therefore, despite its anti-state result, that Chief Justice Rehnquist took the position that Congress could achieve with its purse what it could not achieve with its sword.[177]

---

[177]See, *e.g.*, FCC v. League of Women Voters, 468 U.S. at 403 (Rehnquist, J., dissenting) (Congress may decide to condition public broadcasting grants on funds not being used to subsidize editorialism on non-commercial, educational broadcasts; "I do not believe that

What is surprising, on reflection, is that so many other members of the Court took a position contrary to their votes in the past. Although anything said on that score is idle speculation, the obvious answer is that Chief Justice Rehnquist's opinion in *Dole*, in apparently simple fashion, reached the result the others wished. The majority of the Court simply was unwilling to strike a statute aimed at eliminating drunk-driving deaths. The fundamental issue presented by the case and Chief Justice Rehnquist's superficial analysis, however, never received the careful scrutiny they deserved. Once the implications of *Dole* are understood, no Justice, save Chief Justice Rehnquist, ought to be satisfied with the Court's decision.

---

anything in the First Amendment to the United States Constitution prevents Congress from choosing to spend public moneys in that manner"); Thomas v. Review Bd. of the Md. Employment Sec. Div., 450 U.S. 707, 720- 27 (1981) (Rehnquist, J., dissenting) (disagreeing with entire Sherbert v. Verner analysis).

MAIMON SCHWARZSCHILD

VALUE PLURALISM AND THE CONSTITUTION: IN DEFENSE OF THE STATE ACTION DOCTRINE

I

The search for a united system of values has been a powerful ideal in western thought. From Plato[1] and classical Jewish thought,[2] through Kant[3] and Marx,[4] it has long been an article of faith and hope that all true values are compatible with one another, and perhaps part

Maimon Schwarzschild is Professor of Law, University of San Diego, and Barrister of Lincoln's Inn, London.

AUTHOR'S NOTE: Thanks (and the customary exemption from responsibility) to Larry Alexander, Kent Greenawalt, Sheldon Krantz, Silvia Loza, and to the Institute for Advanced Legal Studies in London, in whose hospitable library this article was mostly written.

[1] Plato, Protagoras, in Hamilton & Cairns (eds.), The Collected Dialogues of Plato 309, 351 (1963). Socrates' point throughout the dialogue is that virtue is "a single whole, knowledge." But Plato characteristically sets the scene so ironically that it is difficult to be sure of Socrates' or Plato's earnestness on the question. For a good recent study of Plato's complex irony, see Seeskin, Dialogue and Discovery: A Study in Socratic Method (1987).

[2] See, e.g., Talmud Babli, Makkot 23b–24a (distilling all the biblical commandments down to one all-embracing precept: "the righteous shall live by faith"). But cf. Neusner, Invitation to the Talmud 291–92 (1984) (the Talmud's extensive debates over the reasons for religious laws "taught the Jews not to be terrified by the necessity to face, and to choose among, a plurality of uncertain alternatives").

[3] See Findlay, Kant and the Transcendental Object 296 (1981) (Kant's categorical imperative "gives expression to the single, ultimate, unconditional imperative of morality").

[4] Tucker, The Marxian Revolutionary Idea 53 (1969) (Marx's philosophy "expressed a search for unity—for a world beyond all antagonisms and therefore beyond justice as the equilibrium of them").

and parcel of a greater good.[5] The implications of this ideal are tantalizing, for if all "goods" are reconcilable, and especially if they constitute facets of one great good, then the discovery or revelation of the ultimate system of goodness promises us the Right Answer about how we should live our lives, individually and collectively.

The English philosopher Sir Isaiah Berlin rejects this ideal. Berlin, a prominent thinker, essayist, and historian of ideas is perhaps best known for his identification with value pluralism: the insistence that human values are many and varied and cannot be made to harmonize. Within every person, says Berlin, and certainly within every community of people, there coexist deeply held values and aspirations that conflict with one another. No ideological formula or verbal sleight-of-hand can reconcile these true conflicts. You cannot have, for example, perfect human equality and perfect freedom, because people often exercise their freedom to differentiate themselves from others and so to make themselves unequal to their fellows.[6] Likewise, you cannot have perfect humility and yet attain fame and glory.[7] Berlin concludes that there is no ultimate principle or philosophical law that can tell people how to reconcile or even how to compromise their conflicting values. It all depends on the concrete situation,[8] and on what people want most at a particular time. Even in theory, there are no tidy "universal solutions."[9]

The theme recurs throughout Berlin's work. Berlin's most famous essay is probably "The Hedgehog and the Fox," which categorizes writers, thinkers, and human beings in general either as "hedgehogs"—who try to fit everything into one unitary vision —or as "foxes" to whom any all-embracing system would be alien.[10]

---

[5]Levi, Philosophy amd the Modern World 5 (1977) ("Western man looks back with longing" to periods of "unity of the fabric of life").

[6]Berlin, Equality, in Berlin, Concepts and Categories 81, 96–102 (1979). Berlin adds that the pursuit of perfect equality can conflict with other human aims as well, including happiness, virtue, and "colour and variety in a society for their own sake." Id. at 96. "It is only the fanatical egalitarian that will demand that such conflicts invariably be decided in favour of equality alone." Id. Likewise, of course, only the fanatical adherent of a conflicting value would always decide against equality.

[7]Berlin, The Originality of Machiavelli, in Berlin, Against the Current 25, 69 (1979).

[8]Berlin, Equality, note 6 supra, at 96.

[9]Berlin, Montesquieu, in Berlin, Against the Current 130, 148 (1979).

[10]Berlin, The Hedgehog and the Fox, in Berlin, Russian Thinkers 22 (1979). The title of the essay comes from a fragment of Greek poetry which says, "The fox knows many things,

Berlin unmistakably prefers the pluralist fox to the single-minded hedgehog. Berlin praises Montesquieu for grasping that "the ends pursued by men are many and various and often incompatible with one another," and that "no single moral system, let alone a single moral or political goal, could provide the universal solution to all human problems."[11] More arrestingly, Berlin attributes to Machiavelli the crucial discovery that "not all ultimate values are necessarily compatible with one another,"[12] since "there exist at least two sets of values—let us call them the Christian and the pagan— which are not merely in practice but in principle incompatible."[13]

Berlin puts it most succinctly in his essay "Two Concepts of Liberty":

> [I]t seems to me that the belief that some single formula can in principle be found whereby all the diverse ends of men can be harmoniously realized is demonstrably false.[14]

> Pluralism . . . seems to me a truer and more humane ideal than the goals of those who seek . . . great disciplined authoritarian structures. It is truer, because it does, at least, recognize the fact that human goals are many, not all of them commensurable, and in perpetual rivalry with one another.[15]

The human and political stakes in all this are high. The unitary vision, says Berlin, points to tyranny; value pluralism, on the other hand, implies that people should be free to choose among competing values. If there is only one harmonious system of values, "then the only problems are firstly how to find it, then how to realize it, and finally how to convert others to the solution by persuasion or by force."[16] But if there are values in profusion, authentically good

---

but the hedgehog knows one big thing." *Ibid.* Berlin's essay describes Lev Tolstoy as a natural fox who desperately works at being a hedgehog, with an "agonised belief in a single, serene vision, in which all problems are resolved, all doubts stilled, peace and understanding finally achieved." *Id.* at 80.

[11]Berlin, Montesquieu, in Berlin, Against the Current 130, 158 (1979).

[12]Berlin, The Originality of Machiavelli, in Berlin, *id.* at 25, 71.

[13]*Id.* at 69. "If what Machiavelli believed is true, this undermines one major assumption of western thought: namely that somewhere . . . is to be found the final solution of the question of how men should live." *Id.* at 76.

[14]Berlin, Two Concepts of Liberty, in Berlin, Four Essays on Liberty 118, 169 (1969).

[15]*Id.* at 171.

[16]Berlin, The Originality of Machiavelli, in Berlin, Against the Current 25, 78. See also Berlin, Two Concepts of Liberty, in Berlin, Four Essays on Liberty 118, 168: "It is, I have no doubt, some such dogmatic certainty that has been responsible for the deep, serene,

yet authentically irreconcilable, then the path is open to toleration and compromise:[17]

> Toleration is historically the product of the realisation of the irreconcilability of equally dogmatic faiths. . . . Those who [perceived the irreconcilability of values] realised that they had to tolerate error. They gradually came to see merits in diversity, and so became sceptical about definitive solutions in human affairs.

Berlin's value pluralism—his insistence that the best human values are many and conflicting and not even in theory harmonizable—embodies an outlook that ought to appeal to lawyers, especially lawyers educated in the common law tradition. As Anthony Kronman points out, common lawyers put a high professional emphasis on the particularities of cases; this makes lawyers suspicious of general ideas and hospitable to "points of view too various and irreconcilable to be accommodated in any single system of ideas."[18]

The object of this article is to explore what the implications might be for legal doctrine if Berlin is right. Specifically, this article will try to apply Berlin's idea of value pluralism to one perennially troublesome and controversial constitutional doctrine: the "state action doctrine." I will suggest that value pluralism implicitly supports the state action doctrine, and affords a much clearer justification for it than is usually offered by the doctrine's defenders.[19]

---

unshakeable conviction in the minds of some of the most merciless tyrants and persecutors in history that what they did was fully justified by its purpose."

[17]Berlin, The Originality of Machiavelli, note 12 *supra*, at 78.

[18]Kronman, Practical Wisdom and Professional Character, 4 Social Philosophy and Policy, 203, 230 (1986) (lawyers' "professional training and subsequent experience is case-centered and hence inevitably corrosive of the faith in abstractions on which all prophetic and revolutionary movements ultimately rest"). *Id.* at 231.

[19]For an impressive scholarly defense of the state action doctrine and an extensive review of the cases, however, see Burke & Reber, State Action, Congressional Power, and Creditors' Rights: An Essay on the Fourteenth Amendment, 46 So. Cal. L. Rev. 1003 (1973) (arguing that the Fourteenth Amendment protects the individual from arbitrary government while promoting private freedom of choice); see also Marshall, Diluting Constitutional Rights: Rethinking "Rethinking State Action," 80 N.W.U.L. Rev. 558 (1985) (if the courts were to enforce the Fourteenth Amendment provisions upon private individuals, the substantive content of those provisions would inevitably have to be diluted).

II

The Fourteenth Amendment to the Constitution provides that "No State shall . . . deprive any person of life, liberty, or property without due process of law; nor deny to any person within its jurisdiction the equal protection of the laws." Ever since the years immediately after ratification, the Supreme Court has generally held that the Fourteenth Amendment does in fact bind only the "state"—in other words, the institutions of government[20]—and not private citizens.[21]

The state action doctrine, then, is the principle that the laws and policies of government must respect due process, equal protection, and free speech,[22] but that there is no constitutional obligation on the private citizen or private organization to do likewise. Laws must be constitutional, but not private acts unless the private act is prescribed by public law—and then it is the law, not the private act, that is subject to challenge. Although the courts have generally insisted upon this "state action" limit to the reach of the Constitution, the limitation has aroused intense controversy.[23]

---

[20]Like the state governments, the federal government is bound by Fourteenth Amendment principles. Bolling v. Sharpe, 347 U.S. 497 (1954).

[21]Civil Rights Cases, 109 U.S. 3, 11 (1883) ("individual invasion of individual rights is not the subject-matter of the amendment"). See also Lockhart, Kamisar & Choper, Constitutional Law 1514 (5th ed. 1980) ("The basic doctrine of the *Civil Rights Cases*—that it is 'state action' that is prohibited by the fourteenth amendment—has remained undisturbed").

[22]The provisions of the Bill of Rights, including free speech, are virtually all held to be "incorporated" by the Fourteenth Amendment Due Process Clause. See Duncan v. Louisiana, 391 U.S. 145 (1968); see also Fiske v. Kansas, 274 U.S. 380 (1927).

[23]For a sample of scholarly articles criticizing or condemning the state action doctrine, see Chemerinsky, Rethinking State Action, 80 N.W.U.L. Rev. 503 (1985); Brest, State Action and Liberal Theory: A Casenote on Flagg Brothers v. Brooks, 130 U. Pa. L. Rev. 1296 (1982); Thompson, Piercing the Veil of State Action: The Revisionist Theory and a Mythical Application to Self-Help Repossession, 1977 Wisc. L. Rev. 1 (1977); Alexander, Cutting the Gordian Knot: State Action and Self-Help Repossession, 2 Hastings Const. L. Q. 893 (1975); Black, Foreword: "State Action," Equal Protection, and California's Proposition 14, 81 Harv. L. Rev. 69 (1966); Henkin, Shelley v. Kraemer: Notes for a Revised Opinion, 110 U. Pa. L. Rev. 473 (1962); Van Alstyne & Karst, State Action, 14 Stan. L. Rev. 3 (1961); Horowitz, The Misleading Search for State Action under the Fourteenth Amendment, 30 S. Cal. L. Rev. 208 (1957). For a sample of the much smaller and generally less impressive scholarly literature supporting the state action doctrine, see Avins, "State Action" and the Fourteenth Amendment, 17 Mercer L. Rev. 352 (1966); McKennery, An Argument in Favor of Strict Adherence to the "State Action" Requirement, 5 Wm & Mary L. Rev. 213 (1964); see also Burke & Reber and Marshall, note 19 *supra*.

It is important to understand at the outset what the controversy is *not* about. It is not about the power of Congress or the state legislatures to enact laws requiring private persons to act in accordance with constitutional values.[24] Legislative bodies unquestionably have the right to do this. In a constitutional democracy, any law can be enacted unless it is prohibited by the Constitution, and the Constitution certainly does not prohibit the extension of, say, egalitarian or proceduralist norms to private persons.[25] The rub is that what the legislature giveth, the legislature can also taketh away: what is enacted by majority vote can be repealed by majority vote.

Critics of the state action doctrine therefore insist that constitutional values ought to govern private institutions as well as public ones, regardless of the possible will of the majority at any given time. Scholarly condemnation of the state action doctrine was especially overwhleming during the 1960s and early 1970s. The moral fuel for this condemnation was the feeling that racial equality should be enforceable as a constitutional norm in the private sector as well in the sphere of government. Charles Black put it with characteristic passion when he attacked the doctrine in 1967: "[T]he state action problem is the most important problem in American law. We cannot think about it too much."[26]

The attacks on the state action doctrine make a powerful conceptual as well as moral point. The conceptual point is based on a Supreme Court case of 1948, *Shelley v. Kraemer*.[27] *Shelley* held that a state court could not enforce a racially restrictive property covenant entered into by private parties, because for a court to enforce the covenant would be state action and a violation of the Equal Protection Clause. The broad principle that the critics of the

---

[24]"Private persons" in this context is shorthand for both "natural persons" and "legal persons." Criticism of the state action doctrine often concedes that natural persons should be exempt (wholly or in part) from the prohibitions of the Fourteenth Amendment, but insists that powerful private organizations should not be exempt. When confronting this issue, I will not use the "shorthand." See notes 40–41 *infra* and accompanying text.

[25]Since 1937, the Supreme Court has consistently upheld the constitutionality of such Acts of Congress. See, *e.g.*, Katzenbach v. McClung, 379 U.S. 294 (1964); NLRB v. Jones & Laughlin Steel Corp., 301 U.S. 1 (1937). Professor Richard Epstein is today virtually alone in suggesting that such legislation might be unconstitutional. See Epstein, Takings (1985).

[26]Black, Foreword: "State Action," Equal Protection, and California's Proposition 14, 81 Harv. L. Rev. 69, 70 (1967).

[27]334 U.S. 1 (1948). For a more extensive discussion of *Shelley*, see notes 96–125 *infra* and accompanying text.

state action doctrine infer from *Shelley* is that state action is always implicit in any private act: for the state to permit the act is itself state action.[28] Thus, if the state permits you to discriminate, the state has acted, and the only remaining question is whether your discrimination can pass muster under the Equal Protection Clause. The argument is very persuasive, at least in the abstract, because you have a "right" to do anything you are not prohibited from doing, and if you have a "right" to do it, then the state will enforce an obligation upon everyone else to respect your "right."[29] And this threat of enforcement is surely state action!

The argument is so good that it makes even its proponents a little uneasy. Their unease stems from the fact that once the state action doctrine is effectively demolished (by showing that everything is state action), the private citizen is left in precisely the same position as an organ of state under the Constitution. Thus, even a person's choice of a marriage partner, if based on race or religion, might be seen as a violation of equal protection under the Fourteenth Amendment. Many critics of the state action doctrine therefore concede that while constitutional norms should in principle apply to everyone, there ought to be an exception for a "small area of privacy,"[30] or as another scholar put it, that "authentically private life" should be "fenced off" from the constitution's commands.[31] This begs at least one important question, however, namely, What is so good about privacy? Why should privacy outweigh the enforceability of explicit constitutional norms?

To be sure, the Supreme Court has said that privacy itself is guaranteed by "penumbras" and "emanations" of the Bill of Rights,[32] or by the Due Process Clause of the Fourteenth Amendment.[33] But the question remains, Is there a principle to justify exceptions to the applicability of such important values as equality and proceduralism?

---

[28]Black, note 26 *supra*, at 93–95. See also Horowitz, Van Alstyne & Karst, Henkin, Alexander, note 23 *supra*.

[29]See generally Hohfeld, Fundamental Legal Conceptions as Applied to Judicial Reasoning (1914).

[30]Henkin, note 23 *supra*, at 498–500.

[31]Black, note 26 *supra*, at 101.

[32]See Griswold v. Connecticut, 381 U.S. 479, 484 (1965).

[33]See Roe v. Wade 410 U.S. 113, 129 (1973).

If there is such a principle, articulating it ought to help in defining how broad (or how narrow) the "privacy" exception should be. What is more, privacy is not expressly provided for in the Constitution, and even as a value it cannot be taken for granted. Radical feminists, among others, insist that privacy is actually oppressive and that there should be no distinction between private and public.[34] Any "privacy" or other limit upon the reach of the Constitution, then, needs a clear justification in principle.

The suggestion of this article is that Isaiah Berlin's value pluralism provides that principle. Pluralism is a principle that justifies not only an exemption for some ill-defined "small area of privacy," however. Rather, it justifies the traditional state action doctrine itself.

III

The Fourteenth Amendment values of equality and proce-duralism are good values, as any pluralist would cheerfully agree.[35] The objection to the state action doctrine is that since these constitutional values are good, they ought to apply to everyone and not just to the government. While conceding that equality and proceduralism are good, a value pluralist would deny that Four-teenth Amendment values necessarily coincide with other human values that are also good.[36] Equality conflicts with values that differentiate people, like meritocracy and tradition (values that conflict with each other, too, of course). Equality has long been recognized as potentially conflicting with liberty.[37] Due process

---

[34]See Mackinnon, Feminism, Marxism, Method and the State, 8 Signs 635, 646 (1983): "[F]eminist consciousness has exploded the private. For women, the measure of the intimacy has been the measure of the oppression. To see the personal as political means to see the private as public." See also Burns, Apologia for the Status Quo, 74 Georgetown L. J. 1791, 1797–99 (1986); Olsen, The Family and the Market: A Study of Ideology and Legal Reform, 96 Harv. L. Rev. 1497, 1561–2 (1983). In general, totalitarian doctrines reject the distinction between public and private and attack the idea of privacy as "immoral," "antisocial," and "part of the cult of individualism." Westin, Privacy and Freedom 23 (1967). For examples from Mao's China, see Hollander, Privacy: A Bastion Stormed, 12 Problems of Communism 1 (1963).

[35]Cf. Westen, The Empty Idea of Equality, 95 Harv. L. Rev. 537 (1982) (arguing that equality is an entirely empty idea because people can only be treated equally with respect to some right or other good extrinsic to equality). See also Chemerinsky, In Defense of Equality: A Reply to Professor Westen, 81 Mich. L. Rev. 575 (1983) (rebutting Westen).

[36]See Berlin, notes 6–15 supra.

[37]See Tocqueville, Democracy in America 113–14 (1974) ("There is good reason for distinguishing [equality and freedom]; the taste which men have for liberty, and that which

conflicts with values like informality and intimacy; often, it may conflict with efficiency as well.[38]

Government, to be sure, cannot coherently pursue conflicting ends at one and the same time. Government is a monopoly. Since there is only one body of government institutions, the Constitution prescribes the values by which that government must govern—in the case of the Fourteenth Amendment, values of equal protection and due process.

If government is one, however, nongovernmental "persons" are many. Certainly the individual citizens are many, with individual tastes, interests and values. Nongovernmental institutions are many, as well: under American law, none—at least in principle— may operate monopolistically unless the monopoly is actually established and regulated by the government.

If Isaiah Berlin is right, and human values are many, conflicting, and irreconcilable, then private persons and institutions should be presumptively free to act in accordance with manifold and differing values, lest some authentic values be submerged altogether. The state action doctrine means that only the government is constitutionally bound in its laws and policies by the Fourteenth Amendment and the Bill of Rights. The doctrine frees private persons to act in accordance with many and competing values, unless legislation—popularly enacted and popularly revocable— intervenes to require private compliance with constitutional values.

On a theoretical level, value pluralism thus implies that privacy is important in principle, and not just a matter of personal taste.[39] The existence of a private sphere within which people are free to choose their values ensures that various and conflicting values will be pursued. If the private sphere were somehow abolished, then only publicly adopted values could be pursued. But public, governmental institutions—there being only one government—

---

they feel for equality are, in fact, two different things; and I am not afraid to add, two unequal things").

[38]See Gellhorn, Byse & Strauss, Administrative Law 445–49 (7th ed. 1979) (quoting various studies of the drawbacks and costs to welfare recipients in general of offering adjudicatory hearings in the field of welfare administration).

they feel for equality are, in fact, two different things; and I am not afraid to add, two unequal things").

[39]Cf. Griswold v. Connecticut, 381 U.S. 479, 510 (Black, J., dissenting) ("I like my privacy as well as the next one, but . . .").

cannot adopt at one and the same time values that conflict with one another. This would be no great loss if all true values were mutually reconcilable and harmonious. But if value pluralists are right that they are not, then some true values would inevitably be lost.

At a more practical level, critics of the state action doctrine frequently make the point that "private" corporate institutions in the twentieth century are often very powerful—virtually the equals, perhaps, of government itself.[40] The observation is no doubt perfectly true.[41] But which particular private powers are "too powerful" is generally a matter of controversy. It is difficult to imagine how "too powerful" could be defined as a matter of constitutional principle. It is not at all difficult, on the other hand, for democratic institutions to impose legal limits on private companies, through statutes enacted by majority vote. Majorities can become minorities, of course, and vice versa, and statutes can be repealed. Hence the possibility of pluralism over time, even if value pluralism is restrained by statute at a given time. But statutory regulation is very different from regulating private bodies by "entrenched" constitutional norms that are practically immune from change by majority vote. Constitutional regulation of private persons and institutions would suppress competing values almost immutably.

The Constitution binds the public monopoly of government to the public values expressed in the Constitution. But there exist many other conflicting values. Private "persons" are also many. The pluralist case for the state action doctrine is that there should be no constitutional bar to diverse persons pursuing diverse values—values that conflict, yet values that are all good in the eyes of at least some people some of the time.

---

[40]See Chemerinsky, Rethinking State Action, 80 N.W.U.L. Rev. 503, 510–11 (1985), citing Unger, Law in Modern Society 201–02 (1976) (corporate power is sometimes virtually indistinguishable from state power). See also Berle, Constitutional Limitations on Corporate Activity—Protection of Personal Rights from Invasion through Economic Power, 100 U. Pa. L. Rev. 933 (1952).

[41]It is true at least in a metaphoric sense. But after all, even the most powerful corporation cannot directly control the armed might of the state. American constitutional government has persisted from 1787 until today, whereas formidable corporate powers have frequently come a cropper, often to the general amusement and relief of the American public.

IV

So much for the theory. How will it work in practice? If governmental monopoly alone is the basis for insisting (at the constitutional level) on conformity to the Fourteenth Amendment, how will this affect the way lawsuits are decided?

Consider four well-known cases in which the applicability of the Constitution to private parties was at issue. The first two could be dealt with relatively straightforwardly under the pluralism theory of state action. The second two are somewhat more difficult.

A. MOOSE LODGE NO. 107 V. IRVIS[42]

Moose Lodge was an all-white private club in Harrisburg, Pennsylvania. The Lodge had never received public funds, although it did hold a liquor licence from the state. The Lodge refused service in its dining room and bar to the black guest of a Lodge member and the rejected guest sued the Lodge (as well as the state liquor licensing authority) for violating the Fourteenth Amendment. The theory of the lawsuit was that it violated equal protection for the private holder of a liquor licence to discriminate on the basis of race.

The Supreme Court dismissed the case on the ground that there was no state action.[43] At an intuitive level, this outcome might evoke some sympathy on grounds of "privacy"—the idea that people (even Moose) should be entitled to socialize with whomever they like without running afoul of the Constitution.[44] It is not clear, however, what precise legal grounds the Supreme Court relied on for its decision. The Court observed that there were 114 other liquor licences—public bars as well as private clubs—in Harrisburg,[45] so that the Lodge's licence fell "far short of conferring . . . a monopoly in the dispensing of liquor" in the town.[46] But the Court also seemed to rely on the idea that the state was not "enforcing" private discrimination,[47] and the Court concluded that

[42]407 U.S. 163 (1972).

[43]*Ibid.*

[44]See Civil Rights Cases, 109 U.S. 3, 59 (1883) (Harlan, J., dissenting).

[45]Moose Lodge No. 107 v. Irvis, 407 U.S. at 182 n. 2 (Douglas, J., dissenting).

[46]*Id.* at 177.

[47]*Id.* at 172, citing Shelley v. Kraemer, note 27 *supra.*

the licence did not "sufficiently implicate"[48] the state in the Lodge's discrimination. The subversive thought arises that if Mr. Irvis had really insisted on being served, the Harrisburg police presumably would have "enforced" the Lodge's racial policy. And the Court certainly does not clarify how "implicated" the state would have to be in order to be "sufficiently implicated."

On the pluralism theory of state action, the court's result in Moose Lodge was right. The value prized by the Lodge—racism, in a word—may be distasteful to most of us today, but in other times and places such values as "ethnic solidarity" might be very desirable—as counterweights, perhaps, to the homogenizing effects of mass society. The Constitution should not be an unalterable bar to the pursuit of such values by private groups like the Moose.[49] By the time the Moose Lodge case was decided in 1972, after all, there were plenty of other places to meet, eat, and drink in Harrisburg, including restaurants and bars integrated by statute,[50] and probably including integrated private clubs as well. In other words, there was a realistic choice among competing values open to blacks and whites alike. Pluralism suggests that constitutional values should be constitutionally obligatory only when there is no such choice.[51]

B. JACKSON V. METROPOLITAN EDISON CO.[52]

Metropolitan Edison was a regulated private utility which cut off Mrs. Jackson's service for alleged non-payment of her bills. This company was the only entity, public or private, licensed to supply electric power to most of the town in which Mrs. Jackson lived.[53]

---

[48]*Id.* at 177.

[49]Legislation, on the other hand, properly can and does bar many kinds of private discrimination, including discrimination in "public accommodations" such as hotels, restaurants, and theaters. *See* Civil Rights Act of 1964, as amended, 42 U.S.C. §§ 2000–2000a-6 (1987).

[50]*Ibid.*

[51]But suppose there were no realistic choices for blacks? Until a few short years before Moose Lodge, blacks were victims of pervasive discrimination, private as well as public: indeed, a black American faced grave difficulties buying a drink in a bar, a meal in a restaurant, or a night's lodging in a hotel. See Heart of Atlanta Motel v. U.S., 379 U.S. 241, 252–53 (1964). For a discussion of that problem, see notes 96–125 *infra* and accompanying text.

[52]419 U.S. 345 (1974).

[53]419 U.S. 345, 366 (Marshall, J., dissenting).

Her service was cut off without notice, without an opportunity to meet with the company, and without any other procedure that would have given her a chance to state her case or settle her account.[54] She sued the company for violation of due process. A government-operated utility in comparable circumstances would certainly have been required as a matter of due process to give notice and at least an informal hearing before cutting off her service.[55]

The Supreme Court dismissed Mrs. Jackson's case on the ground that there was no state action. Justice Rehnquist held that a company's government-guaranteed monopoly does not "necessarily" mean that it is subject to the commands of the Fourteenth Amendment.[56] He concluded that there was not a close enough "nexus" between the state and what the utility did, to justify treating the company's acts as state action.[57]

Now, if power utilities were many, they might ideally compete with each other, some by offering "due process," others by not offering it and attracting customers with lower prices or some other enticement. The possibility that the market might work in this way implies that the Constitution should not require all competing companies to offer due process. Of course, whenever a majority of people think the free market is not working in this way, they are free to impose due process on the companies through legislation. And if the market or people's thinking about the market changes, the legislation can be repealed. But there should be no constitutional bar to pluralism, whether in the economic sphere or in any other.[58]

---

[54]Mrs. Jackson concededly had a long and complex history of not paying for this company's services. *Id.* at 347.

[55]See Memphis Light, Gas & Water Div. v. Craft, 436 U.S. 1 (1978).

[56]Although state law required the utility to obtain a "certificate of public convenience" as a prerequisite of doing business, Justice Rehnquist voiced doubt that Metropolitan Edison was a monopoly guaranteed by the state, since utilities are "natural monopolies." 419 U.S. 345, 351 n.8. Of course, telephone service also used to be considered a "natural monopoly." But *cf.* North Am Tel. Ass'n v. United States, 460 U.S. 1001 (1983) (approving the antitrust consent decree breaking up the telephone monopoly into competing companies), aff'g United States v. American Tel. & Tel. Co., 552 F. Supp. 131 (D.D.C. 1982).

[57]419 U.S. 345, 351.

[58]For a forceful statement of the importance of economic free markets to human choice and human freedom, see Hayek, The Road to Serfdom (1944). See also Friedman, Capitalism and Freedom (1962). Hayek and Friedman are, of course, rather far on the political right. Thinkers on the political left are also increasingly open to the idea that there is a proper

Power utilities, however, are not many. Metropolitan Edison was a licensed monopoly. To put it a little melodramatically, anyone wanting to offer a competing utility service (with due process guaranteed) would have had to face down the implacable armed might of the United States government. Where a monopoly is licensed and regulated by law, there is no pluralism. And where there is no pluralism—where the power of the state ensures that only one body of values will prevail—the Constitution exists to ensure that Fourteenth Amendment values are the ones that must govern. So on the value pluralist theory of state action it was wrong to exempt Metropolitan Edison from the Due Process Clause.[59]

C. FUENTES V. SHEVIN[60]

Mrs. Fuentes bought household appliances under a sales contract that called for monthly payments over a period of time. The form contract provided that if the buyer defaulted on the payments the seller might "take back" the merchandise. Mrs. Fuentes defaulted, and under Florida law the seller obtained a writ of replevin from a small-claims court ordering the sheriff to seize the goods. Florida required no notice to the buyer and no opportunity for a hearing before the seizure; the law simply required the seller to deposit a bond for at least double the value of the property, and to institute a small-claims court action in which the parties' conflicting claims could later be heard. Mrs. Fuentes sued the state of Florida for depriving her of property without due process of law, on the theory that the state must offer her some kind of hearing before the sheriff can seize the goods.

On the face of it, this was an easy state action case. The sheriff was an officer of government. The Supreme Court had already construed the Due Process Clause to prohibit the government from seizing property without some form of prior notice and hearing. In

---

sphere for market freedom. See, *e.g.*, Plant, The Market: Needs, Rights, and Morality, New Statesman (March 6, 1987), 14–15 (socialists acknowledge a legitimate sphere for markets).

[59]Justice Marshall, in dissent, aptly noted that the Court's analysis "would seemingly apply as well to a company that refused to extend service to Negroes, welfare recipients, or any other group that the company preferred, for its own reasons, not to serve. I cannot believe that this Court would hold" a monopoly utility to be exempt from "the constitutional mandate of nondiscrimination. Yet nothing in the analysis of the majority opinion suggests otherwise." 419 U.S. 395, 374 (Marshall, J., dissenting).

[60]407 U.S. 67 (1972).

terms of the pluralism theory of state action, where state agencies are concerned there can be no question of value pluralism; Mrs. Fuentes, after all, had no other sheriff to turn to, and constitutionalism means that the government monopoly must abide by the Fourteenth Amendment. It appears that Mrs. Fuentes ought to have won. And so the Supreme Court held.[61]

But suppose the state law had merely permitted creditors themselves to seize debtors' goods in cases of default. The creditor is not an officer of state, nor acting under state compulsion. Six years after deciding *Fuentes*, the Supreme Court confronted a case of "self-help" repossession in *Flagg Brothers v. Brooks*.[62] Mrs. Brooks had turned her possessions over to Flagg Brothers for removal and storage. There were disputes about the charges, and Flagg Brothers threatened that if Mrs. Brooks did not pay, the company would exercise its rights as a warehouseman under state law and sell the goods. Whereupon Mrs. Brooks sued the company for depriving her of property without due process in violation of the Fourteenth Amendment. But since Flagg Brothers was a private concern, the Supreme Court held that the company was not bound by the due process clause and was therefore perfectly free to act without giving Mrs. Brooks a hearing in advance.[63]

The distinction between the two cases is obviously that in *Flagg Brothers* the private creditor acted on its own, whereas in *Fuentes* a public officer (the sheriff) carried out the seizure. But is there any real difference between summary seizure by the creditor and summary seizure by the sheriff at the behest of the creditor? After all, in both cases it is the creditor who chooses whether to proceed with repossession, and if the creditor invokes the aid of the sheriff, the officer's task is purely ministerial, a matter of routine. Even if the creditor were to act alone, it would surely be constitutional for the sheriff to intervene to prevent mayhem or murder by a debtor resisting repossession. Thus, if Moose Lodge, say, has the right to discriminate against blacks, then the club surely ought to be entitled to call the police if a would-be black guest refuses to leave

---

[61]*Id.* at 96–97. The Supreme Court did not couch the matter in terms of "pluralism," of course. What it did emphasize was that here was a seizure by "state power," *id.* at 79, and that due process is required before "the State authorizes its agents to seize property in the possession of a person upon the application of another," *id.* at 80.

[62]436 U.S. 149 (1978).

[63]*Id.* at 157.

the premises; likewise, an all-black private club ought to be able to call the police to expel white intruders. On the same principle, if a private creditor has the right to repossess without a hearing, it ought to be legitimate for the sheriff to carry out the repossession, if only in order to keep the peace.[64]

From the point of view of value pluralism, there is certainly a strong argument against constitutional prohibition of summary repossession. The argument is that, without a constitutional rule, a debtor like Mrs. Fuentes might have more of a choice among installment-contract sellers when she buys her appliances. In an ideal credit market, sellers might compete with one another, some by disclaiming the right to repossess without a prior hearing in cases of default, others by not disclaiming and charging lower prices.[65] If the market might produce such competition, debtors ought to be free to choose which sort of creditors they borrow from: market pluralism, even if it is only potential, should not be choked off constitutionally.[66] Prohibiting summary repossession would diminish the diversity (at least the potential diversity) of the credit market. It would diminish the range of commercial values that might be adopted by non-monopolists.

If the argument is right thus far, the constitutional permissibility of summary seizure should not turn on whether a public officer or a private "repo man" (or woman) actually carries out the reposses-

---

[64]Critics of the state action doctrine agree that there is no real difference between *Flagg Brothers* and *Fuentes*, and consider this as evidence that the state action doctrine is bankrupt. See, *e.g.*, Brest, State Action and Liberal Theory: A Casenote on Flagg Bros. V. Brooks, 130 U. Pa. L. Rev. 1296 (1982). Brest argues that since Flagg Brothers and Fuentes are not distinguishable, the state action doctrine itself must be condemned as "invit[ing] manipulation and mystification." *Id.* at 1330. Brest's main claim is that all private action is conceptually attributable to the state that permits it; therefore, if one wants to preserve a sphere of private autonomy exempt from public control, one must rely on a kind of "natural law" of privacy. *Id.* at 1301. By accepting the idea of "natural law," however, one must accept that the Supreme Court may generally "protect interests or rights beyond those explicitly mentioned" in the Constitution. *Id.* at 1297. Value pluralism, I would suggest, is a far less nebulous (and manipulable) justification than "natural law" for limiting the reach of public principles.

[65]If this sounds totally implausible, imagine two simple advertising slogans: "Buy It From Joe: Nobody Will Ever Just Take It Back in the Dead of Night," and "Buy from Nancy: If You Pay Your Bills You Can Pay the Lowest Price in Town."

[66]For a similar thought, satirically expressed, see Leff, Economic Analysis of Law: Some Realism About Nominalism, 60 Va. L. Rev. 451, 460–61 (1974) (precluding creditors' remedies can hurt debtors as well as creditors).

sion. The crucial question is whether repossession takes place as a matter of public obligation or as a matter of private choice. It would surely be state action for the law to require summary repossession whenever a debtor defaults. The monopoly power of the state would be making summary repossession a public obligation: no one would have any choice. This would be true regardless of whether the statute required public officers or private creditors to carry out the actual seizures. On the other hand, when the law permits private contracts that call for summary repossession, a choice can be negotiated by the creditor and the debtor. There is a potential for market pluralism—the availability of widely different terms in the credit market. How much choice there really is will depend on the ebb and flow of the credit market, which in turn is subject to regulation by the ebb and flow of legislation. But the question of who carries out contractual repossessions can scarcely affect whether debtors have a realistic choice about what sort of installment contracts to enter into. Thus if value pluralism is the proper basis for the state action doctrine, the conclusion is that summary repossession—however enforced—should not be seen as state action when it is based on private contract.

Value pluralism, in short, suggests a realistic test for whether there is state action under the Fourteenth Amendment. The test is whether the monopoly institutions of government are enforcing their own will, or merely vindicating the private choices— villainous though one might sometimes think them—of private persons. When the state adopts its own policy, there can be no pluralism: the citizens have no choice but to submit, and constitutionalism requires that the government policy must conform to the Fourteenth Amendment. The essence of state action is thus the preclusion of private pluralism. When the state undertakes to enforce private choices, on the other hand, the citizen may potentially enjoy an array of possible choices. Various people may act upon various, conflicting values. And so long as the government is not preempting private pluralism, it makes sense to say that there is no state action under the Fourteenth Amendment.

If this analysis is correct, then the Supreme Court was wrong in *Fuentes v. Shevin*, and the sheriff's repossession ought to have been upheld. Yet the decision in *Fuentes* is scarcely an injustice crying out to heaven for redress. It is perhaps worth reflecting on why not. The equities of the case certainly favored Mrs. Fuentes. There is no evidence that Florida installment-plan sellers were actually competing on the basis of whether they would invoke the summary replevin and seizure laws. The contract in question was a "contract of adhesion": the repossession clause was part of a form contract printed "in relatively small type," and Mrs. Fuentes had no opportunity to bargain over the terms.[67] In short, the pluralism of values in the marketplace here—the range of choices open to Mrs. Fuentes—were practically rather narrow. What is more, the contractual terms themselves were ambiguous. The repossession clause merely said that upon default the seller might "take back" the merchandise.[68] The clause did not say *how* the goods might be taken back—whether by "final judgment, self-help, with a prior hearing, or . . . without a prior hearing."[69] Quite apart from any constitutional question of due process, the summary repossession might have been held unconscionable or simply unenforceable as a matter of contract law.[70] More generally, consumer-credit debtors are often—although by no means always—poor people, easily victimized, good candidates for judicial sympathy.

More broadly, *Fuentes*—even if wrongly decided—has not really had any ill consequences for the state action doctrine because the significance of the case has proved so paralyzingly difficult to understand. The question of whether summary repossession is state action, and what the proper principle of analysis should be, has been a source of almost comic perplexity, creating a considerable scholarly cottage industry.[71] The confusion about what *Fuentes* means for state action has tended to isolate the decision. As a practical matter, therefore, the case has not eroded the Supreme Court's general commitment to the state action doctrine. For a value pluralist, the essence of the doctrine is that it distinguishes between exercises of choice by the monopoly institutions of the state—which must conform to the Constitution—and exercises of

---

[67]407 U.S. 67, 95.

[68]*Ibid.*

[69]*Id.* at 95–96.

[70]See Uniform Commercial Code sec. 2–302 (1982) (contracts may be unenforceable if "unconscionable"). The classic article on the unconscionability clause is still Leff, Unconscionability and the Code—the Emperor's New Clause, 115 U. Pa. L. Rev. 485 (1967).

[71]In 1975, Professor Alexander cited forty-four law review articles and comments on the subject. Alexander, Cutting the Gordian Knot: State Action and Self-Help Repossession, 2 Hastings Const. L. Q. 893, 894–95 n.3 (1975). Connoisseurs will discover many more contributions since that time, including, *e.g.*, Brest, note 64 *supra*.

choice by private persons acting, as private persons always do, with the protection of the state. This is an essential distinction for a society that wants to safeguard the diversity of its own values by limiting the reach of the constitutional norms that govern its public institutions.

D. MARSH V. ALABAMA[72]

The town of Chickasaw, Alabama, a suburb of Mobile, was a "company town." It was wholly owned by the Gulf Shipbuilding Corporation, a private concern. Apart from being owned by Gulf, Chickasaw had "all the characteristics of any other American town."[73] The place had houses, streets, a sewage system, a "business block" where shops were located, and a post office. It also had a deputy of the Mobile County Sheriff, paid by the company, who served as the town's policeman. Mrs. Marsh, a Jehovah's Witness, tried to distribute religious leaflets in the main shopping street of Chickasaw. The deputy sheriff told her that she could not distribute her leaflets there, as it was private property. She persisted, and he arrested her for trespass.

She pleaded that Gulf's prohibition on distributing leaflets violated the free press and religion clauses of the First and Fourteenth Amendments. The Supreme Court agreed, saying that the company was engaged in a "public function" in operating Chickasaw,[74] and that the Constitution therefore forbade Gulf from curtailing freedom of press and religion in the town.[75] The court also concluded that the State of Alabama violated the Constitution by imposing criminal penalties on Mrs. Marsh.[76]

Now, the point of the decision cannot be that it is unconstitutional for a state ever to enforce trespass laws against religious speakers.[77] After all, if I enter your home uninvited and begin to deliver a sermon, I am not constitutionally immune from the

---

[72]326 U.S. 501 (1946).

[73]*Id.* at 502.

[74]*Id.* at 506.

[75]*Id.* at 508.

[76]*Id.* at 509.

[77]See Gunther, Cases and Materials on Constitutional Law 988–89 (1980): "Apparently, the invocation of a state trespass law was not important to the finding of state action. Rather, Marsh rested largely on the nature of [Gulf's] private activity," namely that operating Chickasaw was a "public function."

trespass statutes. Mrs. Marsh's constitutional complaint arose because of Gulf's policy prohibiting the distribution of religious leaflets anywhere in the town. It was Gulf's policy that the Supreme Court found constitutionally objectionable.[78]

The *Marsh* decision intuitively seems right. As the Court said, "had the people of Chickasaw owned all the homes and all the stores . . . all those owners together could not have set up a municipal government with sufficient power to pass an ordinance completely barring the distribution of religious literature."[79] Surely this corporate owner should not have been constitutionally free to do so either.

Analytically, however, the Supreme Court seems to have relied on the idea that when a private person performs a "public function," the person's actions become state action and must conform to the Constitution. This idea is problematic because it begs the difficult question: What, constitutionally, is a "public function"? Not, as we have seen, operating a power utility,[80] although governments sometimes operate power utilities.[81] Not operating a private school, although governments often devote a large proportion of their budgets to operating schools.[82] It is difficult to imagine how there could be a conceptual boundary between public and private functions, because it is virtually impossible to conceive of a function that cannot be carried out either publicly or privately. In the Soviet Union, for example, at least until recently, all lawful economic activity has been the preserve of the state.[83] In a "libertarian" utopia, on the other hand, the legitimate functions of

---

[78]"The managers appointed by the corporation cannot curtail the liberty of press and religion of these people consistently with the purposes of the Constitutional guarantees. . . ." 326 U.S. at 508.

[79]Id. at 505.

[80]See Jackson v. Metropolitan Edison, notes 52–58 *supra*, and accompanying text.

[81]See Memphis Light, Gas & Water Div. v. Craft, note 55 *supra*.

[82]Hence private schools may do things that public schools would be constitutionally forbidden from doing. See Rendell-Baker v. Kohn, 457 U.S. 830 (1982) (there was no state action when staff members were dismissed by a private school that received most of its funding from state sources). See also Evans v. Newton, 382 U.S. 296, 300 (1966) ("While a state may not segregate public schools so as to include one or more religious groups, those sects may maintain their own parochial educational systems").

[83]See Schwarzschild, Variations on an Enigma: Law in Practice and Law on the Books in the USSR, 99 Harv. L. Rev. 685, 688 (1986) ("statutes on the books give the Soviet government a monopoly on economic activity within the country").

government would be vanishingly few.[84] It is scarcely more satisfactory to speak, as the courts sometimes do, of "traditionally"
public functions.[85] American governments today do all sorts of
things, generally accepted as part and parcel of modern government, that would have seemed unthinkably radical to many people
a century ago; on the other hand, American governments in some
parts of the country have long performed functions that are still
traditionally private elsewhere in the United States.[86]

Over the years, the Supreme Court has implicitly recognized the
difficulties that would be created by a "public function" theory of
state action. This recognition has taken the form of a strong judicial
reluctance to classify private activity as public in function. The
company town decision in *Marsh* was handed down in 1946.[87] After
a twenty year hiatus,[88] the Supreme Court experimented with an
extension of *Marsh* by holding that a private shopping center called
Logan Valley Plaza could not, consistently with the First Amendment, bar union picketing on its property.[89] Four years later the
Court refused to apply the First Amendment to a private shopping
center confronted with leafleters protesting the Vietnam War.[90]
And by 1976 the Court announced that *Logan Valley* was overruled

---

[84]See generally Nozick, Anarchy, State, and Utopia (1974).

[85]See Jackson v. Metropolitan Edison Co., 419 U.S. 345, 352–53 (1974).

[86]The State of North Dakota has operated a commercial bank since 1919. See 1B North
Dakota Century Code 6–09–01 (State Law of 1919, Ch. 147) ("the State of North Dakota
shall engage in the business of banking . . . under the name of the Bank of North Dakota").

[87]326 U.S. 501 (1946).

[88]In the twenty years after *Marsh*, Professors Burke and Reber describe the "vitality" of the
decision as having been "doubtful." Burke & Reber, note 19 *supra*, at 1069.

[89]Amalgamated Food Employees Local 590 v. Logan Valley Plaza Inc., 391 U.S. 308
(1968). Justice Black, who had written the majority opinion in *Marsh*, dissented vehemently
in *Logan Valley*. *Id.* at 330 (Black, J., dissenting).

[90]Lloyd Corp. Ltd. v. Tanner, 407 U.S. 551 (1972). The court distinguished *Lloyd* from
Logan Valley on the ground that the picketing in *Logan Valley* was "directly related in its
purposes to the use to which the . . . property was being put." 407 U.S. at 563–64. It is
difficult to imagine what difference this should make under the First Amendment, and
Justice Marshall said in dissent that there was "no valid distinction" between the two cases.
Id. at 584 (Marshall, J., dissenting). More convincingly, the Court pointed out that in *Lloyd*
the leafleters had "alternative avenues of communication" on nearby public streets, so that
there was no need to attribute public function (and thus state action) to the shopping center
in order to vindicate First Amendment values. *Id.* at 566–67. On the same day that it decided
Lloyd, the Supreme Court held in Central Hardware Co. v. NLRB, 407 U.S. 539 (1972), that
shops could ban union soliciting in their parking lots. The company's ban was not state
action because free-standing shops do not have "the functional attributes of public use." *Id.*
at 547.

and that private shopping complexes do not perform a public
function and need not conform to the First Amendment after all.[91]

How would *Marsh v. Alabama* be analyzed on the value pluralism
theory of state action?

Pluralists could agree on the following two propositions:

1. There are authentically good values that are incompatible with
the free speech values of the First Amendment. One such value is
peace and quiet.[92] Another is that there should be private preserves
of orthodoxy. Most people would agree, for example, that a
Communist Party meeting should not be constitutionally required
to entertain a speaker on the virtues of capitalism or—no doubt
worse from the Communist point of view—on the virtues of
Trotskyism. There is value in corporate solidarity, which suggests
that executives at Pepsi headquarters should not have a constitutional right to hang a banner from their office windows saying
"Things Go Better with Coke." Pluralism implies that private
organizations should in general be free to pursue diverse values—
whether consistent or inconsistent with the values implicit in the
First Amendment.

2. Chickasaw's owner, Gulf, was private. In ordinary circumstances, when a private company insists on values contradictory to
the First Amendment there is no erosion of public
constitutionalism—the principle that the Constitution must control
the government's monopoly of public power.

Now, a pluralist critic of the Supreme Court's decision in Marsh
would offer a third proposition:

3. Not only did Gulf's ban on distributing leaflets in Chickasaw
not erode public constitutionalism, it did not significantly infringe
private pluralism either. Concededly, by insisting on peace and
quiet in the town, Gulf restricted the expression of diverse opinions
in Chickasaw. But residents could easily go elsewhere whenever
they wanted to encounter or participate in a robust exchange of
ideas. They could go to Mobile, for example, of which Chickasaw

---

[91]Hudgens v. NLRB, 424 U.S. 507 (1976). Apart from company towns and shopping
centers, the public function theory of state action has arisen most prominently in Terry v.
Adams, 345 U.S. 461 (1953), involving a "private" Democratic county political organization
in Texas that excluded blacks from voting in its primaries. The Supreme Court held that the
"private" primary violated equal protection.

[92]H. L. Mencken praised Calvin Coolidge, only half ironically, for "snoozing away the lazy
afternoons," having "no ideas," and "not [being] a nuisance." Mencken, Coolidge, in Cooke,
ed., The Vintage Mencken 219–23 (1955).

was after all only a suburb. A wide pluralism of choices remained practically open to the people of Chickasaw. Indeed, the existence of the company town side by side with conventional towns served to increase the diversity of municipal atmospheres in which people might choose to live. When private immunity from the Constitution's norms neither erodes public constitutionalism nor precludes private choice, it is an easy case for private immunity from the Constitution's norms. Hence the Gulf Corporation should have won.

At least as strong a pluralist argument can be made in favor of the Supreme Court's result in *Marsh*, however. Accepting propositions (1) and (2) in principle, the situation in Chickasaw was not merely the result of a normal exercise of private choice by a private company. The company employed a deputy of the County Sheriff's Department as its municipal policeman.[93] It is one thing for a company to adopt values at variance with the Constitution. It is another for the company to employ a public officer to enforce those values. Hiring policemen is an act of sovereignty. The presence of the deputy sheriff on the company payroll suggests that Gulf was operating as the government of Chickasaw and not merely as its proprietor. Public constitutionalism requires that governments should conform to the Constitution.

As for private pluralism in Chickasaw, the townfolk's freedom of choice in the matter of exposing themselves to uncensored debate may have been more theoretical than real. The nature of a company town is that its residents work as well as live there. It is not realistic to expect that people who live, work, and do their shopping in a company town will travel beyond the town's borders in order to make themselves available to the distributors of leaflets. Nor have the distributors of leaflets any alternative means of reaching residents who seldom leave the town.[94] A company town does practically infringe the pluralism of private choice for its residents by monopolizing their lives. A company county would do this even more, and a company state, God forbid, still more. It is no defense for such a monopoly to point out that it coexists with conventional

---

[93]326 U.S. 501, 502.

[94]The Supreme Court implicitly acknowledged the importance of these aspects of the situation in Chickasaw when it concluded, "Just as all other citizens, [the residents] must make decisions which affect the welfare of community and nation. To act as good citizens they must be informed. In order to enable them to be properly informed their information must be uncensored." 326 U.S. at 508.

jurisdictions, any more than a conventional jurisdiction could justify its unconstitutional conduct by pointing out that the disaffected are free to live elsewhere. (Or, in the vernacular, "If you don't like it here why don't you go back to Russia?") The Gulf Corporation was the government of Chickasaw in all but name. The lives of the citizens were controlled by Gulf as by a government. The monopoly power of government must conform to the Constitution, and on this view of pluralism Mrs. Marsh's victory in the Supreme Court was proper.[95]

Value pluralism offers no conclusive answer, perhaps, to whether the acts of a company town should indeed be considered state action. The theory does, however, suggest substantive principles upon which the question can be debated. The principles are public constitutionalism and private pluralism: that the monopoly power of government must act in accordance with constitutional values but that private persons, when they are many and various, ought not to be constrained by the Constitution from pursuing many and various values.

V. What about Shelley v. Kraemer?[96]

Shelley v. Kraemer is the key to the moral and intellectual passion aroused by the state action doctrine. *Shelley* involved a house that was sold to a black family in 1945 in defiance of a racially restrictive covenant adopted by the private homeowners in the neighborhood.[97] Nearby owners, parties to the covenant, sued for an injunction against the black buyers' taking possession. The Supreme Court held that private persons are constitutionally free to discriminate on the basis of race or on any basis they please,[98] but that it is unconstitutional state action for a court to enforce a racial

---

[95] This argument supporting the Court's result in *Marsh* suggests that the Court was also correct in refusing to extend *Marsh* to private shopping centers. See Hudgens v. NLRB, note 91 *supra*. A shopping center, however large, does not monopolize the waking and sleeping hours of a body of citizens. *Cf.* Didion, On the Mall, in Didion, The White Album 180 (1979) (an exposition of the author's intense feelings about "shopping-center theory").

[96] Note 27 *Supra*.

[97] The covenant was an agreement, in legally binding form, that the property would not be sold or rented to "people of the Negro or Mongolian race." 334 U.S. at 4–5. Such racial covenants were extremely common at the time. See generally Vose, Caucasians Only: The Supreme Court, the NAACP, and the Restrictive Covenant Cases (1959).

[98] 334 U.S. 1, 13.

covenant by enjoining an interracial sale.[99] Hence the neighbors could not use the courts to stop the sale.

The outcome in *Shelley* was morally right. It would have been indecent, to put it mildly, in the immediate aftermath of the war against Nazism in which black Americans had fought and died, for the Supreme Court to order these black house-buyers out of their new neighborhood because of the color of their skin.

Now, the Supreme Court has steadfastly refused to infer any general principle from *Shelley* other than that racially restrictive property covenants may not be enforced by court order.[100] But if court enforcement of a restrictive covenant is state action, then it is only logical to suggest that private contracts in general should not be enforced if they conflict with constitutional values. The trouble with this suggestion is that it could preclude enforcement not only of racially discriminatory contracts but of contracts supporting religious institutions,[101] or even of contracts that call for something to happen (like liquidated damages) without the need for the parties to give each other hearings on the matter.[102] What is more, contracts are merely one vehicle of private ordering. If contracts conflicting with constitutional values were to be unenforceable, there would be no reason in principle why courts should be permitted to enforce noncontractual "rights" that private citizens might exercise contrary to constitutional values. On this logic, if you bequeath property to one person rather than to another because of the race or religion of the people involved, your will would be unenforceable; so would a simply capricious bequest.[103] If you refuse to welcome

---

[99]*Id.* at 20.

[100]For a summary of cases in which the Supreme Court has refused to erode the state action doctrine by inferring general principles from Shelley, see Burke & Reber, note 19 *supra*, at 1088 n.335. As Burke and Reber observe, the fact that the court has not acted on *Shelley's* implications does not stop controversy over *Shelley* from raging among legal scholars. *Id.* at 1088. For Professor Herbert Wechsler, Shelley v. Kraemer was a prototypically "unprincipled" decision, in the sense that the Court decided the case in disregard of the unwelcome logical implications. See Wechsler, Toward Neutral Principles of Constitutional Law, 73 Harv. L. Rev. 1, 29–30 (1959).

[101]The First Amendment has been interpreted to limit the kinds of financial aid that government can give to religious institutions. See, *e.g.*, Meek v. Pittenger, 421 U.S. 349 (1975).

[102]See Farnsworth, Contracts 895–904 (1982) (a liquidated damages clause is enforceable unless the stipulated amount is so unreasonable as to be a "penalty").

[103]Due process, of course, requires at least "minimum rationality" of state action. See Nebbia v. New York, 291 U.S. 502 (1934); see also Williamson v. Lee Optical, 348 U.S. 483 (1955).

into your home an intruder who wants to deliver a sermon or a
political speech, it would be state action, presumably in violation of
the First Amendment, for the magistrate's court to convict the
intruder of trespassing. Ultimately, state action in the sense of
Shelley is implicit in any private act, so long as the state stands ready
to enforce against all comers your right to do the private act.[104] The
logic implicit in *Shelley* is that private acts are inseparable from
government action, and therefore that the state action doctrine is no
limit at all to the obligatory reach of constitutional values.[105]

   This broad conclusion would certainly be unwelcome to a
pluralist for whom constitutional values are not the only values.
Indeed, the specific decision in *Shelley* seems to contradict value
pluralism, despite one's strong intuition that the decision was right.
Racial equality, so it might be argued, is good, but there are
conflicting values that are also good. One such value is ethnic
solidarity; a related value is community feeling, which may be
strongest among people of similar backgrounds and outlooks. The
Constitution properly requires the government—a monopoly
which must act upon one principle or another—to act upon the
principle of racial equality. But private persons, who are many,
should not be constitutionally precluded from acting upon conflicting values, lest some authentically good values be suppressed
altogether. Private freedom of choice does require public enforcement, else freedom might soon be usurped by whoever is strongest
at the moment. Contracts, for example, are an important way for
private persons to give effect to their choices by entering into
reliable agreements with others.[106] But when courts undertake to

---

[104]See notes 28–29 *supra* and accompanying text. See esp. Alexander, note 23 *supra*, at
897–99 (arguing that in principle it is just as much state action for the state to permit
something as to require or to forbid it).

[105]Then-professor Louis Pollak attempted to derive a more limited principle from *Shelley*,
namely that the Constitution only forbids the courts from enforcing discrimination upon
parties who do not wish to discriminate, but that the courts may enforce a private party's
right to discriminate when the party wishes to exercise the right. Pollak, Racial Discrimination and Judicial Integrity: A Reply to Professor Wechsler, 108 U. Pa. L. Rev. 1 (1959).
Pollak's effort to limit the logical implications of *Shelley* has been effectively criticized in
Alexander, note 23 *supra*, at 904–05 n.35, and in Henkin, note 23 *supra*, at 478 n.10.

[106]The paradox of contract, of course, is that the parties may enter into their agreement
willingly enough, but in order for it to be reliable the agreement has to be enforceable later,
even when a party might be very unwilling to perform. Contract gives effect to free choice,
in other words, by precluding the (later) free choice of noncompliance. For an analysis of
contract as a kind of insurance that makes choice possible, see Friedman, Law in a Changing
Society 91–92 (1959). See also Speidel, An Essay on the Reported Death and Continued

give effect to private choices, the courts are not endorsing, much less imposing, any particular private choices. In *Shelley*, for example, there was no question of the court's imposing a racial covenant on parties who might have been unaware of what they agreed to, or who had been unwilling to agree to it. Indeed, the racial covenant was brazenly clear.[107] Public constitutionalism, the government's commitment to constitutional values, is not eroded when the government enforces the right of private persons to act in accordance with values that conflict with those of the Constitution. Indeed, private pluralism can flourish only when government is prepared to enforce this freedom. Pluralism, in short, seems to imply that the Supreme Court was wrong in *Shelley* and that the racial covenant ought to have been enforced.

There it is. I know that the Supreme Court did the right thing in *Shelley*, that any other outcome would have been hateful and wrong. Yet the decision seems irreconcilable with the state action doctrine, and with the underlying principle of value pluralism. Is there any way of squaring the circle?

Perhaps there is this. Black Americans were the victims of a unique history of injustice in America. Slavery was unique.[108] The obsessive practice of racial segregation (otherwise known as "Jim Crow") for a century after the Civil War was unique.[109] Part of the uniqueness of American racism was its pervasiveness even in those areas of life where it was not legally compelled. In many respects, after all, at least in most parts of the country, white Americans were legally free to associate socially, economically, and politically on equal terms with blacks. It might be expected that many whites would have done so, if only out of pecuniary or other

---

Vitality of Contract, 27 Stan. L. Rev. 1161, 1181 (1975) (contract law affects "the conditions of freedom in a process where a high value is still put on consent").

[107]See note 97 *supra*, quoting Shelley v. Kraemer, 334 U.S. at 4–5. *Cf.* Fuentes v. Shevin, discussed at notes 68–70 *supra* and accompanying text. In *Fuentes*, the contractual provision permitting repossession by the creditor was ambiguous as a waiver of the debtor's right to procedural fairness.

[108]For a sample of the vast literature on American slavery, see Genovese, Roll Jordan Roll: The World the Slaves Made (1974) (emphasizing the informal nonlegal characteristics of the slave system); Stampp, The Peculiar Institution: Slavery in the Ante-Bellum South (1956).

[109]See generally Black, The Lawfulness of the Segregation Decisions, 69 Yale L. J. 421, 424–26 (1960) (segregation was pervasive in the South until at least 1960). See also Myrdal, An American Dilemma (1944); Woodward, The Strange Career of Jim Crow (1957).

self-interest.[110] With few exceptions, in fact, they did not. There was a startlingly broad consensus among white Americans that blacks were to be kept down and kept out.[111] There was no pluralism about race. Blacks were truly a "discrete and insular minority."[112]

In the century after the Civil War, the Supreme Court did intermittently strike down statutes and other official acts that blatantly discriminated against blacks.[113] The impact of those decisions on the racial atmosphere of the country was close to nil.[114] The reason was obvious. Discrimination against blacks was far more than a matter of government policy. It was a disease deeply embedded in American life. American race relations were just the sort of "extreme real-world condition" that would stretch any constitutional doctrine to the breaking point. Unsurprisingly, the state action doctrine looks pathetic in the face of the American racial crisis. A decision in *Shelley v. Kraemer* upholding the restrictive covenant on "state action" grounds would have been blind to reality because it would have relegated blacks to seeking out a nonexistent pluralism about race among white Americans.

So the state action doctrine and the underlying idea of value pluralism are undoubtedly failures if they are judged only against the pathology of Jim Crow racism. But the pathology of Jim Crow was the gravest and longest-running failure of American democracy as a whole. *Shelley v. Kraemer* no more refutes the general validity of the state action doctrine than the shame of Jim Crow refutes American democracy as a whole. The Fourteenth Amendment requirements of equal protection and due process, after all, apply in a wide variety of contexts including many unrelated to race, just as American life in general is more than its history of race relations.

---

[110]Sowell, Markets and Minorities 26 (1981) (discrimination has costs to the discriminator as well as to the victim, and the more competitive the discriminator's environment the higher the costs).

[111]See, *e.g.*, Hill, Race and Ethnicity in Organized Labor: The Historical Sources of Resistance to Affirmative Action, 12 J. of Intergroup Relations 5 (1984) (describing the historically racist policies of labor unions, supposedly a "progressive" force in American society).

[112]U.S. v. Carolene Products Co., 304 U.S. 144, 152 n.4 (1938).

[113]See, *e.g.*, Strauder v. West Virginia, 100 U.S. 303 (1880) (striking down the statutory all-white jury); Buchanan v. Warley, 245 U.S. 60 (1917) (residential segregation).

[114]For a good history of the climate in the years leading up to the school desegregation decision in Brown v. Board of Ed. 347 U.S. 483 (1954), see Kluger, Simple Justice: The History of Brown v. Board of Education and Black America's Struggle for Equality (1976).

In fact, the Constitution itself recognizes the inapplicability of the state action doctrine to the plight of black Americans in the aftermath of slavery. Unlike the Fourteenth Amendment, with its state action limitations, the Thirteenth Amendment absolutely prohibits slavery in the United States, and gives Congress power to enforce that prohibition, without any limitation as to state action.[115] Moreover, since 1883, the Supreme Court has interpreted the Thirteenth Amendment to give Congress power to abolish "all badges and incidents of slavery."[116] Accordingly, in a 1968 case strongly reminiscent of *Shelley v. Kraemer*, the Supreme Court felt no need to invoke the Fourteenth Amendment at all. Instead, in *Jones v. Alfred Mayer Co.*, the court relied on the 1866 Civil Rights Act, enacted under the Thirteenth Amendment, and forbade discrimination by a private property developer who refused to sell to blacks.[117] The decision recognized that pervasive Jim Crow was indeed a "badge and incident" of slavery.[118] And while the decision relied on an old Act of Congress adopted under the Thirteenth Amendment, it would have been a small step—as the Court itself implied[119]—to hold that the Thirteenth Amendment directly prohibits "badges and incidents of slavery," whether imposed privately or by government. In *Shelley v. Kraemer*, in other words, just as in the later *Jones* case, the Supreme Court might have relied on the Thirteenth Amendment to strike at Jim Crow. The Thirteenth Amendment provides a basis for accepting the result in *Shelley* (which one knows was right), while preserving the balance of public constitutionalism and private pluralism implicit in the state action doctrine under the Fourteenth Amendment.

Today, it would be especially perverse to infer a wholesale repudiation of the state action doctrine from *Shelley* and the racial

---

[115]Legislation under the Thirteenth Amendment "may be direct and primary, operating upon the acts of individuals, whether sanctioned by State legislation or not." Civil Rights Cases, 109 U.S. 3, 22 (1883). This contrasts with the Fourteenth Amendment, of course, which binds the government to equal protection and due process in general but imposes these values only on the "state," leaving private persons free to pursue other, conflicting values.

[116]Civil Rights Cases, 109 U.S. 3, 20. Over a powerful dissent by the first Justice Harlan, however, the Court held that "it would be running the slavery argument into the ground" to treat Jim Crow discrimination in public accommodations as a badge of slavery, *id.* at 24.

[117]Jones v. Alfred Mayer Co., 392 U.S. 409 (1968).

[118]"[W]hen racial discrimination herds men into ghettoes and makes their ability to buy property turn on the color of their skin, then it too is a relic of slavery." *Id.* at 442–43.

[119]*Id.* at 439 ("whether or not the Amendment *itself* did any more than" abolish slavery, Congress may certainly abolish badges and incidents).

crisis of its time. Black Americans themselves are now no longer a "discrete and insular minority" excluded from the workings of pluralist democracy.[120] The unique historical failure of pluralism for black Americans was confronted and to a considerable degree overcome in the civil rights revolution of the past generation. To be sure, disproportionately many blacks remain poor and therefore suffer grave social and educational disadvantage. But for black Americans living in two-parent families, incomes now approach those of whites.[121] In general, the achievements of the civil rights movement should not be underestimated.[122] Without suggesting that America has become anything like a racial utopia, it is surely fair to say that America's home-grown apartheid has been dismantled and that racial pluralism has begun to take root in the country. In politics, in employment, and simply in living together as neighbors, substantial numbers of white Americans now accept their black fellow-citizens on equal terms in ways that would have been unthinkable forty years ago. The America of *Shelley v. Kraemer,* disfigured by pervasive Jim Crow discrimination, was a very different place from the more contemporary America of *Moose Lodge No. 107 v. Irvis:*[123] an America in which comprehensive civil rights laws and a changed social climate now ensure that only the occasional private club, under narrowly confined circumstances,

---

[120]Professor Bruce Ackerman, among others, observes that blacks are no longer a discrete and insular minority. See Ackerman, Beyond Carolene Products, 98 Harv. L. Rev. 713, 742 (1985). As he says, "it is no longer visionary to hope" that America will increasingly be a society without any minority groups suffering the sort of persecution that blacks underwent. *Id.* at 717. After a sober analysis of why judicial intervention in behalf of discrete and insular minorities is increasingly unnecessary, however, Professor Ackerman takes off in a flight of rhetoric to the effect that pluralist values are "lesser" values, *id.* at 743, and that the Supreme Court should enforce egalitarian values that are not "specific" in the Constitution, *id.* at 743–4, values appropriate to the politics of "mass mobilization and struggle," *id.* at 743. Professor Ackerman does not specify precisely which egalitarian values he has in mind, what authority the Supreme Court has to enforce them, or what the costs might be in terms of conflicting nonegalitarian values.

[121]See Smith & Welch, Closing the Gap: Forty Years of Economic Progress for Blacks 106 (1986) (Rand Corp. Report No. R-3330-DOL) (as of 1980, black families with both husband and wife present earned 82 percent as much as white families, better than double the income ratio of 1940; and only 15 percent of such families were poor).

[122]In the political sphere, for example, the number of black elected officials increased tenfold between 1965 and 1982, and blacks are now routinely elected to almost every major category of public office. Cavanagh & Stockton, Black Elected Officials and Their Constituencies 1–2 (1983).

[123]See notes 42–51 *supra* and accompanying text.

may still openly discriminate on the basis of race.[124] Racism itself, in other words, is no longer the reproach it once was to the idea of American pluralism.

Indeed, for civil rights advocates who support "benign discrimination" as a way of shrinking the racial disparities that persist, the state action doctrine may actually be a help rather than a hindrance nowadays. While the Supreme Court has sometimes upheld "benign" racial quotas and similar "affirmative action" in the public sector, the court has done so very uneasily. After all, the Fourteenth Amendment forbids the government to discriminate in any way on the basis of race, at least in the absence of a "compelling state interest."[125] Accordingly, the Justices have been bitterly divided over racial quotas imposed by court order or adopted by government agencies; and where such quotas are upheld, it is usually on the basis of "strict scrutiny" and a conclusion by the court that the particular quota is indeed required by a "compelling state interest."[126] Without the state action doctrine, the same stringent conditions would apply to reverse discrimination in the private sector, where most of the jobs and other benefits in the American economy are to be had. In fact, the Supreme Court has been much less troubled about affirmative action carried out by private institutions acting on their own. The state action doctrine means that there can be no *constitutional* objection to such affirmative action: the Fourteenth Amendment only governs the government. The only possible challenge to private-sector affirmative action is therefore statutory, and the Supreme Court —by comfortable majorities among the Justices—has refused to construe the civil rights acts to prohibit "reasonable" reverse discrimination.[127] Whatever the limits on government affirmative action, in other words, the state action

---

[124]See, *e.g.*, the Civil Rights Act of 1964, 42 U.S.C. §§2000 *et seq.*

[125]See Korematsu v. United States, 323 US 214 (1944).

[126]See Sheet Metal Workers v. EEOC, 478 U.S. 421, 485 (Powell, J., concurring) (1986) (court-ordered affirmative action remedy justified by a "compelling governmental interest" in this case; the Supreme Court was divided 5–4 over whether to uphold the lower court's remedy, and Justice Powell was the crucial fifth vote). See also Regents of Univ. of Calif. v. Bakke, 438 U.S. 265 (1978).

[127]See United Steelworkers of America v. Weber, 443 U.S. 193, 209 (1979) (upholding "private sector voluntar[y] . . . affirmative action plans" by a 5–2 vote). See also Local No. 93, Int'l Assoc. of Firefighters v. Cleveland, 478 U.S. 501 (1986) (upholding on statutory grounds an affirmative action consent decree adopted by a government agency, and specifically not confronting the constitutional question because it was not raised in the District Court).

doctrine implies broader latitude for private corporations and institutions. Private institutions are many and competing: the logic of pluralism is that the Constitution should not preclude some of them from opting for aggressive affirmative action, or even—perhaps more realistically—from being privately pressured into it.

Whatever the implications for affirmative action, the moral authority of the struggle for civil rights is no basis today, if it ever was, for repudiating the state action doctrine and its protection for private pluralism—especially in the many areas of life apart from race that might be governed by a Fourteenth Amendment cut loose from the state action requirement.

VI

The fundamental objection to the state action doctrine and to the underlying principle of value pluralism is not that these ideas would have precluded the courts from confronting America's racial crisis. They did not and needed not do so. The true paradox of pluralism is that pluralism itself is but one among many values, and incompatible with some of them. People at times yearn for an all-embracing social unity of purpose which is by definition incompatible with tolerance for a plurality of values. Pluralism is incompatible with radical egalitarianism,[128] and also with a traditionalism that prescribes people's roles instead of confronting them with choices.[129] Yet people at times yearn for equality and at other times for the security of tradition. Pluralism is incompatible with the dream of achieving a "science" of solving political problems, since pluralism denies that human ends can be reconciled with each other into any system of objective laws from which one could derive a unified theory of what is good for people.[130] Pluralism itself, in short, has costs in terms of the fulfillment of other values. Value pluralism thus means that there can be no utopia, that the very idea of utopia is incoherent.

---

[128]See Berlin, Equality, in Berlin, Concepts and Categories 81, 92 (1980) (equality, at least when taken to a fanatical extreme, requires "total uniformity"; only in a society "where people differ as little as possible from each other in any respect whatever, will true equality be attainable").

[129]Jean-Paul Sartre and other existentialists speak of people's "vertigo" at the possibilities offered by free choice. See Sartre, Being and Nothingness 30–31 (1969 ed.). See also Cumming, Starting Point: An Introduction to the Dialectic of Existence 347–48 (1979).

[130]Berlin, Does Political Theory Still Exist? in Berlin, Concepts and Categories 143, 153 (1980).

Utopian critics of "liberalism" and advocates of "community" are therefore always quick to point out pluralism's costs.[131] The writings of Isaiah Berlin are a lucid reminder, however, of the virtues of pluralism. Pluralism recognizes the deep philosophical implausibility of the idea that the values men and women have struggled over throughout history, often violently, are actually reconcilable in some harmonious system embracing all the ends that people legitimately consider "good." After all, most people know from their own lives how their deepest desires sometimes conflict. You want to do good, but also to do well; you want a busy career, but you also want time to raise your children; you want to live in the city, but also to live in the country. Constitutional principles like equal protection and due process of law, likewise, are truly grand principles, but they are not the only legitimate principles for people to base their actions upon.

Moreover, Berlin makes it clear why value pluralism is directly associated with tolerance and freedom, whereas "monism" or the ideal of an all-embracing system of values is associated with fanaticism and tyranny. To admit that the fulfillment of some of our ideals may in principle make the fulfillment of others impossible implies some skepticism, even humility, about how people ought to be governed. The idea that any one value or system of values is supreme, on the other hand, implies that enforcement of the supreme values is legitimate "by whatever means necessary."[132]

Berlin puts it this way:[133]

> So long as only one ideal is the true goal, it will always seem to men that no means can be too difficult, no price too high, to do whatever is required to realise the ultimate goal. . . . But if this is not so, then the path is open to empiricism, pluralism, toleration, compromise.

Value pluralism and the state action doctrine surely do not promise a constitutional utopia. But, as Arthur Leff once wrote, "before agreeing with any 'how awful' critic, one must always ask him the really nasty question, 'compared to what?'"[134]

---

[131]For a sample of "critical legal studies" criticism of legal liberalism, and advocacy of "community," see Critical Legal Studies Symposium, 36 Stan. L. Rev. 1 (1984).

[132]See notes 16–17 *supra* and accompanying text.

[133]Berlin, The Originality of Machiavelli, in Berlin, Against the Current 25, 78 (1981).

[134]Leff, Economic Analysis of Law: Some Realism about Nominalism, 60 Va. L. Rev. 451, 460 (1974).

BARRY D. KARL

CONSTITUTION AND CENTRAL PLANNING: THE THIRD NEW DEAL REVISITED

"Charles Eliot and I agreed that the history of the New Deal starts logically immediately after the termination of the World War, but it has become voluminous only since 1929," Franklin Roosevelt wrote historian Samuel Eliot Morison in February 1938.[1] His bland assertion of a proposition that has generated a certain amount of debate among historians searching for the origins of the New Deal need not be taken as gospel, of course, but it is interesting. Nor ought one misunderstand the importance, perhaps, of the man whose agreement he claimed. Charles W. Eliot II was the executive officer of the planning board Roosevelt had placed, initially, in the Department of the Interior in 1933, and he remained its executive throughout its ten-year history, serving the board's academic and industrial community membership as effectively as circumstances and his own professional commitments allowed.

Eliot was one of the first of his generation to adopt planning as a profession in itself rather than as an adjunct to some other profession. He was part of a group of professionals, some of whom began their careers in various aspects of urban planning, who now sought to establish planning as an overall generic term that could encompass economic, social, administrative, and geographical factors—the list was itself open ended—under a single professional rubric. It was an ambition as central to his generation's social

Barry D. Karl is Norman and Edna Freehling Professor of History, The University of Chicago.

[1]Franklin D. Roosevelt to Samuel Eliot Morison, Feb. 28, 1938, II FDR: His Personal Letters, 1928–1945 761–62 (1950).

science as the search for unifying theories was for the natural sciences they so often sought to emulate.[2]

Eliot fought what must sometimes have seemed to him a losing battle against those who refused to accept planning as a technical pursuit separate from the subjects being planned and the objects toward which planning could be directed. As that first generation of professional planners saw it, such specialization obscured essentials in the range of interests for which planning appropriately could be undertaken and generated needless competition and conflict. The profession had begun to assert a new, comprehensive definition of the governmental role of planning. To the extent that planners were adapting to their new professional conceptions of non-partisan independence and political neutrality their forebears in American public administration had been claiming, they were destined, perhaps, to run into some of the same opposition from those who believed that a truly democratic polity exempted no one from the responsibility of being judged by the traditional criteria of politics.

At the same time, Eliot's approach to planning had increasingly come to involve an acceptance of the political process as an integral part of the planning process. His generation of planners was far more inclined to see the sharp separation of planning and politics as a romantic ideal that in practical terms did more to frustrate the efforts of planners to plan than a more realistic acknowledgment of the interdependence of the two would have. The dignified distance from politics the old Progressives had struggled to maintain forbade them from lobbying for their proposals, but it was a self-restraint that seemed to younger planning enthusiasts an invitation to disaster.

As the New Deal's experiment with planning, the National Resources Planning Board (NRPB) and its various administrative predecessors played a role which has remained curiously unique, given the fact that no President, and certainly no Congress, has seriously considered the reestablishment of the kind of central planning agency for American government the NRPB aspired to become. When Congress abolished it in 1943 over Roosevelt's objections, it did not simply conclude it by refusing to continue its

---

[2] Eliot's activities are best described in Clawson, New Deal Planning: The National Resources Planning Board (1981).

funding but took every step it could to assure that the experience be blotted from the record and not permitted to reappear. Few aspects of the New Deal, save the four-term presidency itself, were subjected to so total and systematic an effort by Congress to protect against any future revival.

By the end of the New Deal planning had become clearly identified as the idea that the government of modern industrial states required systematic projections of future actions based on scientific research, comprehensive collections of data, and objective testing of results in order to build continuous cycles of governmental policy-making. It had in various earlier guises been the practical aim of modern experts on both sides of the Atlantic since the last decades of the nineteenth century. The experience of the two World Wars and the revolutions that transformed the Soviet Union, China, Italy, and Germany in the years that paralleled the American Progressive Era and the New Deal had all contributed to the general sense in Western society that laissez faire, parliamentary democracy, and the ideologies of individualism would have to give way to new conceptions of corporate management and modern statism.

Yet by the end of World War II Americans were rejecting such ideas. To explain so dramatic a transformation, let us first trace the origins of the American idea of planning and its relation to the development of European conceptions of the planned state.

I

The American interest in planning has always posed a problem for those historians who have chosen to examine it, in part because of the contrast between the way Americans have used the term and its origins in modern European thought.[3] In European theory the concept has always been associated with the application of scientific method to descriptions of human development that might have relevance for policies to be determined by the state. But it is in many significant respects an ancient idea. Caesar's Gallic Wars could be considered one of the classical models; and, at least as far back as Marco Polo, detailed descriptions of the climate, social and political behavior, natural resources, and economic

---

[3]Graham, Toward a Planned Society (1976); The Planning Idea from Roosevelt to Post-Reagan, in The New Deal Viewed from Fifty Years (Gelfand & Neymeyer eds. 1983).

development of foreign cultures were employed to determine the future actions of those interested in using them for purposes of deciding commercial and governmental policy. The large descriptive literature that accompanied New World colonization efforts was designed in part for similar purposes of generating public support at home and encouraging new adventures by those disposed to be attracted to the opportunities being described.

Writers since the 1930s have taken the mid-1920s as the beginning point of the American concern with planning. A bibliography entitled "Five Years of 'Planning' Literature" appeared in *Social Forces* in 1932–33 to introduce readers to a wealth of material that had appeared only recently.[4] Shelby Harrison's *A Bibliography of Social Surveys* appeared in 1930. Harrison sought to define the beginnings of the survey movement with the Pittsburgh Survey of 1909 and to celebrate the planning experiments recently completed by the cities of Chicago and New York, separating the modern scientific surveys from their predecessors.[5] Yet the survey movement extended well back into the nineteenth-century in forms not all that different from those Harrison was now celebrating. The sanitarians of the early nineteenth century used statistical studies and population maps to examine the origins and spread of disease. Combining the scientific interests of Belgian statistician Lambert Quetelet (1796–1874) with the reform concerns of British administrative reformer Sir Edwin Chadwick (1800–1890), American reformers like Bostonian Lemuel Shattuck sought to reshape American cities in accordance with the health needs of urban dwellers and the requirements of the industrial work force.[6]

Yet for much of the nineteenth century that industrial side of planning with its emphasis on urban populations and their interests was subordinated to those aspects of European planning that focused on natural resources and the growth of empire. Ever since the dawn of the era of exploration, the collecting of information designed to facilitate exploitation and use of resources by others had

---

[4]Brooks & Brooks, Five Years of Planning Literature, Social Forces 430 (1932–33).

[5]Harrison, A Bibliography of Social Surveys (1930); Kellogg, The Pittsburgh Survey (1909).

[6]Shattuck, An Essay on the Vital Statistics of Boston from 1810 to 1841 (1841); Proceedings and Debates of the Third National Quarantine and Sanitary Convention (1859). A brief history of the formation of the group is given in a letter from Wilson Jewell.

been essential to the making of plans by empires, businesses, and the proselytizing religious groups that moved in the wake of their explorations. To the extent that they acknowledged what they were doing as planning, they cited Old Testament models of population mobility directed by God, who knew where the lands of milk and honey were located and could direct His people to them. For American planners of the 1930s, even those who insisted that planning was a new and modern phenomenon, one of the favorite examples they liked to use was the story of Joseph in Egypt.

What most differentiated American conceptions of planning from European, however, was the root of European theories in a historical past that accepted the primary role of government in the process of planning. In the great age of exploration, governments directed the builders of colonial empires and fully expected to control the resulting wealth. One of the most influential factors in the development of revolutionary ferment in colonial America was the effort on the part of British government to gain a firmer grip on the processes of colonial economic development. The American rejection of that design was destined to play an important role in the growth of the independent nation as former colonies and the newly settled regions resisted efforts by the federal government to control policies in the states.

In the odd and ad hoc way the nation developed, federal policy could reign supreme in the territories as Congress and the Departments of War and Interior superintended the remarkable expansion of the nation; but admission to the Union, paradoxically perhaps, brought national supremacy to an end and left policy-making to state government and local representatives elected to Congress to fight for the interests of the state.

Although the American use of planning ideas has always rested essentially on the need to control the natural resources of a geographically and demographically expanding society, an unwillingness to center that control in the federal government has always posed stumbling blocks to any discussion of planning as a systematic responsibility of government. Thomas Jefferson and Alexander Hamilton have always served as the demigods—yin and yang or Manichean opponents, depending on the way they are used—of the two essentially different concepts of planning, one committed to an essentially physiocratic view of planning as a mixture of individual labor and agrarian resources, the other committed to a view of national and international management that depended on large-scale institutions to govern national self-development and international trade. The research and writing of the German naturalist Alexander von Humboldt (1769–1859) reinforced the interest in the relation between natural resources and physical geography, keeping scientific investigation at the forefront of a younger generation's passion for travel, replacing the role played by religious proselytizing, even combining the two as missionaries collected specimens and descriptions of plant and animal life for naturalists back home.

Although many of the names have been dropped from the planning literature, planners of Franklin Roosevelt's generation referred easily to Hamilton and Jefferson as the planning alternatives of the founding generation. "The Constitutional Convention itself was a large-scale planning board," wrote the authors of the National Planning Board's *Final Report*, 1933–34, and they went on to cite Hamilton, Gallatin, Henry Clay, and John Quincy Adams as stars in the nation's first firmament of planners.[7]

That same generation read Herbert Croly's famous compromise between Jefferson and Hamilton. They saw in Admiral Alfred Thayer Mahan's writings an extension of the planning past that now put the United States in the geopolitical center of the international world, its two oceans a unique resource for the expansion of national power. The fact that they still did not use "planning" to describe what they were talking about may be attributed in part to the fact that the term had not yet come into use—but only in part. Other nations were arguing the issue of centralization in the reformation of their national governments and the bureaucracies required to run them. Americans were talking about civil service reform.

Part of the Progressive debate involved the modernization of federal policy-making and the creation of new modes of federal regulation of national business and banking. Enlightened railroad men in particular were concerned with the need for planning to assure a proper use of the nation's resources. James J. Hill's *Highways of Progress*, which appeared in 1910, is a remarkably interesting commentary on the problem of nonrenewable resources and the need for policy regarding them. But too little agreement

---

[7]National Planning Board, Final Report 1933–34, Historical Development of Planning in the United States, at 19.

existed on the appropriate role of the federal government in such a transformation.

While many of the Progressives who wanted greater federal centralization thought that World War I would bring it about, it was clear in the aftermath of that war that their hopes were mistaken. The Transportation Act of 1920 turned the railroads back to private ownership, thereby sounding the death knell of federal ownership as the way to ensure national transportation planning. Such events received mixed responses from planners like Frederic Delano, who now turned to regional and local planning.

For a nation still half-agrarian in 1920 the Jeffersonian image was particularly useful. The Louisiana Purchase and the Lewis and Clark expedition were cited frequently as examples of the application of scientific knowledge to resource discovery and use. Yet the problem of the twenties was not limited to historic references to an ideal past. The concern with the limitation on expanding and expandable resources had added an urgency that made it difficult to avoid the one element of European planning theories Americans had always managed to avoid: the role of a powerful central government as the arbiter of the management of resources. The fact that the Teapot Dome scandal, like the nineteenth-century railroad scandals, was viewed as an episode of political corruption rather than a problem in the use of federal political power for the distribution of the nation's national resources may only underscore the tendency of American historians to adopt American habits of interpreting their national political system.

The inadequacies of state and local governments to plan coherently was a topic of continuous discussion as states vied with one another to obtain control over state services to citizens and the revolutionary new resources like electricity. Yet the very broadening of the perception of the need to gain rational control emphasized the differences of planning from state to state, and the conflicts that could arise as seemingly antiquated state and city administrative boundaries blocked the effective transmission of new services all citizens were learning to believe they needed.

The years since the end of World War I had been important years for those interested in adapting American government at all levels to a programmatic management of public policy many had only recently begun to call now "planning," and Franklin Roosevelt had clearly associated himself with their interests and concerns. He had shared with them the experience of wartime planning and Wilson's struggle to create for the American war machine a supporting command economy like those backing the war efforts of both friends and enemies in Europe. Wilson had succeeded by evoking concepts of volunteer involvement and dollar-a-year management of war agencies by executives from the private sector who offered their services as citizens committed to supporting the war effort. While "volunteerism" frequently served as the velvet glove that covered the iron fist of administrative command, particularly toward the end of the war, the recollection of patriotic amateur management without federal coercion fueled the dream of cooperative business-government relationships that leaders like Herbert Hoover, Newton Baker, and Owen D. Young were committed to reviving after the war. To call the process "planning" was acceptable in the 1920s, but oddly acceptable and not destined to survive the 1930s. The planning experiments in the Soviet Union and the rise of various corporatist conceptions of the state in Italy, Germany, and France were predicated on a direct governmental role that Americans were committed to rejecting.

If the experience of World War I had emboldened planners eager to use the federal government to manage nationwide programs, it nonetheless increased the fears of those who saw in the federal government a threat to local autonomy and individual control. That same experience had dramatically increased the perception of the need for greater rationality and standardization, not only in industry but in education, health care, the employment of labor, and the quality of administrative services. While the term "planning" was still not used comfortably by everyone concerned with such problems, the elements that came to be associated with the planning idea were all there.

The drama of flood control had helped transform attitudes as people accustomed to accepting such events as natural disasters to which they had to adapt came to see dams, engineering, and electricity as man-made miracles that could turn nature to man's uses. Yet politics intervened. Rivers crossed state lines and interfered with agricultural interests and industrial needs. William E. Leuchtenburg's *Flood Control Politics: The Connecticut River Valley Problem, 1927–1950* brilliantly reconstructs the complexity of state relationships in public works planning.[8]

---

[8](1953).

The relatively brief depression that followed the end of the war and the period of direct American involvement in the reconstruction of Europe had stimulated a whole variety of ideas for dealing with economic recession on a national rather than a local scale. Herbert Hoover's work with the reports on *Waste in Industry* was only part of a movement that included extensive discussion of the use of public works projects as a way of managing what most economists agreed were cyclical problems with employment.[9] While their efforts at counter-cyclical planning were crude by later Keynesian standards and involved little if any of the mathematical models and projections still decades away, the idea of providing for the intervention of public money when private resources dried up was clear. What was not clear was where the public money would come from—state or local government—and what role the federal government might appropriately play, if indeed it had a role to play. The improvement of the national economy after 1923 tended to mute such concerns, but it did not stop them entirely among those economists committed to predicting cyclical change.

At the same time, it is important to point out that the planning dilemma of the 1920s seemed to suggest an untenable choice where sources of funding were concerned: state and local governments bound by traditional political controls, on the one hand, and, on the other, a federal government that moved uncertainly and threateningly into positions of control over the distribution of the nation's resources. The war experience had in many respects reinforced the latter concern dramatically without touching the concern for the former, which had been such an important part of the Progressive Era battles. The regional planning movement of the 1920s arose, in part, as an effort to find some kind of compromise, a less threatening sword with which to cut the myriad Gordian knots tied by governments in the states and cities that reformers still considered hopelessly corrupt. Regional planning suggested, at least, some form of governmental alternative, as temporary, perhaps, as an association or a planning group, or as permanent as a county government or village board.

The effort to create a public-private national nexus that could bypass or entirely avoid the presence of the federal government was part of the system Hoover kept trying to create, first as Secretary

[9]Grin, The Unemployment Conference of 1921: An Experience in National Cooperative Planning, Mid-America, April 1973.

of Commerce and then as President. His industrial conferences preceded his presidency. His Research Committee on Social Trends brought members of the new academic social science professions to Washington to advise him. But whether such programs, supported by private philanthropic foundations and utilizing leaders from industry as well as academia, constituted a search for a new system of national management is itself an important topic of historical debate.[10]

My language up to this point has been designed to communicate efficiently the particular kind of American Jeffersonian base on which the 1920s interest in planning rested. The post-World War I view of planning combined natural resource-agrarian planning ideas with a certain amount of urban-industrial experience to produce a view of planning that confined government regulation to areas sufficiently distant from traditional problems of social management to be safe from criticism by those who considered planning a radical invasion of community privacy. With the exception of *Recent Social Trends* such planning did not attack problems of poverty, the education of the young, or the welfare of the sick and aged, except indirectly. In a version of what would later be called "trickle-down theory," the planning of natural resource use in all its rapidly developing forms was intended as a method of overall benefit that would ultimately reach everyone, a universal panacea similar to, though obviously much more sophisticated than, the availability of free land in the nineteenth century. In a rapidly industrializing nation, the right to a job was destined to replace the right to a plot of land, and with something of the same ambiguity where the inherent opportunities were concerned.

By the 1920s electrical power had come to provide a model for such ideas. What the railroad had done for the development of planning ideas in the nineteenth century, electricity was destined to do for the first part of the twentieth, but on a much higher level of the seemingly miraculous. The railroad had demonstrated the need for thinking that transcended state lines and traditional political boundaries. It had provided an example of a single technological

---

[10]Alchon, The Invisible Hand of Planning: Technocratic Social Science and the Rise of Managed Capitalism, 1910–1933 (1985); Fisher, The Role of Philanthropic Foundations in the Reproduction and Production of Hegemony, 17 Sociology 206–33 (1983); Bulmer & Fisher, Debate, 18 Sociology 573–87 (1984).

entity that affected everything it touched by changing the ways people could live and earn their livings. It transformed opportunities everywhere it went. Government had been forced to intervene on a national scale, even by providing the basic resources with which the industry would be developed. Electrical power offered similar opportunities, and since the nation's waterways, rapidly becoming obsolete as transportation routes, could now be revived as the basic natural resource for electric power development, there seemed a natural symbiosis between technology and nature. Flood control, the traditional relation between flooding and social catastrophe, and the massive hydroelectric dams helped expand the public view of the new technological management. Rapid development of new electrical devices from the electric light to radios and washing machines popularized technology as part of the improvement of the quality of daily life. All such changes throughout the 1920s raised with them basic issues of planning—but planning on a national scale. Electrical lines and the waterways themselves transcended state lines. Radio used airwaves. Airplanes transformed the American sense of place. The federal government, pressed by business leaders like Herbert Hoover, accepted limited managerial responsibility.

While national planning would still have been unacceptable in the 1920s, particularly against the background of planning developments in Italy and the Soviet Union, regional planning movements were based on an acceptance of the fact that even though state and local boundaries were no longer adequate to deal with problems of modern technology there was still an alternative to domination from Washington. A consciousness of the need to define city boundaries led to discussions of the new concept of "metropolitan region," an idea designed in part to get around the older battle over annexation and urban politics to find ways of enlarging services. While Americans were no more agreed on accepting public ownership of utilities than they had been before the war, the search for ways of defining public responsibility was part of the background Franklin Roosevelt took with him when he moved from the Governorship of New York to the White House.

All these matters point to a basic set of issues about planning that predate the onset of the Depression. Among those issues are these: that American planning did not have to be perceived as revolutionary as long as it rested on natural resources, the traditional agrarian base of national planning; that federalism expressed through the traditional political relationships between and among the forty-eight states would have to be made more effective if it were to deal with the increased number of problems that transcended state boundaries; that technological change itself had expanded the number of problems faced by, and opportunities available to, all Americans, regardless of where they lived, problems and opportunities that could only be dealt with effectively by some agency of government; and, finally, that there were specialized forms of knowledge and techniques now available for dealing with common problems. This is not to argue that there were no revolutionary conceptions in American society that saw these issues as requiring major changes in form of government as the only way to deal with the future. It is simply to try to outline a centrist approach that both Herbert Hoover and Franklin Roosevelt could have agreed upon in the decade before the Crash.

Although there was within the industrial community itself a planning idea that was indeed revolutionary in the sense of not having evolved out of a traditional agrarian base, its leaders considered themselves industrial capitalists bent on modernizing capitalism's view of the labor-management relationship. Part of the group Hoover had been involved with in the postwar studies of industry and unemployment, they accepted the existence of business cycles, not simply as scientifically observable events, but as events that could be balanced by counter-cyclical public works planning.

Although they made relatively little headway in the 1920s, they continued to argue vociferously and at length that studies of potentially useful state and local public works could yield a list of projects that could, on the approach of economic downturns, be started as a means of providing employment and lessening the impact of the downturn.

Even before the Crash, journal writers were looking at ways of coping with serious economic downturns. "It is proposed that federal, state, and local governments, in addition to appropriating money the expenditure of which cannot be hastened or postponed, shall make certain credits available, in connection with public works planned well in advance, which credits shall be used only when specified official indexes of economic conditions show that business be headed for a depression," one proposal put it. "Conversely," they continued, "it is proposed that measures shall be taken looking toward *decreased* capital expenditures when business appears to be headed for inflation." Such pronouncements, the authors recognized, required someone to direct; but they dealt with that question just as obliquely as many of their contemporaries did. "Through widespread announcement of such action and the scientific basis for such action, private business shall be afforded the leadership which it now lacks, and which it must have in order that in its own interest it may coordinate its activities with governmental activity."[11]

Such counter-cyclical planning appeared to be a prophecy of Keynesianism except for two significant points. It did not assume a permanent condition of stagnation that required continuous government management, and it sought methods of avoiding deficit spending through elaborate systems of delaying fundable works in good times. Deficit spending and the subsequent unbalanced budgets were still looked upon as the ultimate danger.

The possibility of a new role for the federal government was being debated, again before the Crash and with a stronger emphasis on the required role of government. The idea that government had responsibility for maintaining prosperity even when it was not in any apparently immediate danger was already there. As John B. Andres, Secretary of the American Association for Labor Legislation, put it in March 1929, "We need a permanent policy of long range planning of public works. The new administration is under obligations to establish it securely in the law of the land. The Special Session of Congress opening in April, related directly to the maintenance of prosperity, is an appropriate occasion for the prompt passage of this legislation."[12]

Hoover had indeed accepted that obligation. He had promoted this counter-cyclical planning during his presidential campaign and was committed to continuing it in office. As *The Literacy Digest* put it in the December following his election, "The abolition of poverty—or a job for every worker—was more than once depicted by Mr. Hoover during his campaign as the great aim of the American economic system. Now his proposal to create a $3,000,000,000 reserve fund to be used for public construction work so as to ward off unemployment in lean years is hailed as a

---

[11]Foster & Catchings, The New Attack on Poverty, Review of Reviews, April 1929, at 77.

[12]American Labor Legislation Review, March, 1929, at 4.

step toward that goal."[13] Remembering that the amount, $3 billion, was a far more dramatic sum in 1928 than it is likely to appear today, one can see the public relations value of the announcement as clearly as all the news media saw it.

By the time of the Crash and the onset of the Depression, however, Hoover's mood—and more importantly, his knowledge of the limitations of federal power—had changed. His awareness of the absence of machinery for the planning of public works and of information that could lead to rational planning of even a limited variety, plus the eagerness with which members of Congress fought to gain control themselves of any planning, led him to call for both the machinery and the power to control it. Congress gave Hoover such a planning board in the Employment Stabilization Act of 1931. The bill provided that "whenever, upon recommendation of the board, the President finds that there exists or that within 6 months next following there is likely to exist . . . a period of business depression or unemployment, he is requested to transmit . . . such supplement estimates as he deems advisable for emergency appropriations. . . ."[14] One year later, Congress was again looking to the expansion of public works through the creation of Public Works Administration. Two bills were before Congress, the Williamson Bill and the Cochran Bill. Both would have given the President increased power over public works, but the problems outlined for Hoover by the executive secretary of the American Engineering Council are particularly interesting. The legislation called for major reorganization power for the President, which the Council did not believe he would get. It also gave extraordinary control over public works to the Army Corps of Engineers, which the Council also opposed. The Council's arguments were based on political expediency, but also on the grounds that the Army Corps were already too strong in their ability to oppose public works building. Again, the legislation required greater presidential control over the Comptroller General's authority to block expenditures.

Since all these points are central to the issues that hobbled planning and killed executive reorganization in the New Deal, it is useful to see them emerging even before Roosevelt came to office.[15]

---

[13]Hoover's Plan to Keep the Dinner-Pail Full, Lit. Dig., Dec. 8, 1928, at 5–7.

[14]P.L. 71–616.

[15]Executive Secretary of the American Engineering Council to the President, Feb. 15, 1932, Public Works File, Herbert Hoover Presidential Library (cited below as HHPL).

While Hoover was criticized for not using the extensive materials produced by planning board, the length of time it took him to find a director acceptable to all parties and the new board to produce its plans and the proximity of the presidential election may serve as partial explanation. So does his growing concern over budget deficits as a threat to recovery. It is nonetheless true that the studies, surveys, and plans he insisted that it prepare made possible the initial public works energy of the New Deal. Historians, in a sense, always face the problem of how to interpret the contrast between the ideas Hoover had been so deeply committed to and so articulately supportive of since 1921, and the way he faced those issues after 1929.

One can complicate the matter rather significantly by looking into the administration itself where the examination of the problem of public works planning and unemployment had aroused an interesting dispute. Edward Eyre Hunt, one of Hoover's administrative assistants in Hoover's Commerce years and now a White House assistant in charge of social science advice and other planning projects, had long been an advocate of planning.[16] Hunt, a classmate and good friend of John Reed during their Harvard days, had turned his perspective toward a kind of social Taylorism that used engineering and scientific management to produce the social advances he believed socialism had once advocated. Hunt used the experience of the electric companies and the telephone companies in the 1920s as models of what planning could become without state ownership.

On the other hand, Hoover's Secretary of Commerce, Thomas Lamont, appointed a committee that examined the use of public works to provide employment. That committee came to a conclusion Roosevelt would come to by the end of his first term, namely, that public works construction was not labor intensive, and therefore, if employment was the basic issue, public works construction might not be the way to meet it.[17] But at the beginning of what was turning out to be a general enthusiasm for public works, Lamont's caution did not appear attractive.

It might be worth pointing out that the idea of public works as counter-cyclical planning was, by 1929, a decade old, having

---

[16]See An Approach to State Planning, 6 Social Forces 111– 17.

[17]Report of the Committee on a Program of Federal Public Works, Dec. 16, 1931, Reel 15, Thomas Lamont Papers, HHPL.

emerged in 1919 as a political issue. A United States Emergency Public Works Board had been proposed to Congress. Several significant economists, among them J. M. Clark, had been advocates of various forms of public works planning to provide countercyclical employment. Otto T. Mallery had become a leading publicist of the issue in the *American Labor Legislation Review* and elsewhere.

It seems to me that the problem in attempting to distinguish between investment pump-priming and employment always depends on having Keynesian theory that enables one to turn the two into one another, in a sense, at least theoretically. Hoover did not have such a theory, and neither, really, did Roosevelt. That leaves the other side of public works—the importance of the construction industry to congressional politicians—in fuller view than any of the advocates of systematic planning were able to accept.

Continuing efforts on the part of individual congressmen to introduce specific public works building programs for their districts kept Hoover in a more or less continuous state of rage. In December 1930, he counted up $4.7 billion worth of such projects being debated in the Senate. In his characteristic fashion, he worked out a statement that also reflected his anger at being accused of refusing to act to help the unemployed.[18]

Yet it was difficult for him to see the relation between his rejection of those projects and his earlier support of a $3 billion reserve, at least from the perspective of the public, which was being asked to see a difference. It preserved the idea that public works were essentially useful works, not simply make-work programs. In a sense, however, public works planning was the most revolutionary of the planning ideas of the worldwide Depression of the 1930s and the most consistent with international responses to the Depression. Elsewhere, most notably in Germany, Italy, and the Soviet Union, the political reality and utility of public works building were faced more directly as means of employment, useful or not, than they were in the United States.

Roosevelt's activity in the planning debate in the 1920s took the form of a preoccupation with the organization of state and local government. Even before the Crash he had begun to use his position as Governor of New York to argue for major reorganization

---

[18]Treasury Raid Statement, Dec. 15, 1930, Presidential Papers—Unemployment File, HHPL.

in the structure of state and local governments, pointing out not only the excessive costs of overlapping and antiquated administrative offices, but also the inability to deliver modern services to the public through existing administrative organizations. He had requested the New York Institute for Public Administration to examine the relation between state and local governments in New York and had begun to advocate the consolidation and simplification recommended to him by that survey.

"Why must the American people be inconsistent?" he asked. "In our business life and in our social contracts we are little controlled by the methods and practices employed by our forefathers. . . . Nevertheless, in almost every State in the Union we seem content, in the main, to accept and continue to use the local machinery of government which was first devised generations or even centuries ago."[19]

In 1929 he proposed a statewide survey, declaring: "I have long been interested in the general subject of city and regional planning. The present proposed survey of the whole State is merely an intelligent broadening of the planning which heretofore has been localized. It is a study for a statewide plan which will include the use of every acre in the whole State. So far as I know, this is the first time in the United States that the city or regional plan idea has been extended to take in a whole State. It will, therefore, be of great interest to everyone who realizes the importance of looking ahead and of using our resources to the best advantage."[20]

By 1931 he was repeatedly describing the antiquated local boundary lines that blocked rational allocation of resources, calling for greater centralization in state responsibility for providing government services and asking for more modern methods of establishing working relations among neighboring states. "And yet perhaps in the old days, regional planning could not have been done," he told a New York City group celebrating the regional plan. "We could not have avoided things because we did not know enough about the elements of economics; we did not know enough about the changes in social progress to make any prognostication for the

[19]Address on Reorganization and Consolidation of Function of Local Government and Their Effect on Taxes, Saranac, New York, Sep. 11, 1929, I Public Papers and Addresses of Franklin D. Roosevelt: 1928–1932 The Genesis of the New Deal 281 (Rosenman ed. 1938).

[20]A Proposal for a Survey of Soil and Climatic Conditions, Address at Silver Lake, N.Y., Aug. 15, 1929, *id.* at 477.

future or to lay down a plan that would be worth the paper it was written on for more than a few years to come. One thing we have learned from this work that has been done by this commission, the Chicago commission and the many bodies that have been organized and are carrying on splendid work through the United States. We are learning facts, we are learning something about ourselves, many things perfectly obvious, now that they have been pointed out to us, and others perfectly new. I am wondering if out of this regional planning which is extended so widely throughout the country, we are not going to be in a position to take the bull by the horns in the immediate future and adopt some kind of experimental work basis on a distribution of population."[21]

The following spring he took the occasion of a meeting of the Conference of Governors called to discuss land utilization and state planning to demand greater government involvement in social and economic conditions. "More and more," he told the governors, "those who are the victims of dislocations and defects of our social and economic life are beginning to ask respectfully, but insistently, of us who are in positions of public responsibility why Government cannot and should not act to protect its citizens from disaster. I believe that question demands an answer and that the ultimate answer is that Government, both State and national, must accept responsibility of doing what it can do soundly, with considered forethought, and along definitely constructive, not passive lines."[22]

Thus, a year before his campaign for the presidency he had already begun spelling out the basic issues of regional and national planning his later New Deal planning board would formulate for him in much more detail. However cautious he may have appeared in the actual campaign of 1932, his pronouncements before relevant groups as he approached the presidency reveal elements of a program that the NRPB attempted to carry out. The New Deal's planning inheritance was thus a large one. The assumption that Roosevelt's remarkable position as a committed believer in the full range of the planning tradition would produce a planning revolution in the United States was widely held, not only among those who now identified themselves with the growing professions in the

[21]Extemporaneous Address on Regional Planning (Excerpts), New York City, Dec. 11, 1931, id. at 495, 497.

[22]Address before the Conference of Governors on Land Utilization and State Planning, French Lick, Ind., June 2, 1931, id. at 485, 486.

field of planning, but with many industrial leaders eager to find answers not only to the immediate crisis of the Depression but to the long range problems of industrialization they had been observing for more than three decades.

A group of regional planners who organized the Regional Planning Association of America in 1930, set up a conference on regional planning in Charlottesville, Virginia, in July 1931. Among the guests were Henry Morgenthau, Jr., then commissioner of conservation of the state of New York. Their pro-forma invitation to Governor Franklin Roosevelt was accepted, much to their surprise, and his discussion of regional planning startled many of them.

His speech repeated his views of problems of local government, its costs, the inefficiencies of overlapping jurisdictions and ineffective management of public services. "In the same way the larger units of government have been properly and logically forced to assume functions that once belonged to the lesser units," he told them. "The demands of a different sort of civilization and a different sort of national economy have forced us to redistribute the burdens which the public service imposes."[23] His tone was historical. Times have changed and people must change with them. It would not do to concentrate attention only on the larger theories of efficient government being argued in the world and to ignore the hard details of life around us. "We talk about Russia's five-year plan and the excellence or iniquity of Mussolini's system, in preference to giving consideration to the question whether a town supervisor is good for anything or inquiring what a village health officer does to earn his pay."[24]

The substance and language of the Charlottesville speech more than forecasts the later regional studies of the NRPB. Planning, they were sure, had its leader. The Chairman of the group and one of the organizers of both the conference and the Regional Planning Association of America was Louis Brownlow. In his memoirs he recalls his astonishment later when he realized that he was listening to the ideas that would later eventuate in Roosevelt's backing of TVA.[25]

---

[23]Address at University of Virginia on the Excessive Costs and Taxes in Local Government, Charlottesville, Va., July 6, 1931, *id.* at 288, 299.

[24]*Id.* at 301.

[25]Brownlow, A Passion for Anonymity 268–71 (1958).

Two years later, an industrial planning group that now entitled itself the National Economic and Social Planning Association was organized in Washington and began the following year a monthly journal called *Plan Age* that served as a vehicle for their ideas, but also as a supportive commentary on the planning aims and purposes they were certain they saw in Roosevelt and the New Deal. Their certitude was amply supported by Roosevelt's repeated assertions of his interest in and the need for planning, even though, as their articles frequently suggested, they were having difficulty tracing the implementation of those ideas.

The breakdown of the assumption that a planning revolution was about to take place—indeed, the growing hostility to it in the subsequent history of the New Deal—is thus a problem of some significance. Historians have accepted its demise as something Roosevelt himself helped bring about either through indifference or through his growing preoccupation with international affairs. Since describing the process involves relatively little in the way of new evidence, but a great deal in the way of reorganizing what we know of the period, it might be useful simply to describe the basic events first, and then to attempt to provide some explanation for them.

Roosevelt appointed a planning board in the Interior Department to aid the Secretary in his tasks as Administrator of the Public Works section of the National Industrial Recovery Act of 1933. Within the year he had shifted the board from its position in Interior to a Cabinet board consisting of the Secretaries of Agriculture, War, Commerce, and Labor, as well as Interior, and the three outside members of the initial board as advisory to the Cabinet board. By the spring 1935 he had decided to use that board to provide him with a plan for reorganizing the administration of the executive branch, but changed his mind when he realized that five Cabinet members would be on such a planning group. He considered the idea of turning over the planning of reorganization to an outside group of social scientists, but feared that it would not be under the kind of personal control he now insisted he needed. A series of ad hoc decisions stemming entirely from the desire to find outside funding for such a committee led him finally to create his Committee on Administrative Management, the so-called Brownlow Committee, attaching it to the committee he had created to aid him in the administrative management of the presidency, the

National Emergency Council. That group consisted of administrative appointees who did not hold Cabinet rank.[26]

The point that has been lost historically, however, is the fact that the Brownlow Committee was originally to have been a direct outgrowth of the planning board. Roosevelt had accepted that board's rather remarkable assertion in 1934 that the nation needed a planning board, that the Cabinet had been intended originally as such a board but had failed to become one, and therefore the time had now come. In a telegram designed to subvert an effort by the existing board's Cabinet members to retain control of any reorganization study, the academic members of the board argued that "a joint committee of nine Cabinet and independent members would prove cumbersome and ineffective." The reason the Cabinet envisaged by the founders had failed to become such a board, they continued in their historical voice, was that the idea "proved disappointing despite the high general character of the man and also because the Cabinet men were naturally interested in their own departments." They recommended a board of "not more than five disinterested individuals reporting directly to the President."[27]

In any case, the Brownlow Committee proceeded to do its work, but building somewhat surreptitiously on a report issued by the planning board in 1935. That report, entitled *Regional Factors in National Planning and Development*, had called for a major restructuring of the executive branch to provide regional planning centers under the oversight of a national planning board in Washington. The arguments for so major a reassembling of the nation's basic units of government are remarkably similar to those Roosevelt had used as governor. "Planning" had now been extended to cover a great deal beyond public works, indeed, to cover now the full range of services provided by the federal government. The regrouping of all executive agencies would be under a new system of ten to twelve regional centers. Such centers were not to have fixed boundaries in order to allow the maximum of flexibility in the grouping of services within centers. Although TVA was referred to often as a model, it was in sense the anti-model, indeed, the report decried

---

[26]The chapters covering the history of the origins of the Brownlow Committee in Brownlow's memoirs were taken verbatim from a memorandum he prepared on the subject in 1939. They are as accurate an account as we have.

[27]Telegram, June 25, 1934, File 1092A, Franklin D. Roosevelt Library (cited below as FDRL).

the use of river valleys as models because, again, of their restrictive boundaries. The authors objected, too, to the decentralization of control in TVA, but that point was so counter to their claims that they, too, were decentralizing federal administration, that it received relatively little attention.

Roosevelt's participation in the reorganization study and his awareness of its relation to the regionalism study are made clear in the conference notes from his meetings with the National Resources Committee even before the reorganization study was fully under way. He did not want a report that he disagreed with since "the public effect of a disagreement would make impossible any action because of the difference in the recommendations." He spelled out to them examples of the kinds of study he wanted done, his efforts to provide clearance of legislative proposals through the Emergency Council he had already set up, his concern over the independent commissions, the arrogation of policy powers by the Comptroller General, the proper use of Executive Orders, and the delegation of Congressional powers.[28]

What comes through the notes is Roosevelt's effective grasp of the administrative issues that concerned him. His problems with the emergency agencies and the use of the state representatives of the planning board for coordination of field activities of the federal agencies led directly into discussion of the regionalism report. "The President had in mind 8 District Chairman, or Authority Chairman," the notes continue, "who in the preparation of plans would submit eight reports to the National Resources Board, from which the Board would then make a preferred list of projects to the extent of money indicated by the President as available for the next fiscal year." Roosevelt's acceptance of the connection between the reorganization study and the regional plan is clear.[29]

The Brownlow Committee, nonetheless, recommended the creation of the National Resources Planning Board, but without very clearly identifying its relation to the modernized regional structure of government on which it was going to rest. They also recommended the abolition of all the independent administrative commissions Congress had been creating since 1887 and their repositioning in the relevant departments. This step, bringing to an end a long history of congressional efforts to establish administrative

---

[28]Merriam papers, Regenstein Library (University of Chicago), Box 173, Folder 16.

[29]*Ibid.*

units to which it could delegate executive authority it did not feel
comfortable giving the President, was exceedingly important to the
President who used it as the prime example of reorganization in his
first discussion of the topic with the press.

The independent commissions were not authorized by the Constitution, he explained in his lecture to the press on December 22,
1936, and they might even be in violation of the Constitution by their
usurpation of executive and judicial authority. The President was
the only constitutional executive, he insisted. Speaking off the
record, he took the approach to the Constitution he was going to use
in his later defense of his attempt to reorganize the judiciary. It was
really a very simple document.[30]

Of all the coming recommendations he could have selected, the
consolidation of the independent commissions in the relevant
departments was perhaps the one most likely to arouse the concerns
of political leaders who looked upon the independent commissions
and their own growing relations with the bureaucracies that ran
them as protection of their authority against the President. Congress had always been more willing to share its rule-making
authority with bodies it created and which it could influence with
pressures and demands. If Congress did not see that as a questionable delegation of authority, there were many in the legal profession
who did. Even so, for the President to claim the authority for his
office was an even larger bit to swallow.

It is important to point out Roosevelt's complete commitment to
the report of the Brownlow Committee. He had not only accepted
all its recommendations, he had helped design them. Aware of the
fact that the New Deal had already generated a vast expansion of
administrative responsibilities for the executive branch, he was now
committed not only to bringing them under presidential control,
but to rationalizing their relation to the rest of the executive branch.
It is important to note, too, the relation between the Board's studies
and the programs Governor Roosevelt had persisted in recommend-
ing to the New York legislature.

Roosevelt's conviction that planning was on the horizon is also
clear in his approach to the six-year public works proposal. He
reminded Congress that "in a previous message, I have suggested a
permanent planning agency under the Chief Executive in order
that, among other things, all public works proposals may filter from

---

[30]FDR Press Conferences, microfilm vol. 7, roll 4, Dec. 22, 1936.

the many individual departments and bureaus to a central planning place and thence to the President."[31] His effort in that message to connect national planning and the regionalism study is also clear. "But it is not wise to direct everything from Washington," he explained. "National planning should start at the bottom, or, in other words, the problems of townships, counties and States, should be coordinated through large geographical regions and come to the Capital of the Nation for final co-ordination. . . . Any division of the United States into regions for the husbandry of its resources must possess some degree of flexibility."[32]

In October of 1937 Roosevelt sent to his assistant, James F. Byrnes, a report from Merriam on a conference at the Chateau D'Ardenne in France. The topic of the conference was planning. The memorandum, with marginal emphases provided by either the President or Byrnes (Roosevelt asked Byrnes to return the memo to him and he did), suggests the uniqueness and importance of the American form of national planning. The fact that the American board was a planning board rather than an economic or budget agency was important, as was its use of outside advisers rather than government administrators alone.[33]

There is evidence from a conference on January 8, 1938, that Roosevelt was still looking for a permanent planning board "when the Reorganization Bill was passed," as he so optimistically put it. He had begun to describe a complex system of drawing individuals from various departments into the planning process to discuss such matters as the relocation of industry to areas needing jobs. All of this, of course, was not to be, but Roosevelt was still determined to try.[34]

It is at this point in a simple narration of events that the problems grow complex, but in a special historiographic way. The extraordinary success of Roosevelt's re-election campaign had led him and his supporters to believe that he now had support no previous President could have claimed. It is probable, too, that the character of the election campaign, its highly charged ideological divisions, had given the victory an ideological character as well. Roosevelt

[31]Merriam Papers, Box 193, Folder 11.

[32]June 3, 1937, from printed text in the Merriam Papers, Box 173, Folder 16.

[33]File 1092, FDRL.

[34]Merriam Papers, Box 173, Folder 16.

believed that he now had a mandate to overrule objections from the Supreme Court, as well as a Congress with a Democratic majority sufficient to amend the Constitution, if necessary. Yet, as we all know, the battle with the Supreme Court and the subsequent legislative history of the New Deal are marked by compromise and defeat that, by 1938, had produced a now familiar stalemate between the President and the revived and revitalized congressional opposition.

Historians have adopted a variety of stances with regard to the second term, arguing at times that he really got what he wanted in any case, or that the period proves the inherent triumph of conservatism in American politics, or that the preoccupation with foreign policy and the coming war in Europe eroded interest in domestic affairs. Such interpretations—and I include some of my own earlier ones among them—accept what happened not only as the only thing that could have happened, but somehow as better than what he had actually planned.

It now seems to me that only by comparing what he wanted with what he got and by examining the tactical problems that emerged unexpectedly out of the Supreme Court fight, can one begin to see the problem not only of the New Deal as a reform movement but of the entire role of planning in American government.

II

The key issue takes us back to the original recommendations of the Brownlow Committee. Regional planning authorities were central to their conception of planning and the presidency. Their failure to make that an issue in their report may have been a tactical error of a kind. Even so, by 1938 the dispute over centralization had taken the center of the stage. It was by then a case of being damned either way. Executive reorganization had been identified with Roosevelt's drive for power, the threat of dictatorship. The regional planning system, TVA model or not, rested on a central planning board of some kind if Roosevelt were to be able to control it. The two, executive reorganization and regional planning, were so dependent upon one another that their separation in the final reorganization bill written and passed by Congress spelled disaster.

The point, and it is important one, is this: if my argument is correct—namely, that Roosevelt had a plan for his second term in

office, a Third New Deal, if you will, that rested on his attaining
the aims of the Brownlow Committee—then the failure of the first
reorganization bill is critical to our understanding of what the New
Deal might have become, as well as what it actually did become.
Contrary to what I argued some years ago, the Reorganization Act
of 1939 did not give Roosevelt what he wanted in 1937 by a long
shot. What he wanted in 1937 would have involved a dramatic
transformation in American presidential administration. It would
have placed in the White House a planning board charged with the
responsibility for directing the actions of a regional system of
planning boards. It would have given the President a new echelon
of government to administer federal policies in the states.

While the administrative language invites quibble with all of its
distinctions between advice and command, staff and line, and the
like, such a central board with such a regional system would have
transformed the methods of resource distribution Americans were
accustomed to. The entire political system of state and local
influence on resource distribution would have had to have been
transformed along with it.

The significance of the failure of the first reorganization act has
been seriously understated, particularly as an explanation for the
subsequent failure of the New Deal to establish the rational system
of administrative government Roosevelt had envisaged. Part of that
significance, again, is obscured by our habit of viewing Roosevelt as
a happy pragmatist who resented administrative procedures and
enjoyed secretly duplicating assignments to subordinates and slap-
ping together convenient organizations of various kinds. There is
plenty of evidence, particularly in the latter part of his first term,
that he was seriously worried about such practices. That was the
reason for his appointment of the Committee on Administrative
Management in the first place. Certainly by the middle of the
second term while the reshaped reorganization bill was under study
he was concerned.

The minutes of the President's meeting with his planning board
in October 1939 are particularly notable for the numerous references to avoiding duplication and overlap. Thus, with regard to the
board's investigation of the current state of scientific research, the
minutes note that Roosevelt "seemed particularly concerned that
the NRPB coordinate its work in this field with the work of other
departments or agencies of the Government which were undertak-
ing similar or related work." On the study of energy resources and

power policy, he "indicated that overlapping or possible conflict between the two lines of study should be avoided." Turning to relief and reemployment, he called the board's attention "to the functions of other Departments and agencies in the field and urging that due care be taken not to 'step on the toes' of any." The President also approved a study of industrial-economic conditions but, again, he "enjoined cooperation with his Administrative Assistant Currie, and clearance with Lubin and Henderson, to the end that Board does not, as he put it, 'run crosswise with others' in the study."[35]

The Crash of 1937 and the Special Session of Congress convened that fall also distort our vision of his second-term approach to administration. He had already proposed a six-year public works program to Congress—no great revolution since the idea was one Congress had given to Hoover in 1931—but Congress now saw the consequences of such long-range planning and rejected it. The Special Session was a long series of defeats, most important among them for our purposes here, the bill calling for seven separate river valley authorities similar to TVA. As William Leuchtenburg pointed out some years ago, one can examine Roosevelt's motives in supporting a bill the basic principle of which violated the planning board's whole idea of regional planning, but one cannot arrive at clear conclusions about where, exactly, the President stood.[36]

The NRPB Committee members had been lobbying with the President to try to dissuade him from support of Norris's proliferation of TVAs, and modifications had been made in the bill to include the national planning board. But the problem of the TVA and its congressional constituency had already been finessed by the board's handling of the regionalism report.

Explaining to the Technical Committee's director, John Gaus, why the planning board had revised that particular language in the regionalism report, Merriam had said, "we qualified somewhat further the statements on TVA in order to avoid the implication that we were unfavorable to it. Obviously the TVA is in a very delicate position, with the case pending before the Supreme Court and thousands of sharp shooters ready to shoot on the slightest provocation." Merriam had already begun to be aware of the necessity of moderating the optimism with which he had approached the initial

---

[35]File 1092, Oct. 17, 1939, FDRL.

[36]Leuchtenburg, Roosevelt, Norris and the "Seven Little TVA's," 14 Jo. Politics 418–41 (1952).

work of the planning board. "What I fear," he wrote Gaus, "is that public thought is not yet clearly enough crystallized to make a significant program of advance possible. What I hope is, on the other hand, that we may be able to demonstrate still more significant development in a popularly governed country."[37]

The National Resources Planning Board recommended by the Brownlow Committee would have given the President authority for public works planning called for by the regionalism report of the planning board. While the actual execution of plans would in fact have to be carried out through the departments and the plans negotiated with a whole network of state and regional planning groups the board itself had helped to generate, the first reorganization bill would have given the President a direct line of control over the entire process from the very top. All the efforts to make the new board look like nothing more than a group of responsible citizens selected by the President to serve without pay, as a duty to their country, might have concealed the fact that planning of that order might require the building of a planning bureaucracy of major proportions. But Americans like Merriam and Brownlow believed in a public service administration by interested citizens as the alternative to the development of continental bureaucracy. They had learned their faith from Bryce and Woodrow Wilson. The whole history of the rise of industrial management in the United States had supported those lessons, and they created the field of public administration to teach them to new generations. They had experienced what they remembered as that kind of responsible public service in World War I. They were engaging in it now in the emergency of the Depression. Why should they not believe that it could be permanently institutionalized in the presidency?

Subsequent historical accounts of the NRPB have suggested quite different approaches to the problem, seeing in Merriam's approach in particular something resembling a desecration of the planning idea. As one of those bridge figures who stand between two traditions, Merriam was as committed to retaining those aspects of the past he thought essential, at the same time that he acknowledged, at times a bit ruefully, the coming of a different and potentially troublesome future. Marion Clawson's recent account of the NRPB takes Merriam to task for what seemed to many of the

---

[37]Merriam to Gaus, Nov. 10, 1935, Dec. 4, 1936, Gaus Papers, Harvard University.

younger planners of the era his failure to face the new realities of planning, particularly its political consequences. Albert Lepawsky, one of the same generation and a student of Merriam, follows a similar, though slightly more sympathetic, line of argument, in a recent article on planning in the New Deal.[38] The comparisons with Hoover's efforts at public works planning are largely ignored, even though Merriam himself kept trying to remind students of the connection. By 1940 the NRPB was still concerned with the problem of decentralization, and Merriam commissioned a study of the Federal Employment Stabilization Act of 1931 in an effort to work out some sense of the differences. That act, John Miller pointed out, gave "free rein and little guidance" to the states. Yet decentralization required relationships with state and local governments if the planning of public works were to make any reasonable sense at all, and nothing in the creation of the NRPB in the compromise legislation of 1939 made such relationships possible. The fact that critics of the NRPB were were still citing the Stabilization Act as the basis of what they insisted was the NRPB's very limited authority did not help.[39]

Yet the issue was clear, at least in part, and the problems that had troubled Hoover—indeed, that had enraged him as he surveyed Congress's attempts to run its own public works—had not gone away. Federalism, as Americans understood it, would not allow the federal government to intervene in state and local interests. The lifeblood of congressional power was the distribution of the nation's resources, and when public works became one of those resources it had to come under Congressional control. Indeed, as we now know, not until the programs of the Great Society called attention to the need for federal standards of control of federal programs in the states would presidents from Johnson to Carter feel that the issue had to be raised seriously again.

---

[38]Clawson, New Deal Planning: The NRPB (published for Resources for the Future by The Johns Hopkins University Press, 1981). This is an extremely useful account, although for reasons not intended necessarily by the author. Its research is mostly in secondary materials, but the author, as a kind of participant observer, interviewed the surviving participants in the board's work. It thus embodies all of the conflicts, some of them still bitter, among those who saw the board as a potentially successful endeavor hobbled by personality conflicts. Albert Lepawsky's article on Planning in a recent encyclopedia of the New Deal goes out of its way not to mention Merriam.

[39]Decentralization of Federal Employment Stabilization Act Functions, April 22, 1940, Merriam Papers, Box 252, Folder 15.

The significance of the planning problem thus tends to be overlooked, its failure ascribed to some obtuseness on the part of those responsible for conducting the planning process or some public education that could have taken place if only someone had tried. That it might be tied to some fundamental issues in the character of American democracy is not really raised, at least by historians and political scientists. Yet the very roots of the problem were under discussion in another literature, that of the law.

III

Historians have generally tended to view Roosevelt's battle with the Supreme Court as the political fight it indeed was. Yet underneath that fight and largely obscured by it is an intellectual issue that has been all but forgotten until relatively recently, and its recent reincarnation has taken a form that is not likely to relate it to the issues of the 1930s. Put as directly as possible, the problem is this. Planning requires administration. Administration requires bureaucracy. Bureaucracy threatens legislative control. Anything that threatens legislative controls threatens the American conception of democracy.

The contemporary form of the problem has, in recent years, been couched in critical attacks on the regulatory process. The battle between the President and Congress over control of the various agencies of the executive branch took the form of the legislative veto until the Supreme Court stepped in to question that device, extended as it was well beyond the application to executive reorganization plans to which it had been confined. Congress was searching for a means of controlling actions of federal agencies who issued rules that went against congressional will.

The emergence of de-regulation as the way of coping with the problem has tended to mute the battle. If regulatory agencies have less to regulate, then their rules have less significance. The Reagan administration's sympathy with the reduction of federal power has helped, too, by producing an administrative caution on the part of federal agencies that contrasts sharply with the activism of the Johnson and Carter administrations.

Yet, the problem has its origins in the New Deal. Prior to the New Deal Congress had been coping with the expanded administrative needs of an industrial society by creating commissions as a way of avoiding giving to the executive branch powers that threatened congressional control of administration. The crisis of the Depression created administrative agencies on an unprecedented scale, but Congress continued to refuse the President the authority to control them. Part of Hoover's problem in coping with the legislation given him to use public works stemmed from the fact that Congress still refused him the kind of rational control the President—and particularly a businessman/engineer—needed for proper management. Nor were they willing to give it to Roosevelt. New Deal programs contained little federal control over the way money was to be spent.

To leave it as a battle between the President and Congress over resource distribution, however, may demean it. The Supreme Court, then as now, stepped in to defend separation of powers. The issue then was delegation, but the fact that the issue had been debated in law review circles for the previous two decades has been forgotten. And the fact that the issue of democratic control of complex bureaucratic processes of industrial societies was destined to become one of the major worldwide issues of the twentieth century can get lost in the ideological debates that occupy all modern industrial societies. With that in mind, let us return to the question of planning.

Post–New Deal efforts to justify the emergence of an American administrative state by political scientists like Fritz Morstein Marx and Paul Appleby all have a sound that to present day readers may resemble that of a whistler walking past a cemetery. The regulatory state today is virtually a nonpartisan target, not the device for distinguishing conservatives from progressives that it was for almost a century.

The New Deal played a critical role in the creation of what today appears virtually a separate legal structure to support the administrative system that came out of the New Deal and grew apace. Administrative courts, the establishment of law school curricula in administrative law, the training of lawyers in the legislative process, and the growth of Washington law firms committed to managing the system are all part of a process that the New Deal generated, almost, it sometimes seems, by accident. The young lawyers who seemed to sprout up in agencies at the flick of Felix Frankfurter's wand were destined to become the behind the scenes power in Washington for the next fifty years, as the firms that bore some of their names became permanent fixtures that changes of administration could not affect. Thomas McCraw's sensitive treatment of the career of one of their leaders, James M. Landis, spells out part of the complexity. The administrative state needed a large governmental form for its support. The failure of Congress to include the regulatory commissions in their limited revamping of the presidency helped conceal the change that had taken place.

The fact that the change was recognized, predicted two decades earlier, and worried over by some of the same legal minds who were shaping the New Deal has been overshadowed, in a sense, by the standard historiographical interpretations of the Supreme Court fight. If one accepts even modified doctrines concerning "the nine old men," one pictures a court under justifiable fire from Roosevelt, who, as he puts it, loses the battle but wins the war. The drama is justifiable in political and historical terms. It was quite a drama. But that conclusion may conceal from view a real battle that may tell us more about the problems of historical change than we realize. For the same reason that we are not inclined to see in the New Deal parallels with statist revolutions in Europe during and after World War I we do not take seriously the Supreme Court's vision of a constitutional threat in New Deal legislation. They wisely dropped it, we believe, and so, therefore, should we.

A. A. Berle, Jr., had published an essay in 1917 raising questions about the relation between the administrative process and traditional conceptions of American democracy. He concluded with what can only be described as resignation. Administrative law was here to stay, but we were going to have to become more sophisticated in our control of it. "But we are using these administrative instruments," he admits. "We are creating new ones. We are clutching, sometimes ill-advisedly, at them in an endeavor to use them to solve pressing problems. We are fearing them, lest they become tyrannous."[40]

Administrators were appointed, not elected, and their decisions were not necessarily subject to review by traditional courts and certainly not by the legislative bodies by whom they were initially created. Their function as lawmakers was raised as a problem by Felix Frankfurter in 1927. Calling forth all of the specters of French administrative courts and the *droit administratif* Dicey had castigated so thoroughly, Frankfurter went on to trace the history of the

---

[40]Berle, The Expansion of American Administrative Law, 30 Harv. L. Rev. 430 (1917).

growth of administrative law as "a process, largely unconscious and certainly unscientific, of adjusting the exercise of these powers to the traditional system of Anglo-American law and courts." To make sure his readers sensed the crisis he seemed to foresee he went on to describe how "this illegitimate, exotic, administrative law, almost overnight overwhelmed the profession, which for years had been told of its steady advance by the lonely watchers in the tower." He went on to acknowledge as "watchers" Elihu Root, whose warnings in 1916 he quotes, and Charles Evans Hughes, Justice Sutherland, and William D. Guthrie.[41]

The potential tyranny of the administrative process had been raised at the very beginning of the American consciousness of administration. Woodrow Wilson's essay of 1887 had suggested it, but had certified the safety of the Anglo-American tradition of popular control of executive authority, a tradition he contrasted with the continental origins of executive power.[42] The administrative expansions of the New Deal raised the dark issue of the bureaucratic state, suggesting that defining American democracy in bureaucratic terms was not going to be easy, even if it were possible. And if it was difficult in 1887, the possibility of doing it in 1937 against a background of European dictatorships even more threatening than the monarchies of pre–World War I Europe would make it an especially interesting challenge.

By the 1920s American observers of European political thought were growing increasingly aware of an important range of threats to participatory democracy posed by the modern industrial state. William Yandell Elliott characterized it as "the pragmatic revolt." Leaders of mass democracies sustained their power by feeding the public's desire for emotional gratification and the promise, at least, to satisfy short-range material goals. From Elliott's perspective the tradition of republican virtue embodied in late eighteenth- and early nineteenth-century conceptions of responsible leadership had been transformed in ways that could be destructive to Burkean approaches to public authority. Mussolini and Fascism were the prime example for the 1920s. Mussolini fed such an argument when he cited Nietzsche, Sorel, and William James as his intellectual models.

---

[41]Frankfurter, The Task of Administrative Law, 75 U. Pa. L. Rev. 614 (1927).

[42]Wilson, The Study of Administration, 2 Pol. Sci. Q. 197 (1887).

Although Woodrow Wilson's essay, *Leaders of Men*, was not published in his lifetime, the address reflects a similar Hegelian approach to political leadership, a glorification of practical authority over what Wilson considered literary sensitivity, and a remarkable consciousness of the need for power to control popular will. Mass democracy required an authority Wilson seemed to center in rhetorical persuasion rather than force, but his language was as ambiguous in 1894 as it was, later, in his almost coercively patriotic speeches in World War I. It is well to remember that the nation's first modern nationalist leaders, Theodore Roosevelt and Woodrow Wilson, believed in the exercise of a moral authority by political leaders that justified the users of force when rhetorical persuasion was insufficient. Their generation of leaders understood civil rights, when they understood them at all, very differently from the way we have come to understand it.

Many of the reforms of executive authority and executive management that were characteristic of the Progressive Era were not democratic in any populist sense. Wilson's espousal of the Short Ballot movement, like the increasing attractiveness of the city manager movement, were supports for a new consciousness of the limits of democracy, the virtues of professional specialization, the requirements of controls over the impact of technology on society. William F. Ogburn's introduction of the idea of what he called "cultural lag" was an important way of conceptualizing the need for the polity to adjust itself to the demands of technological change.

By the 1930's American writers were looking at the relation between the centralization of government they saw taking place elsewhere in the world and its threat to the democratic tradition. Leonard White, in his article on Public Administration in the *Encyclopedia of the Social Sciences* pointed to the growing power of central governments in the Western world and the decline of the autonomy of local governments. He echoes Wilson's Anglo-American sense of superiority by taking solace in the fact that this centralization was happening much more quickly in Europe than it was in Great Britain or the United States, but it is solace, not assurance he invokes. Like Frankfurter and Berle in their approach to administrative law, he accepts the inevitable with the hope that something will happen to sustain the commitment to democracy in the face of new methods of government and new demands on the state.

"As these trends move on from decade to decade," White wrote, "they emphasize the decline of the amateur and the dominance of the expert. . . . The reform of English local government in the last decade of the nineteenth century, the establishment of the American city manager plan in the twentieth, are indications of a continuing process by which specialization, permanence, and professionalism are conquering the public services. From another point of view this marks the transition from self-governmental institutions to bureaucracy."[43]

Louis Brandeis had long applied his concern for "the curse of bigness" in industry to his approach to the state. His Zionism, his friendship with the British anti-imperialist Sir Alfred Zimmern, and his romantic attachment to Zimmern's description of the Greek city-state reflect his belief that the self-governing community essential to sustaining democracy had requirements of size, cultural cohesion, and proximity of the citizen to the instruments of government. Brandeis's criticism of the New Deal rested on his profound anti-statism.

The Supreme Court's criticism of the New Deal in its attack on the National Industrial Recovery Act is thus a much more complex statement than accounts of the Supreme Court battle are inclined to make it. The unanimity of the Court properly emphasized the singularity of the issue among the many divided opinions of the opposition between the Court and the New Deal. *Schechter* was a criticism of administrative delegation, the culmination of a problem legal scholars had been worrying about for almost two decades.

Three issues, then, need to be seen in relation to one another if the problem of planning is to be understood: executive reorganization, administrative law, and centralization. The problem is not one of unearthing new documents but of placing what we already have in a different order to show relationships that might otherwise be obscured. There is, in addition, the problem of approaching the issue of counter-factual history, of seeing Roosevelt's plan as real, not just a ploy to get something else from Congress but a far-reaching design for governmental reform that failed. The point may be made more significant when one realizes that the problem has been a recurring one since the New Deal as subsequent presidents faced the problem of expanded governmental services,

---

[43]White, Administration, Public, I The Encyclopedia of the Social Sciences 440, 448–49 (1930).

the growth of administrative delegation, the refusal of Congress to grant executive authority to the President, the opposition of the Court to Congress's efforts to retain executive control itself, and the public's inability to deal with the issues that arise.

Two recent presidents, Lyndon Johnson and Richard Nixon, faced conditions so similar to those described here that it might be useful to look briefly at them in order to suggest some of the underlying issues. Both presidents faced vastly expanded programs of social reform that pressed the federal government into areas it had never before entered and increased involvement in traditional areas. Both worried about the lack of central management of what were rapidly becoming politicized, entrenched bureaucracies. Both began searching for methods of increasing presidential control over executive functions, designing second-term plans for dramatic reorganizations of the presidency.

Both Johnson and Nixon were defeated in their plans by circumstances that appeared to have little to do with executive management, except that both, like Roosevelt, were accused of misusing presidential power. Other similarities might include the fact that both, like Roosevelt before them, believed that their overwhelming victories in the preceding presidential elections entitled them to reorganize the presidency.

Johnson appointed a task force headed by industrialist Ben Heineman. Heineman was part of that generation of post–New Deal Democrats who retained their commitment to the view of the New Deal they shared with Johnson. His report called for increased administrative authority through a semi-decentralized system managed from the White House by an expanded presidency. Industrialist Roy Ash provided Nixon with an even more dramatic revamping of presidential authority that would have moved the Cabinet into the White House through a series of boards or commissions that would have strengthened administrative authority.

The Heineman Task Force on Government Organization was brought into existence in 1966. It issued a series of reports which included the following statement: "(1) The regional coordination of the executive agencies in the field . . . is a problem exceeding in administrative and political difficulty the task of Presidential leadership over the agencies in Washington. (2) When to this problem of federal regional coordination is added the task of direct, authoritative regional relations with state and local governments—

particularly governors and mayors—the difficulties are at least doubled for the President."[44]

One of the basic recommendations of the task force was "To make the President's administrative job manageable, and to improve the coordination of related Federal programs, *we believe that the future line organization of the executive branch should be shaped over time to provide a small number (4–6) of line deputies (Secretaries) to manage the full range of executive departments and agencies short of the President*" (emphasis in original).[45]

That the issues were essentially the same ones Roosevelt faced by the end of his first term is clear enough. As writers describing the Great Society programs have already made clear, administration was a serious problem from the beginning. Other similarities with New Deal problems were also clear, although no one seemed to know. Young Washington administrators brought in to manage programs in the cities and states seemed determined to repeat the problem Roosevelt faced with Harold Ickes and his suspicions of local political managers whose honesty and willingness to carry out program aims he questioned. If there was a Harry Hopkins for Johnson willing to negotiate the deals required by the Mayor Daleys and Southern racial limitations of social programs, it might have been Johnson himself. Yet times had changed. A Hopkins for Johnson would have had considerably less leeway in cutting the necessary deals.[46]

Roy Ash began his report for Nixon with quotations from Heineman. He called for an even greater centralization of authority in the White House. Henry Kissinger's assumption of the dual offices of National Security Adviser and Secretary of State reflected that centralization as did the move to create a domestic council under the authority of presidential assistant John Erlichman.

William Safire's account is thorough and succint. ". . . Nixon learned by the middle of his first term what could be done and what could not be done within the executive branch, and the degree of difficulty in making the monster of government move confirmed his

[44]Some notes on Presidential Leadership of Executive Agencies, (written summary of remarks to the task force on Feb. 26, 1967), Box 1094, Files of Fred Bohen, LBJ Library, quoted in Redford & Blissett, Organizing the Executive Branch: The Johnson Presidency 198 (1981).

[45]Quoted *id.* at 203.

[46]See generally Levitan & Taggert, The Promise of Greatness (1976); Gettleman & Mermelstein eds., The Great Society Reader: The Failure of Liberalism (1967).

worst suspicions." The Ash proposals were presented to what Safire calls "a frigid Cabinet, each member worried about losing access to the President."[47] Thus began Nixon's war against the bureaucracy. By 1972 when, immediately following his reelection, he requested resignations en masse, the war had reached full scale. Yet the problem was a real one for him as it had been for Johnson. All the mechanisms that had worked behind the scenes for his predecessors—including impoundment of funds—had ceased to work for him.

In a study of the federal bureaucracy during the Nixon years, two political scientists pointed out the partisan opposition to presidential policies by career administrators. "Unless a conservative Republican president does act sharply to curtail the activities of administrators in these agencies or to politicize the agencies through extensive changes in personnel, he can expect many of his social policies to be received coldly by administrators there. . . . Under the conditions we have described, therefore," they concluded, "the incentives for an aggressively conservative Republican administration to centralize control in the White House are obviously very substantial."[48]

Even granting such concerns, the tendency of presidents to centralize control of domestic programs in the White House is only partly a problem of partisanship. Twentieth-century presidents of both parties have sought methods of managing the branch of government to which they had been popularly elected. Getting a long-range mandate to support such ambitions has been almost impossible, even after overwhelming election victories. Congress continues to hold the keys to administrative management, while the bureaucracy that holds the locks continue to grow.

The threat of presidential power appears in debates over foreign policy and military authority, while the search for domestic power surfaces in periodic reports of presidentially appointed committees. Only one, the report of the Brownlow Committee, reached a level of public debate that made its final enactment a shadow that no one could fear. In the years after World War II the language of budget control replaced that of planning. Where planning did appear, its

[47]Safire, Before the Fall: An Inside View of the Pre-Watergate White House (1975). See also the excellent account in Graham, Toward a Planned Society, note 3 *supra*, at 206–21.

[48]Aberbach & Rockman, Classing Beliefs within the Executive Branch: The Nixon Administration Bureaucracy, 70 Am. Pol. Sci. Rev. 467–68.

leaders were businessmen whose faith in social science had long been lost—or better still, forgotten. De-regulation and cutbacks became the new answer. Even glorifications of "muddling through" lost currency in such an environment.

The next era of pressure on the federal government to expand its administrative responsibilities will undoubtedly raise the whole range of issues again, particularly if those pressures are generated by a sense of emergency. Undoubtedly, once again, it will seem new and threatening to the constitutional order. We will deal with it pragmatically because we are a pragmatic people, as we keep insisting. That belief enables us to glorify the past or forget it, as we choose, but in either case to render it useless. For planning may indeed to be a threat to the constitutional order. Doing without it, or allowing it to go on in secret, may be our only options; and that may well be the issue we have to face.

DENNIS J. HUTCHINSON

THE BLACK-JACKSON FEUD

Only once in the history of the Supreme Court of the United States has one of its members publicly accused another of unethical behavior and of manipulating the decision-making process for personal ends: on June 10, 1946, Justice Robert H. Jackson—then prosecuting Nazi war crimes in Nuremberg—cabled the judiciary committees of Congress and charged that Justice Hugo L. Black had cast the deciding votes in cases in which he had a conflict of interest and further that Black had pressured the Court to issue a decision prematurely for the benefit of labor. "Jackson's explosion shocked the country";[1] there were suggestions that both Justices resign;[2] and the integrity of the Court was widely viewed as gravely wounded.[3] By the time the new Term of Court began four months later, however, the storm had blown over, and the only enduring damage was to Jackson's reputation.

Dennis J. Hutchinson is Associate Professor in the New Collegiate Division and Lecturer in Law, The University of Chicago.

AUTHOR'S NOTE: An earlier, abbreviated version of this paper was delivered at the 1988 Annual Meetings of the Organization of American Historians in Reno, Nevada. Material quoted from the Robert H. Jackson Papers, now located in the Manuscript Division of the Library of Congress, is cited simply as RHJP without reference to box number; material from transcripts of Jackson's interviews with Harlan Phillips for the Columbia University Oral History Project (abbreviated as "COH") is cited by volume and page number of the multivolume version on file at the D'Angelo Law Library, The University of Chicago Law School (after the style of Sidney Fine's Frank Murphy: The Washington Years 710 n.6 (1984)).

[1] Howard, Mr. Justice Murphy: A Political Biography 393. (1968).

[2] Id. at 393–94. See also Gerhart, America's Advocate: Robert H. Jackson 263 (1958).

[3] See, e.g., Fine, Frank Murphy: The Washington Years 470 (1984); Harper, Justice Rutledge and the Bright Constellation 311–12 (1965).

The event has been recounted in several biographical studies of the period[4] and by now should enjoy the tedium of a twice-told tale. Yet its genesis has been misstated, first by its participants and second by partisans of both Justices; worse, its significance—to the doctrinal development of what has been called the "breakup of the Roosevelt Supreme Court"[5]—has been underestimated. To unpack the Black-Jackson feud is to discover the powerful effect of personality on adjudication, and, to some extent, of politics—in a comprehensive, non-partisan sense—on law.

I

A

The first inside account of the 1946 summer storm appeared in *The Truman Merry-Go-Round*, published in 1950 by Robert S. Allen and William V. Shannon:[6]

> It was Frankfurter who was at the bottom of this tragic affair. Jackson had long been openly ambitious to succeed Harlan Stone as Chief Justice. When [Stone] died in the spring of 1946, while Jackson was away at the Nuremberg war-criminal trials, his hopes skyrocketed. It was known that Truman had spoken of Jackson as one of the ablest men on the bench. But "dope stories" began to filter out of Washington to the effect that Truman was now hesitant about appointing Jackson because of his lack of tact and obsessive feuds with other Justices.
>
> These press reports were well founded. Truman had cooled toward Jackson as a result of information imparted by retired Justices Hughes and Roberts. They had visited the President while he was deliberating on the problem and had bluntly advised against Jackson's selection. Jackson heard these stories and rumors with growing anguish. He fretted and brooded that he should be marooned in far-off Germany at such a crucial time. At this point, Frankfurter wrote him that Black had gone to Truman and declared that he would not serve under Jackson.

---

[4]See, *e.g.*, Fine, note 3 *supra*, at 466–70; Douglas, The Court Years: 1937–1975 28–31 (1980); Dunne, Hugo Black and the Judicial Revolution ch. 11 (1977); Howard, note 1 *supra*, 391–94 (1968); Harper, note 3 *supra*, 310–12; Gerhart, note 2 *supra*, at 235–88; Mason, Harlan Fiske Stone: Pillar of the Law 642, 644–45 (1956). See also White, The American Judicial Tradition: Profiles of Leading American Judges 235–38 (1976).

[5]Harrison, The Breakup of the Roosevelt Supreme Court: The Contribution of History and Biography, 2 Law & History Rev. 165 (1984).

[6]Allen & Shannon, The Truman Merry-Go-Round 366–67 (1950).

That accusation was a lie. There was not an atom of truth in it. Black had neither said nor done anything to influence Truman's decision. The story was solely the product of Frankfurter's scheming and devious imagination. But to Jackson, seething and raging in Nuremberg, Frankfurter's letter was like putting an acetylene torch to a powder keg. All of Jackson's hates, resentments, and frustrations centered on Black and exploded in a shameful letter of unfounded denunciation.

It is true that Jackson harbored hopes of becoming Chief Justice when Stone left the Court: President Roosevelt had all but promised him the job in 1941,[7] but Truman's succession to the Presidency in 1945 converted a promise into an uncertainty. In most other respects, the Allen-Shannon story is wrong. It is unlikely that Hughes or Roberts spoke against Jackson; it was Francis M. Shea—one of Jackson's subordinates—and not Frankfurter who wrote Jackson of Black's alleged intrigues; and the explosive cable to Congress was not dashed off in a fit of pique over being passed over for Chief Justice, but began as a rebuttal to the "dope stories" by Jackson to Truman more than two weeks before the Vinson appointment was announced. Jackson planned to cable Truman that the reported feud within the Court was not over personalities but principles. Vinson was named before the cable could be sent, so Jackson redrafted the plea into an attack, which he sent first to Truman and later to Congress.

Jackson was stung by the criticism of him during the height of the affair, but even more by the Allen-Shannon story and by the treatment in John P. Frank's admiring biography of Black published in 1949. To stem the critical tide, Jackson considered publishing his version of matters under someone else's name; indeed, Eugene Gerhart's rendition in *America's Advocate*, published in 1958 four years after Jackson's death, is taken verbatim from a text prepared by Jackson a few months after the Black biography appeared. Jackson provided his fullest statement of the affair to Harlan Phillips for the Columbia Oral History Project, which was completed a few days before Jackson died. The statement largely tracks the account that appears in Gerhart's book, but adds—at least inferentially—one conclusion that refutes Arthur Krock's subsequent claim that "[u]ntil the day of his death

---

[7]Douglas, note 4 *supra*, at 29; for Jackson's disclaimer of the "promise," see Kurland, Robert H. Jackson, in Freidman & Israel, IV The Justices of the United States Supreme Court 2562–63 (1980), which is drawn from the Columbia Oral History.

he believed that Black . . . was responsible for Truman's appointment of Vinson instead of himself as Chief Justice."[8] Jackson's final edition of the transcripts for Phillips make clear that Jackson believed William O. Douglas, not Black, was responsible for Truman's choice of Vinson; circumstantial evidence confirms the suspicion.

The events of late Spring 1946 between Stone's sudden death and Vinson's appointment are difficult to reconstruct. None of the extant papers of the participants allow definitive conclusions: those of Black[9] and Jackson[10] are obviously incomplete, and biographies of Truman, even those utilizing the holdings of the Truman Library, totally ignore the episode.[11] The most comprehensive examination of the fracas to date finds it "difficult to say [w]here the truth lies in this welter of conflicting accounts."[12]

The conflicting nature of those post hoc accounts highlights a feature of the controversy that is now often ignored because it has become familiar: the quarrels within the Supreme Court during the 1940s were both exacerbated and even shaped by publications in popular periodicals by journalists and legal scholars. The precedent was established during the height of the debate over the Court's role during the second Roosevelt administration with Drew Pearson's Nine Old Men;[13] Wesley McCune's knockoff, Nine Young Men,[14] helped to establish the genre. More importantly, journalists such as Marquis Childs (who was a confidant of Stone),[15] Doris Fleeson (who figured prominently in the Jackson blowup),[16] Pearson (who was socially close to Douglas), Krock, and others began routinely to provide "inside" accounts of intra-Court activities. The reports were unprecedented and had more impact, both inside and outside the Court, for that reason.

---

[8]Krock, Memoirs 303 (1968).

[9]Wigdor, The Personal Papers of Supreme Court Justices: A Descriptive Guide 48 (1986). Not only do Black's papers lack his conference notes, as Wigdor points out, but the case files are much thinner than many of those available for other Justices who sat during the period.

[10]Kurland, note 7 *supra*, at 2570.

[11]Compare Tom C. Clark's dubious account in Heller, ed., The Truman White House: The Administration of the Presidency, 1945–1953 30–31 (1980).

[12]Fine, note 3 *supra*, at 468.

[13]Pearson & Allen, The Nine Old Men (1937).

[14]McCune, The Nine Young Men (1947).

[15]See Mason, note 4 *supra*, at 472–76, 700–701.

[16]See text at notes 68–72 *infra*.

Black was one of the earliest victims of the genre: Childs published reports of Black's dubious judicial competency, and Stone was the obvious source.[17] Admirers of Black retaliated with articles extolling his virtues at the expense of his colleagues;[18] one of those articles infuriated Jackson.[19] The Justices, in effect, were put—or put themselves—in the position of arguing their judicial philosophies both in their opinions and in the popular press.

There is an additional factor which contributed to personality conflicts among the Justices during the period, most bitterly between Frankfurter and Douglas[20] and most publicly between Black and Jackson. At stake was nothing less than the leadership of an institution whose agenda was up for grabs once Roosevelt had filled seven of its nine seats by 1943 and the constitutionality of the New Deal was firmly entrenched. After that primary goal had been accomplished, there was nothing philosophically that united the Roosevelt Court.[21] Several of the new appointees—certainly Black, Frankfurter, Douglas, and Jackson—hoped, if not expected,[22] to lead the Court. Yet even the putative leaders made false starts and changed directions as World War II distorted both the issues and the stakes of the game. It is no wonder that feuds developed among the individuals involved. The ultimate question is what difference it made to the decisions and doctrine the Court made.

The feud between Black and Jackson provides a prism through which to view that question. Before turning to the larger question of why feelings between the two were so strong and of what effect it had on the Court's work, it is worth taking a few moments to tidy up the record of Jackson's eruption over the Vinson appointment.

B

Jackson's unprecedented denunciation of Black from Nuremberg was obliquely foreshadowed a year before. On June 18, 1945, the

---

[17]Mason, note 4 *supra*, at 472–76.

[18]See, *e.g.*, Rodell, Mr. Justice Black, 49 The American Mercury 135 (Aug. 1944); Rodell, Supreme Court Postscript, The Progressive, May 27, 1946, p. 5.

[19]*Cf.* Gerhart, note 2 *supra*, at 241.

[20]See generally Urofsky, Conflict among the Brethren: Felix Frankfurter, William O. Douglas and the Clash of Personalities and Philosophies on the United States Supreme Court, 1988 Duke L. J. 71.

[21]See generally Harrison, note 5 *supra*.

[22]See Hutchinson, Felix Frankfurter and the Business of the Supreme Court, O.T. 1946–O.T. 1961, 1980 Supreme Court Review 143, 151–52.

last day of the October 1944 Term, the Court denied a petition for rehearing in *Jewel Ridge Coal v. Local No. 6167, United Mine Workers.*[23] Jackson filed a two-page concurrence in the denial, which looked innocuous on its face but which privately enraged Black.[24] The Court had ruled, 5–4, the month before that "portal- to-portal" time was covered by the Fair Labor Standards Act in the bituminous coal industry.[25] The losing coal company based its petition for rehearing on the ground that the miners were represented by Crampton P. Harris, who was Black's former law partner (and personal lawyer),[26] and thus that Black should have disqualified himself for a conflict of interest. Black wanted a simple *per curiam* denial of the petition; Jackson objected; Stone tried unsuccessfully to negotiate a compromise; and Jackson filed his statement, nominally dissociating himself from the merits of the ruling and implicitly criticizing Black for hiding behind the denial and not facing the music.[27]

Although the conflict of interest issue later became the focal point of the Nuremberg cables, and of subsequent debate among supporters of both Justices,[28] it was not the primary source of Jackson's contempt for Black. As Jackson later wrote privately, "[t]he really sinister thing for the Court and the nation, if true, was thus stated in the cable:"[29]

> While Mr. Justice Murphy was preparing his opinion a strike of the mine workers and negotiations with the operators was proceeding. It was proposed to hand down the decision, in favor of the miners, without waiting for the opinion and dissent. The only apparent reason behind this proposal was to announce the decision in time to influence the contract negotiations during the coal strike. Chief Justice Stone protested such proposed irregular treatment vigorously. I do not believe Mr. Justice Murphy favored it. In all events, it was abandoned. But the conduct of this case . . . created uneasiness in my mind.

[23]325 U.S. 897 (1945).

[24]See, *e.g.*, Mason, note 4 *supra*, at 644.

[25]325 U.S. 161 (1945).

[26]Hearst v. Black, 87 F.2d 68 (Ct. App., D.C. 1936).

[27]See 325 U.S. 897 (1945) (Jackson, J., concurring in denial of rehearing). *Cf.* Gerhart, note 2 *supra*, at 253.

[28]Compare Frank, Mr. Justice Black: The Man and His Opinions (1948); Frank, Disqualification of Judges, 56 Yale L. J. 605 (1947), with Gerhart, supra, at 265–73.

[29]Memorandum, RHJP, 1/7/47, quoting cable.

Jackson suspected that Black was pressuring Murphy, and the others in the bare majority in *Jewel Ridge*, to supply a bargaining chip for John L. Lewis in the growingly bitter strike whose negotiations broke down a day after Murphy circulated his proposed majority opinion.[30] To Jackson, the rush to judgment was simply a nakedly "partisan"[31] manipulation of the Court's decision-making process by Black to suit his own ideological agenda.

The disposition of the rehearing petition was publicly ignored as the Court adjourned for its summer recess. Jackson left with a staff for London to begin negotiations for the war crime trials. He expected to be able to return by the beginning of the October Term, but he grossly underestimated the time that would be consumed in hammering out the terms of the trials with the allies involved, in collecting and preparing documents, and in arranging logistics for—let alone conducting—the trials. He was absent from Washington for more than a year.

For Jackson, Nuremberg was a golden opportunity with twin benefits: he could get back in the action in a non-subordinate role and he could walk out the front door from a situation he was finding increasingly distasteful.[32] He later told Phillips that he "accepted this task because in the first place there was a relief from the frustration at being in a back eddy with important things going on in the world. I'd be less than candid if I didn't admit that influence."[33] More candidly, he told Phillips: "If internal matters at the court had been pleasant and agreeable, and if I had not already considered leaving the court, I probably would not have undertaken it. All things considered I didn't know but that it might prove to be a good exit from the court, and I wasn't at all sure that if I took it on I ever would return to the court."[34]

---

[30]The strike was voted by the Union March 29; the contract expired two days later; John L. Lewis agreed to a thirty-day extension of the agreement on April 1; negotiations collapsed April 6 (one day after Murphy's draft majority opinion circulated within the Court to the others Justices); negotiations resumed April 7; the mines were seized April 10 and a new agreement was signed April 11. RHJP.

[31]Memorandum, note 29 *supra*, at 8.

[32]Kurland, note 7 *supra*, at 2569.

[33]VIII COH at 12.

[34]*Ibid.* Jackson also claimed that he had twice offered Truman his resignation from the Court. See Kurland, note 7 *supra*, at 2569.

Jackson's prolonged absence from the Court did little to ease tensions among the Justices,[35] and, ironically, he exacerbated the problem by leaving. In the first place, Stone disapproved of extrajudicial work in general and the Nuremberg project in particular, which Jackson knew[36] but underestimated.[37] Second, and more important for the Court institutionally, Jackson's absence posed the risk of 4–4 votes and the guaranteed burden on the other members of the Court of Jackson's share of majority opinion assignments. Both problems materialized during the Term.[38]

During the summer between terms, Owen J. Roberts decided to retire, and the intra-Court feuds reached their shameful nadir over the content of the traditional letter from the Court to a retiring colleague.[39] This time, Frankfurter and Black were the antagonists, with Stone caught in the middle and Jackson—away in London working on terms of the trials—largely aloof from the bickering. Jackson offered what Stone's biographer called "common-sense advice"[40] to resolve the squabble, but Stone could not move Black and no letter was sent.

The affair struck Jackson as the last straw, and, perhaps secure in his new challenge, he offered Truman his resignation from the Court as he later recalled to Phillips:[41]

> I came back to Washington for one week that September [1945] and found conditions here at the court perfectly terrible. It was that week I talked with Truman and told him I would just as soon resign. I had gotten the agreement for the Nuremberg trials signed at London and some of my friends urged me that that was a good time to get out of the Nuremberg thing and avoid the risks of failure in the trial. But I was determined to see the matter through and I took the whole subject up with the President. He rejected the suggestion of resignation from the court and said he wanted me to stay.

---

[35] *Ibid.*

[36] "I knew he [Stone] would disapprove of my doing it. I didn't have to ask him to know that. I knew that I would disapprove it if anyone else were doing it." VIII COH at 13.

[37] See Mason, note 4 *supra*, at 714–19, esp. 716; see also Biddle, In Brief Authority 374–75 (1962).

[38] See generally Mason, note 4 *supra*, at 717.

[39] See generally *id.* at 765ff.

[40] *Id.* at 768.

[41] VIII COH at 519–20.

The beginning of the October 1945 Term coincided, Jackson remembered, with "reports that some of the members of the court were very indignant that I was not there attending to my business. These leaks got into the gossip columns of columnists I knew were intimate with some members of the court. There were intimations that the project was political and intended to build us up politically. Some of those were plainly inspired from the court."[42] Jackson tried to meet at least half of the problem by writing Stone that he could return to Washington for the April sitting to dispose of cases that were held up by equally divided votes. Stone, chafing at reports that the Nuremberg Tribunal took a generous holiday vacation, wrote Jackson January 2 that he had worked on both Christmas and New Year's Day, that the rest were behind, too, but that Jackson should stay put.[43]

A few days after he received Stone's letter, Jackson received from a staff member in Washington a newspaper clipping entitled "Stymied Court," which referred to the "severe handicap that has been imposed on the court" and complained "that the court is seriously embarrassed by Justice Jackson's absence. . . . On Tuesday it had to order three important cases to be reargued all over again after Mr. Jackson's return."[44] The staffer's cover letter noted: "In announcing an opinion last Monday the Chief Justice ended with this formulation, 'of course, Mr. Justice Jackson took no part in the consideration or decision of this case.'"[45]

Jackson was now absorbed in the trials, but he repeated to Stone his offer to return in April. Stone again rejected the offer, in letters March 1 and 21, because he apparently felt, according to his biographer, "that it might be charged that Jackson had returned for certain politically delicate cases and for these only."[46] The message was unmistakable to Jackson: "I gave up the idea of returning that spring. That was the way matters stood. They couldn't get out a letter to Roberts. Stone thought it wasn't advisable for me to come

[42]*Id.* at 520.

[43]Mason, note 4 *supra*, at 717.

[44]New York Times, 1/16/46.

[45]Alderman to RHJ, 1/16/46, RHJP.

[46]Mason, note 4 *supra*, at 717.

back. Between the lines, it was perfectly clear to me that he was saying, 'When you get here, you better stay on the job.'"[47]

At the same time Jackson was corresponding with Stone, the trials reached their most dramatic moment. Jackson had been widely praised for his eloquent opening remarks,[48] but his greatest challenge came on March 18 when he began cross-examination of Herman Goering—who, with Hitler dead in the bunker, was the personification of Nazidom and thus the symbolic focal point of the trial. Norman Birkett, one of the British judges, neatly captured the stakes in his diary: "If the leader of the surviving Nazis could be exposed and shattered, and the purposes and and methods of the Nazi government revealed in their horrible crudity, then the whole free world would feel that this trial had served its useful purpose."[49] Anything short of that, thought Birkett, would confirm "the fears of those who thought the holding of any trial to be a mistake."[50]

Jackson cross-examined Goering for two days, but those in the courtroom thought Goering won the battle—at least rhetorically—in the first ten minutes.[51] Two factors, one within his control and one without, confounded Jackson. First: He was ill-prepared on—and thus imperfectly understood—the documents he used. So, as Sir David Maxwell-Fyfe—the deputy chief British prosecutor—later shrewdly observed, "although in fact the documents put by Jackson drove home Goering's complicity . . . , Goering scored heavily in the verbal encounters."[52] Second: The Tribunal ruled that Goering could supplement his "yes" or "no" answers with explanations, which Goering provided bombastically at length. Jackson lost his temper over the ruling,[53] the interrogation foundered, and, in Maxwell-Fyfe's words, "Jackson's prestige was sensibly lowered at both Nuremberg and in America."[54]

---

[47]VIII COH at 522. The message was not as interlineal as Jackson later recalled. See Mason, note 4 *supra*, at 717.

[48]Tusa & Tusa, The Nuremberg Trial 154–58, esp. 157 (1983).

[49]Quoted in Hyde, Norman Birkett: The Life of Lord Birkett of Ulverston 509 (1964).

[50]*Ibid.*

[51]*Id.* at 510.

[52]Viscount Kilmuir (Sir David Maxwell-Fyfe), Political Adventure: The Memoirs of the Earl of Kilmuir 112 (1964).

[53]"I was quite indignant about it, too. There were suggestions that I lost my temper, which, to some extent, were justified." VIII COH at 335. See also Biddle, note 37 *supra*, at 410.

[54]Kilmuir, note 52 *supra*, at 112.

Some would later argue or strongly hint that the Goering fiasco, as it was widely perceived, caused an enormous emotional strain on Jackson and helped to precipitate his outburst scarcely two months later against Black. Norman Birkett's bathetic diary entry for April 9 provides the most extreme contemporaneous view: "[T]he manner of Jackson's appearance was revealing and disturbing. He is a thoroughly upset man because of his failure in cross-examining Goering from which so much was expected. He has taken it very badly indeed and his instinct is to run away from the scene of his failure."[55]

Jackson was extremely disappointed in the popular perception of the episode,[56] but he looked back more in anger than in sorrow. He told Phillips:[57]

> [Goering] left the stand with no delusions. He hadn't been able to break the case against him. The things he'd been obliged to admit were so mean and petty that he looked very small in the eyes of his colleagues. . . . They realized, and he realized, that he had made admissions that bore on the conspiracy point during the period when he felt so expansive and so flattered at his pre-eminence that it would be hard to get away from when the verdict was handed down. . . . Goering's boldness in admitting, in fact his boasting of his aggressiveness had appeared to the galleries like a fine performance, but it made a very damaging record.

Although Jackson was a master of his own defense, especially in hindsight (as his Oral History repeatedly shows), his retrospective assessment of the costs of mishandling Goering ring true. Jackson knew that the concessions Goering made when faced with the documents were critical (a view later vindicated by the Tribunal's judgment);[58] Maxwell-Fyfe's completion of the cross-examination was widely perceived as highly effective;[59] and Jackson was buoyed by reports he received that the other defendants were depressed by

---

[55]Frank, Mr. Justice Black note 28 *supra*, at 131.

[56]Birkett, in Hyde, note 49 *supra*, at 513; Biddle, note 37 *supra*, at 411; see also Tusa & Tusa, note 48 *supra*, at 290.

[57]VIII COH at 339–40.

[58]See, *e.g.*, Harris, Justice Jackson at Nuremberg, 20 The International Lawyer 867, 892 (1986); Conot, Justice at Nuremberg 343 (1983). *Cf.* Tusa & Tusa, note 48 supra, at 288–92, esp. 291.

[59]See *id.* at 285–88; Lord Shawcross, Robert H. Jackson's Contributions During the Nuremberg Trial, in Mr. Justice Jackson: Four Lectures in His Honor 127 (1969) ("made his reputation"). For Maxwell-Fyfe's views, see Kilmuir, note 52 *supra*, at 113–15.

the net effect of Goering's performance.[60] The press may have seen the debate as a field day for Goering, but Jackson—ever the lawyer judging events by lawyer's standards—saw it as an intense irritation and a temporary blow to his pride but not his case, which was what ultimately counted.

Rebounding vigorously from the setback with Goering, Jackson spent the next two months developing plans for the final arguments and working on the cross-examination of Hjalmar Schacht, the banker later acquitted by the Tribunal, and Albert Speer. Biddle thought in late March that Jackson was "unhappy and beaten,"[61] but Jackson's energetic agenda in April and May strongly contradicts the impression. On April 28, Jackson wrote Frankfurter that "Goering's speeches did us a good deal of harm but his misbehavior and other events make up for it."[62] He added, perhaps in a pep talk to both, "the case is moving perfectly" and "I am willing to close my career on the record made here."[63] Jackson's nerves may have been "frayed"[64] in early May, as Birkett recorded, but by then there was a new cause.

Stone died April 22, and the funeral was scheduled for April 25. He later recalled: "That, of course, revived the stories that Roosevelt had promised to appoint me chief justice and revived all the gossip about that. I got advice from many of my friends, all very well-meaning, I'm sure, to fly home to the Stone funeral. Then I got telegrams that I ought to come back to Washington, that there were things going on that I should be there for. But I had never in my life gone seeking a job, and I wasn't going to seek this."[65]

Jackson's decision to stay put and go "about my work"[66] was understandable but costly. His retrospective explanation sounds in pride, which is, of course, credible, but there was probably more to the decision. He had been pummeled in the press for being away and deadlocking an overworked Court; how could he now plausibly find time to return for a funeral, especially where his selflessness

[60]VIII COH at 340–41.

[61]Tusa & Tusa, note 48 *supra*, at 290.

[62]RHJ to FF, 4/28/46, RHJP.

[63]*Ibid.*

[64]Birkett, quoted in Hyde, note 49 *supra*, at 516.

[65]VIII COH at 522–23; compare Kurland, note 7 *supra*, at 2569.

[66]VIII COH at 523.

would immediately be drawn into question? In addition, the press would be likely to turn his appearance into a sideshow that would detract from Stone's funeral to Jackson's detriment. On the other hand, if he did not return to Washington at least briefly, he could not monitor "things going on." So Jackson took the publicly less objectionable course, and the price was that he was quickly outmaneuvered.

No notes of the advice or the telegrams to which he referred survive in his papers, but it did not take long for him to feel at a comparative disadvantage—isolated and poorly informed overseas, outflanked in the Capitol. He recalled later: "Pretty soon the President was asked something about it and gave the press an intimation that he was thinking of appointing me. Immediately there came out a column by Drew Pearson announcing that if I was appointed two members of the court would resign. Everyone knew who they were—Black and Douglas. The commentator was on notoriously close terms with both these men. Things dragged on. Time dragged on."[67]

The Pearson column was published April 24, one day before the funeral. On the same day, Doris Fleeson wrote a column speculating that Truman would fill Stone's chair with Secretary of State Byrnes (who had served on the Court for the 1941 Term) and put Jackson in Byrnes's place at State, thus strengthening Truman's hand at State and still leaving him with one seat to fill on the Court.[68] More speculative newspaper columns appeared daily, eventually making their way into Jackson's hands. On April 26, Ernest Lindley speculated that "many clews . . . point to the elevation of Jackson," although Byrnes and Secretary of the Treasury Vinson—formerly a federal appeals judge—were also mentioned.[69] Two days later, Scripps-Howard reported that two-thirds of its staff expected Jackson to be named Chief Justice; a distant second and third were Black and Byrnes, respectively.[70]

---

[67]*Ibid.*

[68]Pearson's column is discussed in Fine, note 3 *supra*, at 467. Fleeson's column, Byrnes a Chief Justice Possibility, was published April 24, 1946, and the New York Post version was sent to Jackson in Germany. RHJP.

[69]Linley, Chief Justiceship: Many Factors Temper Selection, April 26, 1946, Washington Post, RHJP.

[70]Robert H. Jackson Is Favorite to Head U.S. Supreme Court, April 28, 1946 (clipping sent by B. C. Andrus to Jackson May 7, 1946), RHJP.

Things and time continued to wear on for two more weeks, with more of the same speculation in the press until May 16, when a new slant appeared in Doris Fleeson's column in the *Washington Star*. Jackson's later description of the column is both accurate and revealing of his reaction:[71]

> [S]he said [it] was the inside story of the Jackson-Black battle, as laid before a harassed President. It was very circumstantial. It described the conference on the petition for re-hearing in the Jewel Ridge Case and nobody could doubt that it came from somebody present at that conference, which meant from a Justice. It called the differences of the court a "blood feud," and quoted the President as telling about the feud as he had learned it. It related some of the facts from the rehearing petition and the opinion in the Jewel Ridge Case, with a slant favorable to Black. It didn't recite the fact that Crampton Harris was his counsel when he was sued. It told how Black "reacted with fiery scorn" to what he regarded as an insult and a slur on his judicial honor. It said the President, being a southerner, knew how to understand this affront to Black's honor.

Fleeson also reported that the President "has confided to a Senator: 'Black says he will resign if I make Jackson Chief Justice and tell the reasons why. Jackson says the same about Black.'"[72]

At the same time that Jackson received a copy of the Fleeson column, he received a letter that appeared to confirm his worst suspicions. Written on personal stationery, the letter was dated May 17, the day after the column was published, and came from Frank Shea, who had served on Jackson's negotiations team in London and who had been in the Justice Department before that. Shea assumed Jackson knew the details of recent events, but he spelled them out nonetheless: "I understand that for a few hours it seemed a sure thing for you. Then, Black got word to the President that there would be a row if you were appointed. At this he began to make wide inquiries and to appreciate, perhaps exaggerate, the rifts in the Court."[73] Shea went on to speculate that Hughes and Roberts, whom Truman had consulted in late April, probably gave "no advice" and "some support," respectively. Shea thought the

---

[71]VIII COH at 523–24. And see Fleeson, Supreme Court Feud: Inside Story of Jackson-Black Battle Laid Before a Harassed President, Washington Evening Star, May 16, 1946, p. 15, cols. 4–5, quoted at length in Gerhart, note 2 *supra*, at 259–60.

[72]Quoted in Gerhart, note 2 *supra*, at 260.

[73]FMS to RHJ, 5/17/46, RHJP.

President was leaning outside the Court for the appointment, with Byrnes the leading candidate, notwithstanding recent editorials in the *Post* identifying dangers in that course. Shea guessed that the President "is torn by conflicting considerations and is likely to let the thing drift for a time. If that happens, he might well get back to you." Shea closed by stating what had been obvious since Jackson had decided not to return for Stone's funeral: "There does not seem to be anyone really directing this for you here. I think it suffers from that. Your friends are likely to hesitate about making any important moves without being in a position to consult you."

Shea could not have made it more clear that time was of the essence for Jackson, if he still entertained hopes for the appointment. Then Jackson made a characteristic decision that did nothing for his cause and became a loaded weapon lying about and waiting to go off. Always the loner, Jackson consulted no one in Washington or on his staff in Nuremberg for advice. Instead, he drafted a four-page memorandum for Truman that laid out, in lawyerly fashion, his view of the "case." There is no clue in his papers whether he seriously planned to send the memo to the President, or whether he was simply trying to see how his argument looked in print—a technique he frequently used on the Court for testing ideas about which he had some doubt; although cast in the form of opinions, these memos were more private sounding boards than preliminary drafts for a public audience.[74]

Jackson tried to convey a dutiful tone in the memorandum, but resentment and self-interest bubble at the surface:[75]

> Publications just reaching me, especially the Fleeson column, . . . suggest that advantage is being taken of my absence to convey a distorted view of differences among the Justices. If the only effect of this were personal to me, I should never answer them. But the real problem before you is not whether some present Justice will sit in the center instead of the near end of the bench—the real question is will you advance or retard by the new blood you must add. On this subject I think

---

[74]During his twelve terms on the Supreme Court, Jackson wrote draft opinions or opinion fragments in approximately 100 cases that were never published. By now, the most famous is his draft in Brown v. Board of Education, 347 U.S. 483 (1954), discussed in Kluger: Simple Justice: The History of Brown v. Board of Education and Black America's Struggle for Equality 869–73 (1975); Schwartz, Chief Justice Rehnquist, Justice Jackson, and the Brown Case, 1988 Supreme Court Review infra.

[75]RHJP.

it is very important that you know that the differences are not
petty personal ones but go to matters which seem to me if they
become public to affect the credit of the Court as now
constituted. If I do not give you this information, no one else
seems likely to do so. I think I owe it you you to submit these
facts before you make a new appointment lest you act without
information which coming out afterwards would prove embar-
rassing as once it did with President Roosevelt.

Jackson then turned to the "merits." He said his opinion on
rehearing in *Jewel Ridge* was "not a gratutious reflection on Black"
but was self-protection "against what appeared to be a hook-up
between Black and John L. Lewis which might result in a scandal."
Jackson then spelled out his version of the disposition of the
rehearing petition and turned to the merits of the case, which he
argued was a reversal by Justice Black of the position taken by
Senator Black when he drafted the controlling statute. "On the face
of the record, the decision is one of the most shocking to me in the
Court's history." After quoting a supportive authority on labor law,
Jackson turned to Harris's role in the litigation and then to the
pressure within the Court for an early announcement of the
decision. "This would have been highly irregular and I could never
see any purpose to it except to influence the negotiations between
the miners and companies which were then pending. In any event,
Chief Justice Stone protested such proposal so vigorously it was
abandoned, though but for him it probably would have prevailed."
Jackson then circled back to the conference discussions on the
rehearing petition, quoted Black's threatened "declaration of war"
if there were more than a simple denial, reported that he "could not
yield to this bullying and keep my self-respect," and stated drily "I
filed the opinion." The draft memo concluded: "Now I do not know
enough about the Black-Harris-Lewis relationship to condemn
Justice Black's conduct any more than I know enough to approve it.
I do know that such a victory will not present the appearance of
disinterested justice that people like to think is the function of the
Court. I do not think you would want to be seeming to give
approval to these conditions as might unwittingly be done if I failed
to inform you of them."

Jackson did not send the draft cable, but scribbled "not used" at
its top and pitched it into his growing file on the affair. He left no
explanation of his decision, but two are possible. He may have
simply been overtaken by time: No more than two weeks could

have elapsed between the date he received both Shea's letter and the Fleeson column and June 6, when Truman announced Vinson's nomination.

Or Jackson may have realized that the draft would fail—either rhetorically as written, or, even if redone, politically. The draft claims to show that the "feud" with Black was not personal, but the evidence is so speculative and the argument so undeveloped that the claims sound like those of a sore loser. More fundamentally, no argument or plea from Jackson could ameliorate his problem with Truman, because any contact with him would appear to confirm the gravity of the intra-Court rift. Jackson was a spellbinding campaigner and a partisan loyalist, but he had no experience in political infighting; he always tended to see arguments in logical, lawyerly frameworks. Had he been politically astute, he would have realized that his chances were finished once Black and Douglas tapped their political contacts and their newspaper allies. Unless Truman were convinced that he owed Jackson the Chief Justiceship for services rendered at Nuremberg—for which there is absolutely no evidence—the first material hints of intra-Court bickering over the seat guaranteed as a political matter that no sitting Justice could be elevated.

At first, it may seem striking that Black and Douglas, who were politically savvy, would so readily sacrifice their chances for promotion. Black had nothing to lose, however, because he never had any reason to covet the center chair; his dominant influence within the Court required no further emolument. Douglas, who had already turned down an offer from Truman to be Secretary of the Interior[76] and whose name had already been linked with the Vice-Presidency,[77] had higher aspirations. Jackson, who had nurtured hopes of the Chief Justiceship for a half-decade, was politically neutralized before Stone was in the ground.

All of the speculation and intrigue ended on Thursday, June 6, when Truman announced Vinson's nomination as Chief Justice. Jackson hastily re-drafted his unsent cable for dispatch to "President Truman only" the following day. Only his son, who was on his staff at Nuremberg, and his secretary knew he was working on the cable.[78] As he told Phillips: "I consulted nobody. Nobody knew

---

[76]Simon, Independent Journey: The Life of William O. Douglas 270 (1980).

[77]See generally *id.* at 257ff.

[78]Gerhart, note 2 *supra*, at 261.

that I was issuing it. If anybody had been consulted, they probably would have urged me not to do it."[79] Except for rehearsing the details of *Jewel Ridge*, including the conflict of interest charge, the cable was pure spleen. Jackson obligatorily congratulated Truman on the Vinson appointment, then went for the jugular. He pointed to the rumors of Black's threat to resign if he was named and snarled: "I would be loath to believe that you would concede to any man a veto over court appointments."[80] He continued: "The alternative impression . . . is that something sinister has been revealed to you which made me unfit for Chief Justice. If that were true, I am also unfit for Associate Justice." He explained—and perhaps revealed why he had not sent the draft cable earlier—"I could not volunteer information on this subject without giving the impression of being a petitioner for appointment." After telling his side of the *Jewel Ridge* story, he closed with a veiled threat: "[I] cannot discharge my duties as Chief Justice Vinson's associate if I allow the impression either that an associate 'has something on me' which is disqualifying in your eyes, or that my opinion in the Jewel Ridge case was a 'gratuitous insult' to an associate. Unless you can suggest some better method of making my position clear to the public and to the bar of the country or unless you think it preferable that I release this cable myself from here, I am compelled to ask you to release it."

Truman received Jackson's cable on Saturday, June 8, and replied by coded cable late that night:[81]

> I am afraid that you have been grossly misinformed. I have not discussed the question of the appointment of a new chief justice with any member of the court. I received no information from anyone that even insinuated that you were unfit for promotion. There may have been some newspaper comment regarding differences existing within the court, but I took no notice of them, nor did they enter into my decision in any way. I did not see the article in the *Star* you refer to, nor had I ever heard of it before. Justice Black has given me no information, either orally or in writing, on this subject. The reputation and position of the court are of paramount interest to me and no purpose can be served by making this controversy public.

---

[79] COH at 525.

[80] RHJP, quoted in part in Fine, note 3 *supra*, at 468.

[81] VIII COH at 525–26; RHJP; quoted in part in Fine, note 3 *supra*, at 468.

Truman closed with a compliment to Jackson's work at Nuremberg. Jackson, not surprisingly, viewed Truman's answer "as
manifestly dishonest: [it] made me more determined than I had
been."[82] Jackson received Truman's message on Sunday, June 9,
and worked all day on a new cable—based on what he had sent
Truman—addressed to the chairmen of the Congressional judiciary
committees. Monday morning, June 10, he sent off the cables, held
a press conference, and departed for a vacation in Denmark. The
public cable emphasized the conflict of interest charge against
Black, said he "wanted the practice stopped," and warned darkly
that "[i]f it is ever repeated while I am on the bench I will make my
Jewel Ridge opinion look like a letter of recommendation by
comparison."[83] He justified revealing what transpired in the conference room on the ground that the Fleeson column had already done
so and that he needed to set the record straight.

Washington was, of course, thunderstruck by Jackson's blast.
Newspaper columnists attacked both justices, although Jackson
took most of the fire;[84] there was some talk of a congressional
investigation, but nothing developed;[85] and Black, throughout the
affair, said nothing. Vinson was confirmed by voice vote June 20,
took office four days later and the sensation swirling about the
Supreme Court disappeared from the headlines abruptly by
month's end.

Jackson delivered his widely praised closing argument at Nuremberg on July 27, returned to Washington August 2, and paid a
courtesy call the following morning on Vinson. Six years later he
recalled: "When I came back to the Court, Vinson, of course, was
Chief Justice. From that day to this, Justice Black has treated me
with respect as one gentleman to another. We've never had a word.
Relations were never as harmonious between us as they have been
since. I don't know what they would have been without the
[cable]."[86]

---

[82]VIII COH at 525. Based on Truman's performance at a subsequent press conference,
some journalists also doubted the denial. See Gerhart, note 3 *supra*, at 264–65; Dunne, note
4 *supra*, at 246.

[83]Quoted in Fine, note 3 *supra*, at 469. For the full text of the cables, see 92 Cong. Rec. 6724
(June 12, 1946) or New York Times, Text of Jackson's Statement Attacking Black, June 11,
1946, at p. 2, col. 3.

[84]See, *e.g.*, Harper, note 3 *supra*, at 311–12.

[85]See Fine, note 3 *supra*, at 470.

[86]VIII COH at 532.

Privately, Jackson gloated over the eventual fallout from his blast. He pointed out both to his biographer and to Phillips that Congress "rebuked"[87] the Court for *Jewel Ridge* when it amended the Fair Labor Standards Act and essentially adopted Jackson's dissent.[88] He also noted that Congress amended the Judicial Code in 1948 "to provide that a judge shall disquality himself if his relationship with the attorneys involved warrants it."[89] Black had learned his lesson, according to Jackson's statement to Phillips in 1952: "There has been no more sitting in questionable cases. There has been no disposition to overbear those who disagree with him."[90] And, incidentally, "Mr. Crampton Harris has never appeared in Court since."[91]

C

From the day he returned from Nuremberg in August of 1946 until he died in 1954, Jackson was unrepentant for his role in what he called at its height "the disgraceful brawl."[92] Indeed, he told Phillips: "I have every reason to feel that if I were in the same situation again, I would do just what I did, even though it brought a lot of criticism."[93] He expressed one regret: "The only mistake I made, I think, was in not making a more complete and unequivocal statement from Nuremberg when I made it. It was a mistake shooting from such a long distance. It was a foolish thing, probably, to have done it from that distance because I didn't make the best of my case."[94]

Jackson's regret is revealing. He had the instincts of an advocate, not a politician. When he received the Fleeson column, he reflexively responded by drafting his side of the case. But his real objective at that point was not Black but the Chief Justiceship. Had he thought more clearly or had better advice—or any advice—he might have served his cause better by simply releasing a public statement condemning the gossip-mongers and praising Black as a

---

[87]*Id.* at 531; Gerhart, note 2 *supra*, at 273f.

[88]61 Stat. 84.

[89]VIII COH at 531; Gerhart, note 2 *supra*, at 273. See 28 U.S.C. §455.

[90]VIII COH at 534.

[91]*Id.* at 532.

[92]Fine, note 3 *supra*, at 469.

[93]VIII COH at 533–34.

[94]Gerhart, note 2 *supra*, at 276.

dedicated Justice with whom he disagreed only on matters of principle. The statement might not have made any difference, since Truman was being lobbied hard by those who saw Jackson as an enemy of labor,[95] but it would have been a better gambit than a poorly conceived brief that would have backfired by appearing to confirm the feud. Jackson was no stranger to press conferences in Nuremberg,[96] and a statement would not have seemed as extraordinary there as it would have back in Washington. On the other hand, even if the idea of a statement had occurred to Jackson, words praising Black would probably have stuck in Jackson's throat. "Feud" may be an overstatement of their relations, but not by much. Moreover, Jackson never liked to retreat from a position. He would have seen the diplomatic disingenuousness of publicly praising Black as a confession of error on the *Jewel Ridge* rehearing petition, and emotionally that was too high a price even with the Chief Justiceship at stake.

After Jackson returned to Washington in the summer of 1946, he and the other members of the Court treated the cables and the brawl as if they had never happened. Within two years, the controversy entered a second stage that mocked the first. John P. Frank, a former Black clerk, published an adoring biography and selection of Black's opinions in 1948.[97] Frank, who had been outraged by the cables,[98] had published an article in 1947 entitled "Disqualification of Judges,"[99] which explicitly—and at times unpleasantly[100]—rebutted Jackson's position on recusal and concluded "[h]ad Black disqualified [himself in *Jewel Ridge*], he would have departed from the traditions of 150 years."[101] Jackson paid little attention to the article, but he fumed over the book—especially its "answers" to the question why Jackson made the public charge against Black in the cables: "[F]irst, that Jackson was a virtuous

---

[95]See, *e.g.*, Irving Brant to Black, n. d., Box 61, Hugo L. Black Papers, Library of Congress.

[96]See Tusa & Tusa, note 48 *supra*, at 214.

[97]Frank, Justice Black: The Man and His Opinions (1948).

[98]Frank, then teaching at Indiana University in Bloomington, telegraphed Black: "This outburst begins the final triumph. Congratulations on winning a real if bloody victory in the unmasking of a bad man." Frank to Black, 6/11/46, Box 61, Hugo L. Black Papers, Library of Congress. See also Fine, note 3 *supra*, at 469.

[99]56 Yale L. J. 606 (1947).

[100]*Id.* at 607 & n.5.

[101]*Id.* at 636.

man, revealing an evil situation; second, that Jackson sought to wreak a personal vengeance on the man he thought responsible for barring his path to the Chief Justiceship; and third, that the enormous strain of the Nuremberg trial, a serious failure both in publicity and in results from a prosecutor's standpoint, caused an irresponsible act for which there is no rational explanation."[102]

Shortly after the book was published, Jackson prepared a detailed memorandum—expanding on a shorter version prepared in January of 1947—laying out his side of the story. The memo was written in the third person, and apparently Jackson contemplated having it published under someone else's name. In the autumn of 1949, he sent a copy of the memo, which eventually went through four drafts, to Gordon Dean, who had been a special assistant to Jackson in the Justice Department and at Nuremberg and who then was at the Atomic Energy Commission. Dean had volunteered in late June of 1946 to write a story for a national magazine to help defuse criticism of Jackson's cables from Nuremberg, but Jackson had declined.[103] Dean now wrote Jackson that the "manuscript is persuasive and illuminating,"[104] but cautioned that the story could not be told fully without disclosing the details of Black's alleged manipulation of the outcomes in the portal-to-portal cases— disclosures Dean felt could not be made for two more years without causing a new controversy. Jackson evidently took Dean's four pages of very detailed criticism to heart: The memo, styled "The Black Controversy," was not published during Jackson's lifetime.

After Jackson's death, his own biographer, Eugene Gerhart, used the memo as the basis—to put it mildly—of his chapter 15, "The Black Controversy." Indeed, more than twenty pages[105] of the thirty-two-page chapter is taken verbatim—with inconsequential word editing and reparagraphing—from Jackson's 1949 memorandum. Gerhart acknowledged the memo's existence,[106] but did not

---

[102]Frank, Mr. Justice Black, note 28 *supra*, at 131.

[103]Dean to Jackson, 6/29/46. Jackson replied by cable through an intermediary: "Please advise Gordon Dean appreciate his cable but am too far removed to have much judgment on its contents. Would prefer that he use his own judgment." Jackson to Morgan, 7/10/46. RHJP.

[104]Gordon Dean to RHJ, 11/25/49. RHJP.

[105]Gerhart, note 2 *supra*, at 239–48, 249–50, 251–59, 260–61, 266–67, 270–71, 272–73, 275–76.

[106]*Id.* at 490 n.19.

reveal that the bulk of his chapter was simply an edited and factually amplified revision of his subject's own words.

Jackson apparently intended the memo to be the "more complete and unequivocal statement" that he wished he had made from Nuremberg. As one now may read it in Gerhart's book, the argument is no more convincing than the cables were; it is merely more detailed. Although Jackson adds some illuminating—if incomplete—insights into the early wartime personality clash between the two men, the argument retains the same gravamen of the cables: that Black was improperly "controlling" the results and timing of the portal-to-portal decisions, and that his relationship with Harris required disqualification. Even in its expanded form, the argument sounds like special pleading. On the first point, Jackson simply did not produce convincing evidence that Black acted improperly with respect either to his vote or to the aborted early announcement of *Jewel Ridge*. On the recusal point, Jackson failed to show that Black's link with Harris was any more damning than other instances in which Justices had declined to disqualify themselves. Sherman Minton, who had been a colleague of Black in the Senate and now was a federal appellate judge, probably best captured the common evaluation of the issue in a letter to Black shortly after the cables were released:[107]

> Why the hullabaloo? Did Owen J. Roberts get off the bench when Geo. Wharton Pepper came in to argue the *Butler* case, when everyone whose brains were as thick as buttermilk knew he was employed to bring Roberts in! He brought him with his voice filled with sobs & tears & Roberts wrote his opinion & Stone made him look like a justice of the peace & made himself immortal by his great dissent! Did Pierce Butler come down as his railroad pals argued? Hell no! He wrote the opinion usually—probably some of the railroads were his former clients.

Minton's hearty common sense further makes Jackson look like a pit bull who could not let go of an argument once he had made it and it had been criticized in terms.

The Jackson account is a doubly curious rhetorical failure. Not only did Jackson repeat his twofold mistakes from the cables, but—despite frequent and pointed references to "Black's

---

[107]Sherman Minton to Hugo L. Black, 6/?/46, Box 61, Hugo L. Black Papers, Library of Congress.

biographer"—he never directly dealt with Frank's final two "answers": resentment and mental imbalance. Jackson apparently assumed as he drafted the memo that the merits would refute Frank's implications. Weak cases on both the points that Jackson chose to emphasize had the effect of strengthening instead of rebutting Frank's dark explanations.

Perhaps sensing this, Jackson tried to undercut the resentment theory by telling Harlan Phillips that he never really wanted to be Chief Justice:[108]

> Of course, it was the easiest thing in the world for them to say, and the most difficult thing in the world to meet—I never attempted to meet it—that I was personally disappointed and bitter about the appointment. Unless one knows the inner workings of the court, you can't probably realize that one is really better off as an associate justice of the court in everything except kudos than he is as chief, because the chief has alot of trivial details to attend to. There was no use in answering that, however.

In other portions of the oral history, however, Jackson seethed over what he saw as behind-the-scenes efforts to keep him from the center chair of the Court. Those remarks not only belie his denial, but they reveal that by 1952 Jackson had come to believe that Douglas more than Black had been responsible within the Court for his defeat.

Jackson recalled that early in the planning for Nuremberg, he had been visited by Robert E. Hannegan, the former chairman of the Democratic national committee and Truman's first cabinet appointee. Hannegan asked Jackson to appoint Mark Eagleton, an obscure St. Louis lawyer, as chief assistant in the war crime trials. Jackson vetted Eagleton, concluded he was too inexperienced, and told Hannegan he could not make the appointment. James F. Byrnes, then Secretary of State, visited Jackson—presumably at Hannegan's behest—and urged Jackson to appoint Eagleton. According to Jackson, Byrnes said: "Bob, you may need Hannegan some day. He's very close to the President. He's a power over the President. You don't know what day you may have something happen over here in the court and you will find it very awkward if

---

[108]VIII COH at 527; Kurland, note 7 supra, at 2569. Cf. Gerhart, note 2 supra, at 266 (Jackson's words reworked).

you have Hannegan against you."[109] Jackson rejected Byrnes's advice, to his rue: "Hannegan went out [of my office] rather hurt. I knew it wasn't pleasant at all, but I didn't know that I would ever have any occasion to feel his vengeance."[110] But Jackson did: "Hannagen did take occasion later to get good and even with me because he was most active in persuading the President against appointing me after Chief Justice Stone's death."[111]

What Jackson unquestionably discovered after he returned to Washington in the summer of 1946 was that Hannegan had joined Truman on a weekend party aboard the Presidential yacht April 27 and 28, less than a week after Stone's death. The announced purpose of the trip was to view naval exercises, but the Washington press corps speculated that the Supreme Court vacancy was the real object of the trip.[112] The suspicion appeared to be confirmed the following day when Truman invited former Chief Justice Hughes to give his views on the appointment at the White House, which Hughes did for a half-hour on April 29.[113]

What Jackson also must have heard after he returned was that Douglas had visited Justice Murphy and asked him to have the Dean of the Catholic University law school, a Murphy friend, "reach the White House in opposition to Jackson."[114] Murphy refused to do so, and Douglas reportedly said that he "guessed there were other ways of getting it done."[115] Two of those ways were the columnist Drew Pearson, who was one of the first to report of threatened resignations if Jackson were appointed and who was close to Douglas,[116] and Hannegan. At the 1944 convention, it had been Hannegan who had engineered President Roosevelt's agreement to run with either Truman or Douglas;[117] Douglas, in Jackson's view, certainly had access to Hannegan. Douglas's memoirs contain a careful denial of his or Black's involvement:

---

[109]VIII COH at 62.

[110]Id. at 65.

[111]Id. at 63.

[112]Miscellaneous press clippings, RHJP.

[113]See Gerhart, note 2 supra, at 278f.

[114]Lash, From the Diaries of Felix Frankfurter 301 (1975) (entry for 11/19/46).

[115]Ibid.

[116]Gerhart, note 2 supra, at 258 & 493 n.82.

[117]See Simon, note 76 supra, at 263–65; cf. Douglas, The Court Years, note 4 supra, at 283–84.

"Truman never broached this matter with either of us, and neither of us sent any message to Truman."[118] From Black, who kept silent on the affair, there is only one piece of evidence corroborating Jackson's later suspicions. Black told one of his ex-clerks, Jerome Cooper, that "another Justice, whom he did not name," had played the "role" of "having opposed and possibly prevented Jackson's appointment as Chief Justice."[119]

Jackson's bitter resentment of what he assumed to be Hannegan's work against him, with or without Douglas's encouragement, substantially discredits the story Jackson gave Phillips about the Chief Justiceship. Jackson was probably more hurt—or at least more sensitive—to Frank's implication that the Nuremberg cables were the product of mental imbalance. Jackson told Phillips: "Then they put out the story in Pearson's column, and Black's biographer, Frank, picks that up, that I was under the enormous strain of the Nuremberg trial, which resulted in an irresponsible act for which there is no rational explanation. Well, I may have been mentally irresponsible."[120] When Phillips transcribed the tape and sent the manuscript to Jackson for approval, Jackson penciled through the final sentence,[121] thus deleting what could later be read carelessly as a confession. It was a poor choice of words: Jackson was not Lear but, if anyone, Othello. Throughout the entire episode, both while it was happening and later when it was being reargued, Jackson's customary rhetorical skills failed him. Perhaps the stakes were so high and the isolation so great during the fading days of the trials that Jackson could not compose himself to the task. One of the most revealing insights into his frame of mind when the cables were sent comes from a partial paragraph of his memo that was not used by Gerhart. Referring to the fact that he consulted no one before sending the cables, he stated: "This seems a capital blunder; for accepting the policy of making a statement, some mind not so close to the events it dealt with should have clarified and strengthened the statement. Perhaps little time was given to its preparation, contrary

[118]Douglas, id. at 29.

[119]Cooper, Sincerely Your Friend: Letters of Mr. Justice Hugo L. Black to Jerome A. Cooper 4 (1973).

[120]VIII COH at 528; see also Arthur Schlesinger, Jr., The Supreme Court: 1947, 35 Fortune 78 (Jan. 1947).

[121]RHJP.

to his usual practice; perhaps it suffered from the necessity of adapting it to cable transmission. But there were deeper defects."[122] The next paragraph implies that those "deeper defects" were that the cables would be seen as "due only to personal disappointment" and that the "personal phases of the message almost completely overshadowed the underlying principles which caused disagreement."[123] Despite his repeated rhetorical failures to make his case, Jackson continued to believe that his feud with Black was primarily over principle and only secondarily due to personality. That judgment is simplistic.

II

A

Because of the cables, *Jewel Ridge* appeared in hindsight to be the flash point of the Black-Jackson feud, but in fact the hostilities began during the first term that the two sat together on the Supreme Court, October Term 1941. Jackson's memories of the term are recorded in an early version of his memorandum on the feud—a version more candid and revealing than the ultimate account that found its way into Gerhart's biography:[124]

> Soon after I went on the Court I discovered that I was in the midst of a struggle for power and a political atmosphere, the like of which I had never experienced even in the President's cabinet which was forthrightly political. There were some held-over cases which were equally divided, and Black had written opinions which he hoped to have become the opinion of the Court. In some I joined him. In others I did not. And I promptly saw that this judgment as to the merits of the cases was not what was expected of me as a Roosevelt appointee. . . . When I failed to vote with him with Party regularity there was no doubt in my mind that he cherished great resentment, partly because he believed intensely that I was wrong in my votes and partly because my vote was important to his leadership of the Court.

Jackson obviously disliked the rivalry, but his most acerbic objection was to what he saw as Black's total disregard of the judicial

---

[122]*Ibid.* (Memo at p. 29).

[123]*Id.* at 30.

[124]Undated memo, RHJP, at 1–2.

function: "With few exceptions, we all knew which side of a case Black would vote on when he read the names of the parties."[125]

Jackson's self-styled loss of innocence developed throughout the 1941 Term, but three otherwise unrelated cases amplify the perceptions he later recalled of Black. All three cases were contorted to some extent by the country's plunge into war.

The first case was *United States v. Bethlehem Steel*,[126] which was argued two days after the Japanese attack on Pearl Harbor. The Government sought recovery of what it claimed were excess profits—more than 20 percent—on ships built for World War I under a contract that it now claimed was made under duress. Stone, Roberts, and Jackson recused themselves, and Black wrote for a 4–2 majority that rejected the Government's position. Jackson hyperbolically wrote Douglas that the decision was "the dirtiest day's work the Court has ever done and a defeat for the Government worse than Pearl Harbor."[127] Later Jackson told Phillips that Black thought the company's position was "outrageous, but he was going to vote to affirm it and if he had a chance would try to write an opinion which would show that this was simply the usual thing that happened under these contract systems. He was going to try to knock out the contract system and have the government build its own ships."[128] Jackson added: "[I]t was one of the shocks of my experience on the court that this case was treated this way. I never got over it. It seemed to be that the Supreme Court, at a time when we were beginning another great construction program, would have rendered a great service to the American people if it had said without equivocation that profits so great as to be unconscionable could not be obtained either by robbery or fraud."[129] Frank's biography of Black contended that "the opinion was so written as to come close to inviting Congress to take comprehensive action to control profits,"[130] which Congress soon did.[131]

---

[125]*Id.* at 2.

[126]315 U.S. 289 (1942).

[127]Quoted in Fine, note 3 *supra*, at 349.

[128]VII COH at 28.

[129]*Id.* at 28–29.

[130]Frank, Mr. Justice Black, note 28 *supra*, at 205.

[131]Renegotiation Act of 1942, 56 Stat. 245; 982.

The second case displayed traces of neither Black nor Jackson in the official reports, but the issue and their differing approaches to it then and later is telling. *Hill v. Texas*[132] presented the recurring issue of racial discrimination in the selection of grand juries. Since *Pierre v. Louisiana*[133] in 1939—a unanimous opinion by Justice Black—the Court had held that the remedy for racial discrimination in the selection of grand juries was the quashing of the indictment, even if the selection of the petit jury was not similarly tainted. In 1940, Justice Black again spoke for a unanimnous Court in *Smith v. Texas*,[134] which invalidated a conviction and ordered the indictment quashed where the only constitutional challenge was based on systematic exclusion of blacks from the grand jury. *Hill* presented the identical problem from the same county as *Smith*. The Supreme Court voted to reverse, Stone assigned the opinion to himself, and Jackson circulated a three-page dissent that argued, rather dismissively, that the remedy was a nonsequitur: whatever racial evil took place at the grand jury stage was irrelevant to guilt determined by an untainted trial jury. "The negro case for equal treatment, which is our concern because it is embodied in our Constitution, will not be helped by making this guilty negro its symbol."[135] He concluded: "I would affirm this conviction and would right race wrongs in a cause more representative of the race grievance."[136] Jackson withdrew the dissent, because he became convinced that it would have "a bad effect on race relations" during wartime,[137] and *Hill* was unanimous.[138] Black nonetheless must have viewed the draft dissent as an (attempted) personal rebuke—aggravated by a flip regard for well-settled precedent—and as evidence of Jackson's sterile insensitivity to a just cause.

Jackson's strain with Black reached its high point late in the term over the latest round of cases involving the Jehovah's Witnesses. In

---

[132]316 U.S. 400 (1942).

[133]306 U.S. 354 (1939).

[134]311 U.S. 128 (1940).

[135]Draft opinion, RHJP.

[136]*Ibid.*

[137]Quoted in Fine, note 3 *supra*, at 391.

[138]Jackson finally published his views on the issue in 1950. See Cassell v. Texas, 339 U.S. 282 (1950). The Jackson position acquired three adherents as late as 1979. Rose v. Mitchell, 443 U.S. 545 (1979).

June of 1940, in *Minersville v. Gobitis*,[139] Justice Frankfurter had written for an 8–1 majority (with only Stone dissenting) that the Free Exercise Clause did not immunize children of the Witnesses from regulations requiring public school children to salute the flag of the United States each school day. The decision was roundly condemned in the press, with *The New Republic* pointing out that a German court had recently punished members of the Witnesses for refusing the "Heil Hitler" and hoping the Frankfurter majority "would be embarrassed" by the similarity of judgment.[140] That, and other, editorials apparently had the desired effect on Black, according to Frankfurter:[141]

> In the fall of 1940, after returning from the summer vacation, on the first meeting with Douglas this colloquy took place:
> Douglas: "Hugo teels me that now he wouldn't go with you in the Gobitis case."
> FF: "Has Hugo been re-reading the Constitution during the summer[?]"
> Douglas: "No—he has been reading the papers."

Jackson, who was Attorney General when *Gobitis* was decided, was "bitter" about the decision and scolded Frankfurter for writing it, according to Harold Ickes.[142] Jackson felt the decision was fueling mob action ("[p]eople breaking into other people's house[s] and confronting them with a flag demanding they salute it")[143] and hysteria against aliens; he gave two speeches within a month of the decision condemning the mob lawlessness.[144] Jackson stopped short of explicitly criticizing the decision, and contented himself with a disapproving footnote in his book, *The Struggle for Judicial Supremacy*,[145] which was published January 20, 1941, six months before he joined the Court.

---

[139] 310 U.S. 586 (1940).

[140] Manwaring, Render unto Caesar: The Flag Salute Controversy 154 (1962).

[141] Hirsch, The Enigma of Felix Frankfurter 152 (1981).

[142] Ickes, III The Secret Diary of Harold Ickes 199, 211 (1953).

[143] *Id.* at 211.

[144] See Sharp Limit Is Set on Entry of Aliens, New York Times, June 15, 1940, at p. 9, col. 5 (speech on occasion of formal incorporation of Immigration and Naturalization Service into Department of Justice); A Program for the Internal Defense of the United States, June 29, 1940 (speech to New York State Bar Association).

[145] Jackson, The Struggle for Judicial Supremacy 294 n.48 (1941).

During Jackson's first term, a trio of cases styled *Jones v. Opelika*[146] presented the question whether non-discriminatory municipal ordinances requiring licenses and taxes were unconstitutional as applied to the door-to-door proselytizing and sales by the Witnesses. The Court voted 5–4 to uphold the ordinances, and Justice Stanley F. Reed, as the senior member of the majority, assigned the opinion to himself. Reed, who was generally a friend of organized religion but never a friend of door-to-door salemen,[147] drafted a straightforward opinion rejecting the Witnesses' claims. Stone drafted a biting dissent dimissing Reed's analysis as "irrelevant;"[148] Murphy prepared an impassioned dissent which saw the decision as a dagger in the heart of the Free Exercise Clause;[149] and Black prepared a statement, to be joined by Douglas and Murphy, announcing, rather gratuitously, that they thought *Gobitis* "wrongly decided."[150] Jackson was offended by the unprecedented repentence, which must have smelled of grandstanding, and of what he viewed as the dissenters' mischaracterization of the unobjectionable and non-discriminatory ordinances as samples of the mob hysteria he had condemned earlier. He drafted a two-page concurrence which framed the case as he saw it, left the door open to invalidating such ordinances if they were later proved to be discriminatorily applied, and observed acidly: "My concurrence is to be taken neither as approval or rejection of *Minersville v. Gobitis* decided before I became a member of the Court. It appears factually dissimilar and only remotely similar in doctrine. And to admit that one has formerly been wrong falls short of proving him presently to be right."[151] Jackson apparently did not circulate his draft, which was never published, but his contempt for the dissenters—especially Black—was clearly hardening. At the end of the 1942 Term, during which relations between all of the Justices

---

[146]316 U.S. 584 (1941).

[147]See Reed's opinion for the Court, rejecting both First Amendment and Commerce Clause challenges to "Green River Ordinances" banning door-to-door sales, in Breard v. City of Alexandria, 341 U.S. 622 (1951); *cf.* O'Brien, Justice Reed and the First Amendment: The Religion Clauses (1958).

[148]See 316 U.S. at 604.

[149]See *id.* at 611.

[150]See *id.* at 623–24.

[151]RHJP.

seemed to be sharp,[152] Wiley B. Rutledge joined the Court *vice* Byrnes, rehearing was granted in *Jones v. Opelika*,[153] the earlier decision was reversed 5–4,[154] and then Jackson issued a tirade against the Witnesses in another case for their pressure tactics and vulgar treatment of the beliefs of others.[155]

The most important decision of the 1942 Term, and one of the most pivotal of the period in terms of leadership within the Court,[156] was *West Virginia Board of Education v. Barnette*,[157] in which Jackson wrote an eloquent and oft-quoted opinion for a 6–3 majority that overruled *Gobitis*. Black and Douglas together issued a concurrence,[158] as did Murphy;[159] Frankfurter wrote the only dissent.[160] The cases came down, coincidentally, on Flag Day, 1943. In the light of his opinions in cases involving the Witnesses both before and after[161] *Barnette*, Jackson was an odd choice to be *Gobitis's* undertaker. Stone's biographer does not explain why the assignment went to Jackson, but the reasons are not difficult to imagine. Stone was undoubtedly offended by Black's unprecedented about-face on *Gobitis* in the first round of *Jones v. Opelika*; after *Barnette*, he privately observed that he wished the issue would have been properly resolved "in the first place without following such a devious route to the desired end."[162] By choosing Jackson, he accomplished two objectives: he avoided rewarding behavior he did not respect, and he papered over the Court's *volte face* with an eloquent opinion that reframed the issue as a free speech case instead of a religion clauses case.

---

[152]Hirsch, note 141 *supra*, at 162ff.

[153]318 U.S. 796 (1943).

[154]319 U.S. 103 (1943).

[155]Douglas v. Jeanette, 319 U.S. 157, 166 (1943). See Hirsch, note 141 *supra*, at 166–68. For a discerning interpretation of Jackson's views toward the Witnesses, see Schubert: Dispassionate Justice: A Synthesis of the Judicial Opinions of Robert H. Jackson 69–70 (1969). For a contemporary account of the Witnesses and the tactics they used, and which Jackson condemned, see Stroup, The Jehovah's Witnesses (1945).

[156]See Hirsch, note 141 *supra*, at 171ff.

[157]319 U.S. 624 (1943).

[158]*Id.* at 643.

[159]*Id.* at 644.

[160]*Id.* at 646.

[161]Prince v. Massachusetts, 321 U.S. 158, 176 (1944) (separate opinion of Jackson, J.); Saia v. New York, 334 U.S. 558, 566 (1948) (Jackson, J., dissenting).

[162]To Charles C. Burlingham, quoted in Mason, note 4 *supra*, at 601.

To Black, the opinion assignment represented a failure to acknowledge his leadership role, although he never said so himself. In August of 1944, Fred Rodell published an admiring portrait of Black in *The American Mercury*.[163] Rodell called Black "the nation's most influential legal figure,"[164] the "acknowledged leader of the majority faction"[165] of the Court and the "ablest judge and the most brilliant legal mind among them."[166] Jackson was accused of "unconcealed jealousy of Black's intellectual leadership," the product of "dwindling hope of being named Chief Justice, an honor he once missed by a hair," but "smart enough to see Black the biggest threat to his ambition."[167] Jackson bitterly resented the Rodell essay, as the fierce marginal notes on his copy demonstrate and his references in his later memo on the Black affair attest.[168] A portion of the memo as printed in Gerhart states:[169]

> Black, the senior Roosevelt appointee, particularly disliked the thought that Jackson might be moved over him, perhaps because that might be construed as confirmation of the criticism of his original appointment. Black's friends began to build him up against such a contingency. One of the most virulent of these wrote in a popular magazine that Black, not Stone, was the acknowledged leader of the majority faction of the Court, and declared Black the biggest threat to Jackson's dwindling prospects of gaining the Chief Justiceship. These attacks were repeatedly made by sources close to Justices Black or Douglas. Jackson believed, with some reason, that they were judicially inspired.

By the beginning of the 1944 Term, Jackson saw himself in a state of barely concealed war with Black, and Douglas to a lesser extent. The stakes were nominally the Chief Justiceship, but as the feud intensified, each discrete battle, or case, was a test of strength.

Jackson wrote two opinions during the 1944 Term that both stemmed from strong conviction but which also were direct challenges to what he construed to be Black's asserted leadership of

---

[163]Rodell, Mr. Justice Black 135 (Aug. 1944).

[164]Ibid.

[165]*Id.* at 136.

[166]*Id.* at 137.

[167]*Ibid.*

[168]RHJP.

[169]Gerhart, note 2 *supra*, at 242.

the Court, a dissent in *Korematsu v. United States*,[170] the infamous Japanese exclusion case, and the majority opinion in *Cramer v. United States*,[171] which narrowly construed the Treason Clause of the Constitution—thus reversing Cramer's conviction—and which provoked an angry dissent from Douglas, joined by Black and others, complaining that the "result makes the way easy for the traitor, does violence to the Constitution and makes justice truly blind."[172] It is a curious opinion from someone, as David Currie recently remarked, "not generally perceived as hostile to the rights of the outcast."[173]

The Term ended June 18, 1945, which was the day the denial of rehearing in *Jewel Ridge* was announced. Two interrelated incidents shortly before that provided Jackson with damning evidence of what he was growing to view as Black's raw partisanship. One was *Jewel Ridge* itself. The other was trivial—a dinner April 3 in honor of Justice Black—but was magnified in Jackson's mind into an exercise of brazen injudiciousness on the honoree's part. The dinner was a testimonial sponsored by The Southern Conference for Human Welfare, at which Black was to receive the Thomas Jefferson Award. More than 900 guests were expected, with a head table of twenty-four presided over by Senator Alben W. Barkley. The principal speaker was Fred Vinson, then Federal Loan Administrator. Mrs. Roosevelt also spoke. The other eight Justices had been invited, but four did not attend: Stone, Roberts, Frankfurter, and Jackson. Jackson's objection, as he later wrote in one of the four drafts on the Black controversy, was that "[a] number of the leading sponsors of the dinner were at that moment litigants before the Court."[174] Jackson singled out three: the counsel for the C.I.O. (who had argued that day before the Court),[175] counsel for the A.F. of L., and Crampton Harris, who was on the brief in the C.I.O. case[176] and who had argued *Jewel Ridge* less than a month before and was awaiting its decision. All three were listed as sponsors for the

[170]323 U.S. 214, 242 (1944).

[171]325 U.S. 1 (1945). See generally Howard, Advocacy in Constitutional Choice: The Cramer Treason Case, 1942–1945, 1986 A.B.F. Res. J. 375.

[172]325 U.S. at 48, 67.

[173]Currie, The Constitution in the Supreme Court: The Second World War, 1941–1946, 37 Cath. U. L. Rev. 1, 24 (1988).

[174]Memo at 3, RHJP.

[175]Lee A. Pressman. See C.I.O. v. McAdom, 325 U.S. 472 (1945).

[176]*Ibid.*

dinner. Jackson evidently thought that the facts spoke for themselves, or so his later memo elliptically suggests.

The dinner is really a coincidental footnote to the *Jewel Ridge* case, whose decision was being fought out while Black was being toasted. At issue was whether the Fair Labor Standards Act, which Black had sponsored in the Senate, covered traveling—or "portal-to-portal"—time between the portal and working face of bituminous coal mines. Custom and collective bargaining agreements had excluded pay for travel time, but the unions now claimed §7 of the Act covered portal-to-portal work. The case was argued March 9, 1945, and the Court voted the next day 5–4 against the the unions. Stone asked Jackson to write the opinion, but the next day—Sunday—Reed changed his vote and Black now had the opinion assignment, which he gave to Murphy. On April 5, a Thursday, Murphy circulated his draft opinion for the Court.

Jackson later claimed repeatedly that at this point Black was trying to manipulate the Court to issue its decision in *Jewel Ridge* the following Monday, April 9, in order to provide the United Mine Workers with a bargaining chip in their ongoing negotiations for a new contract in the bituminous coal industry. (A strike had been voted March 29; the old agreement expired March 31; John L. Lewis—the union chief—agreed April 1 to a thirty-day extension of the agreement.) It is true that Murphy told Jackson he was under pressure to issue the decision April 9, but neither of Murphy's exhaustive biographers have identified the source of the pressure.[177] Jackson assumed, of course, it was Black and Douglas. But Murphy resisted the pressure and told Jackson to take as much time as he wished writing his dissent. The pressure eased on Murphy, presumably because an agreement was reached April 11. The decision was eventually issued May 7, and "broke the anthracite deadlock and led to a settlement incorporating portal-to-portal pay as well as to the War Labor Board's approval of the bituminous agreement"[178] of April 11.

Jackson's charges that Black was manipulating the decision-making process in *Jewel Ridge* for purely partisan ends are unsubstantiated. His conclusion testifies to how distorted his vision of Black had become by the Spring of 1945. The most that can be said critically of Black's behavior in *Jewel Ridge* was that he continued to

---

[177]See Fine, note 3 *supra*, at 325; Howard, note 1 *supra*, at 389–94.

[178]Fine, note 3 *supra*, at 325.

vote the view of the Act he had first embraced in *Tennessee Coal Company v. Muscoda*[179] more than a year before, that he may have tried to rush Murphy but that he failed. Jackson's real objection to Black was to Black's judicial philosophy, which he saw as having less to do with conventional legal techniques than with personal preferences. When Jackson tried to recast the criticism—to which he himself was not wholly immune—into a charge of judicial impropriety, he entered a rhetorical thicket from which he never successfully emerged. The petition for rehearing in *Jewel Ridge* was filed May 31, Jackson flared at Black's insistence on a routine denial, and the denial was accompanied by Jackson's tart concurrence the final day of the term. Thus was sown what was reaped a year later in Nuremberg.

B

Recollected in tranquility, the Black-Jackson feud makes one wonder why the heathen raged so. There were other strong personalities on the Supreme Court during World War II, and there were other personality conflicts, but Black and Jackson had the most pitched and, ultimately, explosive, relationship. Why? and, in the end, what difference did it make to the work of the Court?

The answer lies, in large measure, in two factors: how the two men translated for themselves the legacy of the New Deal into their judicial offices, and how the force of personality exacerbated the conflict that emerged from those translations. Consider the second point first. It may be hyperbolic to portray the Supreme Court, as Alexander Bickel sometimes did to his students, as nine scorpions trapped in a bottle, but the personal strain inherent in the nature of the institution is easy to underestimate. Justice Brandeis provided then-professor Frankfurter with a rich portrait of the force of personality on deliberations in the Supreme Court, where "passion"[180] and "finesse"[181] trump legal reasoning.[182] The World War II Court was no different from the Taft Court in that respect, and Jackson was especially susceptible to being influenced by the personal style of his colleagues. One of his most discerning clerks

[179]321 U.S. 590 (1944).

[180]Urofsky, The Brandeis-Frankfurter Conversations, 1985 Supreme Court Review 299, 306.

[181]*Id.* at 328.

[182]*Ibid.*

wrote Frankfurter in 1955 that Jackson's "faults" included "that the *personalities* of others affected him strongly, often influenced his thinking. I think how he felt about Justice Douglas had *some* effect in some of his votes."[183] Jackson was always a loner, and a bit of a prima donna, dating from his days in the Department of Justice. He argued forcefully, sometimes acidly, and it should be no surprise that he was flint ready to strike stone in the conference room of the Supreme Court. Black, and later Douglas more often, provided the occasion for the spark.

The legacy of the New Deal played a more complicated role in the feud. To some extent, Jackson failed to accept—or to appreciate the full consequences of—his oft-quoted conversation with Justice Cardozo when Jackson's name had surfaced for an appointment to the New York Court of Appeals: "He said, 'Jackson, if you have a chance to go on the New York Court of Appeals, go on the New York Court of Appeals. That's a lawyer's court. Those are the kind of problems you'll enjoy. Over on this court there are two kinds of questions—statutory construction, which no one can make interesting, and politics.' "[184] Jackson could say to Phillips by 1952: "Of course he didn't mean politics in the sense of party politics, but in the sense of public policy. There's a great deal of truth in that observation. Many of our cases really turn on your views of political policy, governmental policy."[185]

The portal-to-portal cases are a handy example of the concrete implications of Jackson's theme and of the different shadows the New Deal cast over the Supreme Court. The precise issue was whether §7 of the Fair Labor Standards Act covered only face-to-face work time, as the unions had historically bargained, or the longer portal-to-portal time, which the unions now claimed under the section. Murphy's opinion for the Court adopted the union view, which to Jackson was not required by the statute and, worse, which stripped the collectively bargained agreements of their hard-won sanctity.[186] Jackson's final paragraph bristled: "We doubt if one can find in the long line of criticized cases one in which the

---

[183]E. Barrett Prettyman, Jr., to Felix Frankfurter, 10/13/55, Felix Frankfurter Papers, Reel 42.

[184]VII COH at 23, quoted in Jackson, Full Faith and Credit: The Lawyer's Clause of the Constitution 2 (1945); Jackson, The Supreme Court in the American System of Government 54 (1955). *Cf. id.* at 53ff.

[185]VII COH at 23.

[186]See 325 U.S. at 195.

Court has made a more extreme exertion of power or one so little supported or explained by either the statute or the record in the case. Power should answer to reason none the less because its fiat is beyond appeal."[187]

The depth of Jackson's feeling was the product of positions he had developed and defended in speeches while he was in the Justice Department. He hailed the Wagner Act as "labor's new Bill of Rights,"[188] but emphasized the *quid pro quo* for the new power conferred by the Government: "Labor's new powers impose new responsibility. Organization discipline must prove equal to the task of keeping its collectively-bargained contract. Its faith and credit must be guarded from within by self-discipline."[189] His view was that intervention in labor could only be justified politically by emphasizing the "rights and responsibilities" of both labor and management.[190] Decisions such as *Muscoda* and *Jewel Ridge* could be seen as turning back the clock to the days when labor relations were a function of raw power; this time, it was the Court, not an abusive employer or a menacing union, who was disturbing the new labor peace.

Black's views on the portal-to-portal issue were no less a function of his own New Deal politics. The author of the Black-Connery Bill, which became the FLSA, had passionate sympathy for the working man. When runaway inflation radically devalued the agreements Jackson revered so aggressively, it is no surprise that Black saw both the urgency and the opportunity to ameliorate the problem when the cases reached the Court. Like Jackson, he translated his politics into his votes and opinions on the Court. In fact, Black had said in 1937 that "there is no charge against the integrity of any prospective judge that with reference to economic predilections after he goes on the bench he will still be the same man that he was before he went there."[191]

At bottom it was this attitude of Black that rankled Jackson more than any other. "Something does happen to a man when he puts on a judicial robe," Jackson told Phillips, "and I think it ought to. The change is very great and requires a psychological change within a

---

[187]*Id.* at 196.

[188]Labor's Non-Partisan League: A New Fight for Peace (6/11/38) at 6, RHJP.

[189]Labor's New Rights and Responsibilities (8/24/37), printed in Vital Speeches 718, 719.

[190]*Ibid.*

[191]81 Cong. Rec. 2828 (1937).

man to get into an attitude of deciding other people's controversies, instead of waging them. It really calls for quite a changed attitude. Some never make it—I am not sure I have."[192] In Jackson's mind, Black never left the Senate and his constituents. The transfer of Black's New Deal politics wholesale into his judicial work was thus illegitimate. Yet Jackson was astute enough to recognize, as the final sentence of of statement to Phillips reveals, that he could commit the same sins. He worried, for example, that his opinion for the Court in *Wickard v. Filburn*,[193] while vindicating the New Deal, crossed a constitutional line between state and federal power.[194] His memorable opinion for the Court in *Barnette* had much of its impetus in his fears as Attorney General over *Gobitis*. He was hardly the model of detachment he wished to be.

Both men spent much of the war period searching for a theory to define more clearly their views and their roles. They were impeded in that effort by the war itself, which distorted their priorities. Every major decision had to be seen more for its symbolic effect than for its theoretical significance, as the cases involving blacks and the Witnesses demonstrated. Underlying *Cramer and Korematsu* were the awful questions of whether the Constitution was safe in wartime—at least when civil liberty threatened the war effort. In large measure, neither Black nor Jackson fully developed their constitutional theories until after the war. Black's greatest achievement was his Phyrric defeat in *Adamson v. California*[195] in 1947, which came exactly a decade after he had concurred in its antithesis, *Palko v. Connecticut*,[196] during his first year on the Court. Jackson was more erratic, and with less reason. He came to the Court six months after publishing a sustained study of the proper theory for judicial review. One of the final pages of his book proclaimed: "The Supreme Court can maintain itself and succeed in its tasks only if the counsel of self-restraint urged most earnestly by members of the Court itself are humbly and faithfully heeded."[197]

---

[192]VII COH at 13.

[193]317 U.S. 111 (1942).

[194]See Mason, note 4 *supra*, at 593–96, and see 81 Cong Rec. 306–7 (Appdx.) (1937) for Black's views.

[195]332 U.S. 46 (1947).

[196]302 U.S. 319 (1937).

[197]*Id.* at 321.

Jackson did not return explicitly to the book's teachings until well after the war, probably for several reasons. In the first place, he took responsibility for the book, but much of it was crafted—as were some of Jackson's more scholarly speeches while at the Justice Department—by Paul A. Freund.[198] The book was Jackson's emotionally more than intellectually. The war, the feud, and Nuremberg kept Jackson from working his way back to the book, but in 1950 he mentioned it privately in a letter to Professor Charles Fairman. He consulted Fairman for advice on the history of the Fourteenth Amendment as it bore on the impending segregation cases, as they were then called,[199] and he was skittish about the propriety of the extra-judicial counsel, but he nonetheless observed:[200]

> What is the function of the Court in this matter? I am clear that I would support the constitutionality of almost any Congressional Act that prohibited segregation in education. . . . But I really did, and still do believe the doctrine on which the Roosevelt fight against the old Court was based in part, that it had expanded the Fourteenth Amendment to make an unjustified judicial control over social and economic affairs. We insisted that a majority out of nine appointed life-tenure men should not settle such issues. I enlarged on that subject in *The Struggle for Judicial Supremacy*. I find a good many who were associated in that fight now abandon that position but think the Court should decide such questions provided it will decide their way. The problem in my mind is not merely should we nine decide this case but should such an institution decide such questions for the Nation.

Jackson had come to realize that his anxieties over the direction in which the Court was moving were functionally the same at a theoretical level as those that he had identified with respect to the "old Court" almost a decade earlier. He did not put his hand to elaborating the argument until just before his death, and the posthumous Godkin Lectures were the result.[201]

Jackson appears to have been tempted to make one feint at spelling out his views in 1951, when the *Washington Post* invited him

---

[198]See Kurland, note 7 *supra*, at 2555; RHJP.

[199]See Hutchinson, Unanimity and Desegregation: Decision-Making in the Supreme Court, 1948–1958, 68 Geo. L. J. 1 (1979).

[200]Jackson to Charles Fairman, 3/13/50, RHJP.

[201]See note 184 *supra*.

to review the recently published two-volume biography of Charles Evans Hughes by Merlo J. Pusey. However, the final published version is little more than an elegant star turn from someone who obviously has more to say. There is one striking editorial change which perhaps suggests that the feud and the furor over the Stone vacancy still stung in Jackson's memory. The first paragraph of the review was structured around the image of Hughes outliving the controversy through which he lived so that Washington was "little stirred"[202] when Hughes died in retirement. Jackson's original first sentence, which he cut before publication, read: "Washington adores a funeral—especially if it ushers in a vacancy."[203]

---

[202]Jackson, Warm Portrait of Austere Hughes, 11/18/51, Washington Post, §1B, col. 1.
[203] RHJP.

BERNARD SCHWARTZ

CHIEF JUSTICE REHNQUIST, JUSTICE JACKSON, AND THE *BROWN* CASE

Chief Justice Rehnquist starts his recent book on the Supreme Court by telling how he began his legal career as what Justice Douglas termed "a member of the so-called Junior Supreme Court"[1]—as a law clerk to Justice Robert H. Jackson.[2] The book does not, however, say anything about the most controversial episode of Rehnquist's clerkship—the memorandum Rehnquist wrote on the *Brown* school segregation case,[3] which came before the Court during Rehnquist's clerkship. That memo became an important factor in the Senate debate on the nominations of Rehnquist himself both to the Supreme Court and as Chief Justice.

I. "WHR" ON BROWN

The Rehnquist memo on *Brown* consisted of one-and-one-half typed pages. It was headed, *A Random Thought on the Segregation Case*, and signed "whr."[4] It compared judicial action to

---

Bernard Schwartz is Edwin D. Webb Professor of Law, New York University.

AUTHOR'S NOTE: The author acknowledges the generous support of the Filomen D'Agostino and Max E. Greenberg Research Fund, New York University School of Law.

[1] Urofsky, ed., The Douglas Letters 147 (1987).

[2] Rehnquist, The Supreme Court: How It Was, How It Is, ch. 1 (1987).

[3] Brown v. Board of Education, 347 U.S. 483 (1954).

[4] The memo is reprinted in Nomination of Justice William Hubbs Rehnquist, Hearings before the Committee on the Judiciary, United States Senate, 99th Cong., 2d Sess. 324 (1986). The original is in the *Brown* file, Robert H. Jackson Papers, Library of Congress.

invalidate segregation to the Court's "reading its own economic views into the Constitution" in cases such as *Lochner v. New York*[5]—"the high water mark in protecting corporations against legislative influence." According to the memo, "In these cases now before the Court, the Court is, as Davis[6] suggested, being asked to read its own sociological views into the Constitution." For the Court to hold for plaintiffs here, the memo asserted, would be for it to repeat the error of the *Lochner* Court. "If this Court, because its members individually are 'liberal' and dislike segregation, now chooses to strike it down, it differs from the McReynolds court only in the kinds of litigants it favors and the kinds of special claims it protects."

The memo declared that appellants were "Urging a view palpably at variance with precedent and probably with legislative history." More than that, the memo urged, their argument was contrary to the Constitution itself. "To the argument made by Thurgood, not John, Marshall that a majority may not deprive a minority of its constitutional right, the answer must be made that while this is sound in theory, in the long run it is the majority who will determine what the constitutional rights of the minority are." According to the memo, the cases seeking to establish "minority rights of any kind . . . have been sloughed off, and crept silently to rest. If the present Court is unable to profit by this example it must be prepared to see its work fade in time, too, as embodying only the sentiments of a transient majority of nine men."

The Rehnquist memo stated flatly that the separate-but-equal doctrine, which the *Brown* decision was eventually to overrule, was correct and should be followed. This was, indeed, the memo's categorical conclusion: "I realize that it is an unpopular and unhumanitarian position, for which I have been excoriated by 'liberal' colleagues, but I think *Plessy* v. *Ferguson*[7] was right and should be re-affirmed. If the Fourteenth Amendment did not enact Spencer's *Social Statics*,[8] it just as surely did not enact Myrdal's *American Dilemma*."[9]

---

[5] 198 U.S. 45 (1905).

[6] John W. Davis, who argued the case in favor of segregation for South Carolina.

[7] 163 U.S. 537 (1896).

[8] This, of course, is from the dissent by Justice Holmes in Lochner v. New York, 198 U.S. 45, 75 (1905).

[9] Myrdal, An American Dilemma (1944).

Justice Rehnquist has maintained that his *Brown* memo "was prepared by me at Justice Jackson's request; it was intended as a rough draft of a statement of *his* views at the conference of the justices, rather than as a statement of my views."[10] The Rehnquist explanation has been challenged, particularly during the hearings on his judicial nominations.[11] It is hard not to conclude, as Richard Kluger did in his monumental book on the *Brown* case, that "one finds a preponderance of evidence to suggest that the memorandum in question—the one that threatened to deprive William Rehnquist of his place on the Supreme Court— was an accurate statement of his own views on segregation, not those of Robert Jackson."[12]

To the evidence so convincingly summarized in the Kluger book,[13] one must now add the draft concurrence which Justice Jackson prepared, but never issued, in *Brown*. It has long been known that Jackson worked on a draft which he intended as the basis for a concurring *Brown* opinion. That draft, which has become available in the Jackson papers at the Library of Congress, appears inconsistent with Rehnquist's assertion that his memo was intended to state Jackson's rather than Rehnquist's view on the constitutionality of segregation.

The key sentence in the Jackson draft states categorically, "I am convinced that present-day conditions require us to strike from our books the doctrine of separate-but-equal facilities and to hold invalid provisions of state constitutions or statutes which classify persons for separate treatment in matters of education based solely on possession of colored blood."[14]

II. Squire of Hickory Hill

But the Jackson *Brown* draft has a significance broader than what it tells us about the present Chief Justice's account of the memo he wrote as a Jackson law clerk. It enables us to see in detail the views held on the *Brown* issue by one of the most gifted men ever to serve on the Supreme Court, who played an important role

---

[10]Washington Post National Weekly Edition, July 28, 1986, 8.

[11]See, *e.g.*, note 4 *supra*, at 322, 328–33.

[12]Kluger, Simple Justice 609 (1975).

[13]*Id.* at 606–09.

[14]MEMORANDUM BY MR. JUSTICE JACKSON, March 15, 1954. *Brown* file, Robert H. Jackson Papers, Library of Congress.

in the *Brown* decision process. It also raises the question of what might have happened had the Jackson draft actually been issued as a concurring opinion in the *Brown* case.

Robert H. Jackson was termed by Justice Frankfurter, "by long odds the most literarily gifted member of the Court."[15] As a stylist and phrasemaker, Jackson can be compared only with Justices Holmes and Cardozo. It was Jackson who aphorized the reality of the Supreme Court's position: "There is no doubt that if there were a super-Supreme Court, a substantial proportion of our reversals of state courts would also be reversed. We are not final because we are infallible, but we are infallible only because we are final."[16]

Jackson's sardonic attitude toward his colleagues was expressed in both his opinions and private comments. "The black hole of Columbia"[17] was the way he came to refer to the Court. Frankfurter's diary tells of Jackson's taking him off into a corner at the wedding of Dean Acheson's daughter and saying, "Do you feel as depressed as I do after these Saturday [Court] Conferences?"[18] "Congratulations," Jackson wrote Frankfurter another time, "on your absence from today's session. Only if you have been caught playing the piano in a whorehouse can you appreciate today's level of my self respect."[19]

Lincoln once said that Chief Justice Chase "had the Presidential maggot in his brain," and he "never knew anybody who once had it to get rid of it."[20] Justice Jackson himself harbored ambitions to be President or, at the least, to occupy the Court's central chair. His lack of success in this regard poisoned his whole outlook and made him, in his last years on the bench, increasingly embittered.

The Jackson bitterness surfaced in his famous feud with Justice Black, which continued until Jackson's death a half year after the first *Brown* decision. Jackson once sent Justice Frankfurter a note in which, referring to Black, he declared, "I simply give up understanding our colleague and begin to think he is a case for a

---

[15]With Phil Kurland, n.d. Felix Frankfurter Papers, Library of Congress.

[16]Brown v. Allen, 344 U.S. 443, 540 (1953).

[17]Robert H. Jackson–Felix Frankfurter, July 30, 1954. Felix Frankfurter Papers, Library of Congress.

[18]Lash, From the Diaries of Felix Frankfurter 173 (1974).

[19]Robert H. Jackson–Felix Frankfurter, September 20, 1950. Felix Frankfurter Papers, Harvard Law School.

[20]Quoted in Schwartz, From Confederation to Nation: The American Constitution, 1835–1877, 225 (1973).

psychiatrist."[21] Black, on the other side, wrote a former law clerk that a copy of the *Macon Telegraph* had been sent him that contained an editorial entitled, "Jackson is an Unmitigated Ass." On the same page, Black went on, "appeared an article by John Temple Graves on the same subject. I have nothing but sympathy for John Temple."[22]

Justice Jackson's bitterness also stemmed from an inner feeling of insecurity on his part. Few would have sensed this in a man of Jackson's patrician bearing, whose manners and way of life bespoke the upstate New York squire, transplanted to the Hickory Hill estate that was later to be owned by John and then Robert Kennedy. But Jackson had earned his position through a lucrative practice; he had come from a poor family and had only had one year of education at a second-rate law school. He never got over a sense of inferiority in the face of graduates of the great national law schools, particularly Harvard and Yale, a factor that may have contributed to his bitterness at those he felt had kept him from the highest judicial office.

III. JACKSON AND THE BROWN DECISION PROCESS

What we know of Justice Jackson's role in the *Brown* decision process also casts doubt on the Rehnquist assertion that his controversial memo was a statement of Jackson's own views, rather than those of Rehnquist himself. Jackson's attitude toward the Constitution was summed up in handwritten notes in his file on the Steel Seizure Case:[23] "The Constitution as a blue print. Not a photograph of present structure. Powers never contemplated."[24] The organic text, in other words, is to be interpreted only as a foundation upon which the constitutional structure is to be built. It is to be interpreted to meet the changing needs of different periods of the nation's history. Powers never contemplated by the Framers may be valid when demanded by the "felt necessities"[25] of a later day.

---

[21]Robert H. Jackson–Felix Frankfurter, September 20, 195[?]. Felix Frankfurter Papers, Library of Congress.

[22]"Sincerely your friend": Letters of Mr. Justice Hugo L. Black to Jerome A. Cooper (n.d.).

[23]Youngstown Sheet and Tube Co. v. Sawyer, 343 U.S. 579 (1952).

[24]Steel Seizure case file, Robert H. Jackson Papers, Library of Congress.

[25]Holmes, The Common Law 1 (1881).

In this respect, Jackson agreed with the view of his closest colleague and friend on the Court. In written notes headed *Segregation*, designed to help his own thinking on *Brown*, Justice Frankfurter had recognized that "The equality of laws enshrined in the Constitution is not a fixed formula defined with finality at a particular time. It does not reflect as a congealed formulation the social arrangement and beliefs of a particular epoch." Instead, "It is addressed to the changes wrought by time and . . . must respond to transformation of views as well as to that of outward circumstances. The effect of the change in men's feelings of what is right and just is equally relevant in determining whether discrimination denies the equal protection of the laws."[26]

But Jackson shared with Holmes[27] a horror of absolutes and extremes. The constant danger Jackson feared was, as he put it, to "make up for colliding with Scylla by heading for Charybdis."[28] Despite Chief Justice Rehnquist's contrary assertion, Justice Jackson's actions during the *Brown* decision process indicate that he did not "think *Plessy v. Ferguson*[29] was right and should be re-affirmed."[30] What did concern Jackson was the question of how a proper opinion striking down segregation could be written. Jackson was also troubled by the enforcement issue: how would a decision invalidating segregation be enforced?

But Jackson never expressed the view attributed to him by Rehnquist—that the "separate but equal" doctrine should be reaffirmed, much less that it was "right." On the contrary, from the beginning of the *Brown* decision process, Jackson indicated that he would support a properly written decision striking down segregation. This can be seen, first of all, from Jackson's statements at the Court conferences on *Brown*.

The first *Brown* conference was held on December 13, 1952, a few days after the argument in the case had concluded. It was presided over by Chief Justice Vinson, who spoke in favor of affirming the lower-court decisions upholding the constitutionality of segregation. We know what went on at the conference from notes

---

[26]Felix Frankfurter Papers, Harvard Law School. This is an earlier draft than that quoted in Kluger, note 12 *supra*, at 685.

[27]See Schwartz, Some Makers of American Law 81 (1985).

[28]Box 57, Robert H. Jackson Papers, Library of Congress.

[29]Note 7 *supra*.

[30]Rehnquist memo, note 4 *supra*.

taken by Justices Burton and Jackson.[31] Jackson's own comments were, of course, not included in his notes, so that we know what he said at the conference only from the Burton notes which are unfortunately rather cryptic and, in part, illegible.[32]

So far as can be seen from Burton's notes, Jackson told the conference that he "finds nothing in hist[ory] that says it is unconst[itutional]—nor in courts." On the basis of history and precedent, then, the Justice said, he "would have to say it *is* constitutional." Jackson also asserted that Thurgood "Marshall's brief is sociology not legal issue." Jackson then conceded, "I don't know the effect of segregation," but he did say that one "can't ease this situation by putting children together."

These conference statements did not, however, mean that Jackson favored reaffirmance of *Plessy*. On the contrary, though the Justice did stress the need to give the states a reasonable time to adjust to the decision, he stated specifically that, as far as invalidating segregation was concerned, he "wouldn't object to a holding with a reasonable time element."[33]

Another point should be noted on the first *Brown* conference, so far as Jackson's role in the *Brown* decision process is concerned. Chief Justice Warren is rightly given credit for suggesting, at the outset of his first *Brown* conference, that the Justices discuss the case informally, without taking any votes. Thus, in the 1970 conference on the *Swann* school busing case,[34] Chief Justice Burger began by proposing that the precedent set by his predecessor at the *Brown* conference be followed and that the Justices have a round-table discussion without any vote.[35]

In actuality, the precedent of what Justice Frankfurter later called "a reconnoitering discussion, without thought of a vote"[36] had been set at the December 1952 *Brown* conference presided over by Chief Justice Vinson. More important for purposes of this paper, the precedent was set at the suggestion of Justice Jackson. Accord-

---

[31]Harold H. Burton and Robert H. Jackson Papers, Library of Congress. The conference quotes are from these notes.

[32]Compare Kluger, note 12 *supra*, at 589.

[33]Compare *id.* at 608–09.

[34]Swann v. Charlotte-Mecklenburg Board of Education, 402 U.S. 1 (1971).

[35]See Schwartz, Swann's Way: The School Busing Case and the Supreme Court 101 (1986).

[36]Frankfurter, Memorandum, September 29, 1959. Felix Frankfurter Papers, Library of Congress.

ing to the Burton notes, Jackson began his conference presentation by saying, "If we are going to take time, it is better not to take a vote." Justice Burton's diary indicates that this suggestion was adopted. It states that, at the *Brown* conference, "We discussed the segregation cases thus disclosing the trend but no even tentative vote was taken."[37] Thus, when Chief Justice Warren began his first *Brown* conference by urging a discussion without any vote, he was simply following the precedent set a year earlier at Justice Jackson's suggestion.

In addition, Justice Jackson made another suggestion which had important practical effects. He urged that the Attorney General of the United States be formally invited to take part in the oral reargument before the Court (no such invitation had been extended for the first argument in December 1952) and to file a new brief. In a letter to Chief Justice Vinson, Justice Frankfurter stressed the importance of the invitation. "The reason for having the Government appear," Frankfurter wrote, "was not a matter of tactics or 'public-relations.'" He noted "the point which Bob Jackson made very early in our deliberations, that the new [Eisenhower] Administration, unlike the old, may have the responsibility of carrying out a decision full of perplexities; it should therefore be asked to face that responsibility as part of our process of adjudication."[38]

The next indication of Justice Jackson's *Brown* posture came during the reargument in December 1953. He asked J. Lee Rankin, who argued for the Government, how a decision outlawing segregation would be enforced. Rankin answered that the district courts would do the enforcing, "according to criteria presented and set out by this Court."[39] Jackson was troubled by the question, "What criteria are we going to lay down?" The district courts, he said, should have the enforcing role: "but what are we going to tell them?"

And then, Jackson asked, what about the time that might be needed for enforcement? The Justice said, "there are some conditions that should postpone [enforcement]. Now, what is to be taken, financial conditions, unwillingness of the community to vote funds? What are the conditions that the lower court should consider?"

---

[37]Kluger, note 12 *supra*, at 608.

[38]Felix Frankfurter–Chief, June 8, 1953. Felix Frankfurter Papers, Library of Congress.

[39]49A Landmark Briefs and Arguments of the Supreme Court of the U.S. Constitutional Law (Kurland & Casper eds. 1975).

It was the enforcement problem above all that troubled Jackson. "I foresee a generation of litigation," he told Rankin, "if we send it back with no standards, and each case has to come here to determine it standard by standard."

Jackson's concern with the enforcement problem was to lead him to make what may have been his most important contribution to the *Brown* decision process—the suggestion at the January 16, 1954, conference that the case be set for reargument on the enforcement issue. Before then, however, Jackson took part in the December 13, 1953, conference after the *Brown* reargument, the first important conference presided over by Chief Justice Warren, who had taken his place on the Court two months earlier. We know what went on at that conference from the detailed notes taken by Justice Burton[40] as well as sketchy ones by Justice Frankfurter.[41]

Once again, the Jackson conference comments were inconsistent with the Rehnquist assertion that the Justice thought "that *Plessy* v. *Ferguson*[42] was right and should be re-affirmed."[43] Jackson started his conference presentation by noting, "Cardozo said the work of this Court is partly statutory construction and partly politics. This is a question of politics." What he meant by this is shown by the Jackson gloss on the Cardozo statement in a posthumous work: "Of course [Cardozo] used 'politics' in no sense of partisanship but in the sense of policy-making."[44]

In this sense, Jackson told the conference, a decision against segregation would be "a political decision." The segregation issue was "a question of politics." The Justice also said that the decision "for me personally is not a problem, but it is difficult to make it other than a political decision. . . . Our problem is to make a judicial decision out of a political conclusion"—and to find "a judicial basis for a congenial political conclusion." The clear implication was that he would support a properly written decision striking down segregation. "As a political decision [I] can go along with it."

Interestingly, in view of his reargument suggestion at the next *Brown* conference, Jackson opposed the proposal by Justice Douglas

---

[40]Harold H. Burton Papers, Library of Congress.

[41]Felix Frankfurter papers, Harvard Law School. These notes are erroneously dated "Dec. 16/53." The conference quotes are from the Burton and Frankfurter notes.

[42]Note 7 *supra*.

[43]Rehnquist memo, note 4 *supra*.

[44]Jackson, The Supreme Court in the American System of Government 54 (1955).

at the December 12 conference that the Court decide only the basic principle now and leave the problem of enforcement for later. Jackson told his colleagues, "[I] don't think it wise to just throw in the hopper the abolition of segregation and leave the rest to another fight."

Despite this statement, it was Jackson who, at the next *Brown* conference, on January 16, 1954, resolved the enforcement dilemma by urging postponement of the issue. The January 16 conference is known to us only through brief notes taken by Justice Frankfurter.[45] According to them, Jackson suggested to the conference that the Court needed more time to consider the remedial issue. As Frankfurter's notes quoted him, "let's have a reargument on terms of a decree!!"

Jackson's suggestion for reargument on the terms of the decree was supported by Justices Clark and Black at the conference, and ultimately adopted by the Court. As it turned out, postponing of the enforcement issue, together with a conference consensus on the need for flexibility in enforcement, were crucial to the *Brown* decision process.

IV. Jackson Draft: Introduction

Writing Judge Learned Hand about *Brown* in 1958, Justice Frankfurter stated, "The fact of the matter is that Bob Jackson tried his hand at a justification for leaving the matter to §5 of Art. XIV, 'The Congress shall have powers to enforce, etc.' and he finally gave up."[46] Justice Jackson did not, in fact, give up in his attempt to draft an opinion. The draft referred to near the beginning of this paper indicates that the Justice had done most of the work involved in the writing of a *Brown* concurring opinion. This draft does not conclude that the matter should be left to Congress under the Enforcement Clause of the Fourteenth Amendment. Instead, it deals directly with the constitutional issue and concludes that segregation is invalid. Indeed, from all we know of Jackson's *Brown* views, it is difficult to see the basis for the Frankfurter statement

---

[45]Felix Frankfurter Papers, Harvard Law School. The conference quotes are from these notes, which have not been used by other writers on the *Brown* case.

[46]Felix Frankfurter–Learned Hand, February 13, 1968. Felix Frankfurter Papers, Library of Congress.

that he was for "leaving the matter to" Congress, much less was writing an opinion to that effect.

The collection of the Justice's papers at the Library of Congress contains several drafts of the Jackson proposed concurrence. The latest of these is dated "3/15/54." It is headed MEMORANDUM BY MR. JUSTICE JACKSON and consists of twenty-three legal-size typed pages. Since this draft has never been published,[47] it is worthwhile to analyze it in some detail, if only because it contains the only detailed statement of views on the case by an Associate Justice on the *Brown* Court.

But the Jackson draft is more than the usual judicial statement. It was composed by the greatest master of legal prose since Holmes and Cardozo; so felicitous is the style at times that it makes the reader overlook weaknesses in the substance.

The Jackson draft is divided into four parts.[48] Part I is an untitled introduction, containing four pages. It begins with a typical Jackson literary touch, this time a paraphrase of a line by Matthew Arnold: "Since the close of the Civil War, the United States has been 'hesitating between two worlds—one dead, the other power-less to be born.' Constitutions are easier amended than social customs, and even the North never fully conformed its racial practices to its professions."

As one who had gone to school "where Negro pupils were very few" and there was no segregation, Jackson wrote, he "is predis-posed to the conclusion that segregation elsewhere has outlived whatever justification it may have had. The practice seems marked for early extinction. Whatever we might say today, within a generation it will be outlawed by decision of this Court because of the forces of mortality and replacement which operate upon it."

The draft then pointed out that "Decision of these cases would be simple if our personal opinion that school segregation is morally, economically or politically indefensible made it legally so." But segregation "is deeply imbedded in social custom in a large part of this country. Its eradication involves nothing less than a substantial reconstruction of legal institution [*sic*] and of society. It persists because of fears, prides and prejudices which this Court cannot eradicate."

---

[47]Kluger, note 12 *supra*, at 688–90, quotes from an earlier version, which leaves out important parts, particularly the holding on the invalidity of segregated schools.

[48]The draft quotes are from note 14 *supra*.

Jackson next demonstrated a conciliatory attitude toward the South: "However sympathetic we may be with the resentments of those who are coerced into segregation, we cannot, in considering a recasting of society by judicial fiat, ignore the claims of those who are to be coerced out of it. We cannot deny the sincerity and passion with which many feel that their blood, lineage and culture are worthy of protection by enforced separatism of races and feel that they have built their segregated institutions for many years on an almost universal understanding that segregation is not constitutionally forbidden."

The draft noted the prevalence of separatism among all races and cultures. "But, in the South," it said, "the Negro appears to suffer from other antagonisms that are an aftermath of the great American white conflict. The white South harbors in historical memory, with deep resentment, the program of reconstruction and the deep humiliation of carpetbag government imposed by conquest." Thus, Jackson went on, "I am convinced the race problem in the South involves more than mere racial prejudice. It is complicated emotionally with a white war and white politics."

Jackson wrote that he could not judge "Whether a use of the power of this Court to decree an end of segregation will diminish or increase racial tensions in the South." But, the draft asserted, "I am satisfied that it would retard acceptance of this decision if the Northern majority of this Court should make a Pharisaic and self-righteous approach to this issue or were inconsiderate of the conditions which have brought about and continued this custom or should permit a needlessly ruthless decree to be promulgated."

The Jackson draft's introduction ended with emphasis upon the crucial importance of the case: "The plain fact is that the questions of constitutional interpretation and of the limitations on responsible use of judicial power in a federal system implicit in these cases are as far-reaching as any that have been before the Court since its establishment."

V. JACKSON DRAFT: EXISTING LAW AND SEGREGATION

The second part of the Jackson draft, six pages in length, is headed, "II. DOES EXISTING LAW CONDEMN SEGREGATION?"

The draft's negative answer began by pointing out, "Layman as well as lawyer must query how it is that the Constitution this morning forbids what for three-quarters of a century it has tolerated or approved." Jackson also noted that this "reversal" of the Constitution's meaning is "by the branch of the Government supposed not to make new law but only to declare existing law." The draft then asked, "Can we honestly say that the states which have maintained segregated schools have not, until today, been justified in understanding their practice to be constitutional?"

The draft stated that, from the beginning, the "majestic and sweeping generalities of the Due Process and Equal Protection Clause of the Fourteenth Amendment were capable of being read to require a full and equal racial partnership in all matters within the reach of the law." Yet the texts did not have "such meaning to the age that wrote them." The constitutional clauses themselves did not specifically mention segregation of education. "Thus, there is no explicit prohibition of segregated schools and it can only be supplied by interpretation."

Jackson then turned to the doctrine of original intent: "It is customary to turn to the original will and purpose of those responsible for adoption of a constitutional document as a basis for its subsequent interpretation." But the problem was that too often associated with the original-intent approach—that of ascertaining the intent of the draftsman. In *Brown* the order setting the case for reargument[49] had asked counsel to discuss five questions, two of which focused on the original intent of the Framers of the Fourteenth Amendment. The Warren *Brown* opinion summarized the result of the researches on the matter by stating, "At best, they are inconclusive."[50] The Jackson draft put it a little differently: "Their exhaustive research to uncover the original will and purpose expressed in the Fourteenth Amendment yields for me only one sure conclusion: it was a passionate, confused and deplorable era."

At the same time, it was clear to Jackson that there was not "any influential body of the movement that carried the Civil War Amendments [that] had reached the point of thinking about either segregation or education of the Negro as a current problem, and harder still to find that the Amendments were designed to be a solution." The same, according to the draft, was true, "If we turn from words to deeds as evidence of purpose." There was "nothing to show that the Congress which submitted these Amendments

---

[49]345 U.S. 972 (1953).

[50]347 U.S. at 489.

understood or intended to prohibit the practice here in question."
Similarly, if we "look to the behavior of the states, we find that
equally impossible to reconcile with any understanding that the
Amendment would prohibit segregation in schools." Segregated
schools were widespread in the states when the Fourteenth Amendment was ratified.

The judicial decisions, the Jackson draft noted, also "shared the
understanding that these Clauses of their own force do not prohibit
the states from deciding that each race must obtain its education
apart rather than by commingling." Indeed, the case law during the
past century "is almost unanimous in the view that the Amendment
tolerated segregation by state action."

The draft also stressed the principle that "The custom of a people
has always been recognized as a powerful lawmaker. . . . This
Court, in common with courts everywhere, has recognized the
force of long custom and has been reluctant to use judicial power to
try to recast social usages established among the people." Despite
this, Jackson asserted, "Today's decision is to uproot a custom
deeply embedded not only in state statutes but in the habit and
usage of people in their local communities."

Jackson's conclusion, which ended Part II of his draft, was that
he could not say that segregation had been unconstitutional before
the *Brown* decision itself: "Convenient as it would be to reach an
opposite conclusion, I simply cannot find in the conventional
material of constitutional interpretation any justification for saying
that in maintaining segregated schools any state or the District of
Columbia can be judicially decreed, up to the date of this decision,
to have violated the Fourteenth Amendment."

VI. JACKSON DRAFT: ENFORCEMENT POWER LIMITS

Part III of the Jackson draft, seven pages in length, deals
with enforcement of the Equal Protection Clause.[51] It began by
noting the Fourteenth Amendment's Enforcement Clause, which
gives Congress the power to enforce the amendment. There was no
doubt, Jackson wrote, "that it gives Congress a wide discretion to

---

[51]Part III is headed, "III. DOES THE AMENDMENT CONTEMPLATE CHANGED
CONDITIONS?" and Part IV, "IV. THE LIMITS AND BASIS OF JUDICIAL
ACTION." From the text, however, the headings seem erroneous and Part III should be
headed as Part IV is in the manuscript, and vice versa.

enact legislation on that subject [segregation and education] binding on all states and school districts." In light of the Congressional power, the draft went on, "The question is how far this Court should leave this subject to be dealt with by legislation, and any answer will have far-reaching implications."

Here Jackson dealt with the question of "leaving the matter" to Congress to which Justice Frankfurter had referred in his already-quoted note to Judge Learned Hand.[52] But the Jackson draft did not, as Frankfurter implied, justify leaving the matter to Congress. It is true that the draft did express doubts about the effectiveness of judicial enforcement power. But its ultimate conclusion was the same as that in the Warren *Brown* opinion—that school segregation was unconstitutional—and the draft specifically agreed with the Court decision to that effect.

As indicated, the Jackson draft indicated skepticism about the effectiveness of judicial enforcement in this area. As Jackson saw it, "in embarking upon a widespread reform of social customs and habits of countless communities we must face the limitations on the nature and effectiveness of the judicial process." In fact, the draft asserted, "The futility of effective reform of our society by judicial decree is demonstrated by the history of this very matter. For many years this Court has pronounced the doctrine that, while separate facilities for each race are permissible, they must be equal. Our pronouncement to that effect has remained a dead letter in a large part of the country."

The draft then asked, "Why has the separate-but-equal doctrine declared by this Court so long been a mere promise to the colored ear to be broken to the hope?" The draft's answer was, "It has remained an empty pronouncement because the courts have no power to enforce general declarations of law by applying sanction against any persons not before them in a particular litigation."

The same might well be true of the *Brown* ruling that segregation was invalid. "I see no reason," wrote Jackson in his draft, "to expect a pronouncement that segregation is unconstitutional will be any more self-executing or any more efficiently executed than our pronouncement that unequal facilities are unconstitutional. A law suit must be maintained in every school district which shows persistent recalcitrance to lay the basis for a contempt charge. That

---

[52] Note 46 *supra*.

is an effective sanction in a private controversy, but it is a weak reed to rely on in initiating a change in the social system of a large part of the United States. With no machinery except that of the courts to put the power of the Government behind it, it seems likely to result in a failure that will bring the court into contempt and the judicial process into discredit."

Only Congress, the draft urged, possessed the necessary resources, financial and otherwise, to bring about the widespread reform needed in this field. On the other hand, "A Court decision striking down state statutes or constitutional provisions which authorize or require segregation will not produce a social transition." That was particularly true where segregation had become the dominant feature of the society. Thus, Jackson wrote, "Our decision may end segregation in Delaware and Kansas, because there it lingers by a tenuous lease of life. But where the practice really is entrenched, it exists independently of any statute or decision as a local usage and deep-seated custom sustained by the prevailing sentiment of the community. School districts, from habit and conviction, will carry it along without aid of state statutes. To eradicate segregation by judicial action means two generations of litigation." Because of this, Jackson's draft asserted, "It is apparent that our decision does not end but begins the struggle over segregation."

The draft then went into some of the "problems of adjustment" that would be involved in enforcement of a decision condemning segregation. Jackson's conclusion on them was, "It is impossible now to anticipate all of the difficulties or to determine the time necessary in any particular area to overcome them. While our decision may invalidate existing laws and regulations governing the school, the Court cannot substitute constructive laws and regulations for their governance. Local or state or federal action will have to build the integrated school systems if they are to exist. A gigantic administrative job has to be undertaken."

The draft referred to the Government's suggestion "that the courts assume this task and that we remand these cases to the District Courts under instructions to proceed with enforcement as rapidly as conditions make it appear practicable." This suggestion greatly disturbed Jackson. "I will not be a party," his draft declared, "to thus casting upon the lower courts a burden of continued litigation under circumstances which subject district judges to local pressures and provide them with no standards."

Part III of Jackson's draft concluded by stressing the Justice's concern over the enforcement issue. "Nothing has raised more doubt in my mind," Jackson wrote, "as to the wisdom of our decision than the character of the decree which the Government conceives to be necessary to its success. We are urged, however, to supply means to supervise transition of the country from segregated to nonsegregated schools upon the basis that Congress may or probably will refuse to act. That assumes nothing less than that we must act because our representative system has failed. The premise is not a sound basis for judicial action."

VII. JACKSON DRAFT: CHANGED CONDITIONS

There is an undated note, written on a Supreme Court memo pad in Justice Frankfurter's handwriting, that reads, "It is not fair to say that the South has always denied the Negroes 'this constitutional right.' It was NOT a constitutional right till May 17/54."[53] Part II of his draft, which has already been summarized, indicates that Justice Jackson shared this view. In Part IV, however, Jackson specifically stated his concurrence in the *Brown* decision, which made the right to attend nonsegregated schools a constitutional right.

Part IV of Jackson's draft,[54] six pages in length, started by going back to the point made in Part II—that, before the *Brown* decision, segregation had been ruled constitutional. Hence, the draft conceded, "Until today Congress has been justified in believing that segregation does not offend the Constitution." Nor, in Jackson's opinion, was it "necessary or true to say that these earlier judges, many of whom were as sensitive to human values as any of us, were wrong in their own times."

The pre-*Brown* cases, in Jackson's view, were based upon two assumptions. The draft did not dispute the first of these: "With their fundamental premise that the requirement of equal protection does not disable the state from making reasonable classifications of its inhabitants nor impose the obligation to accord identical treatment to all, there can be no quarrel."

But the second pre-*Brown* assumption, according to the draft, "was not a legal so much as a factual assumption. It was that there

---

[53]Harold H. Burton Papers, Library of Congress.

[54]See note 51 *supra*.

were differences between the Negro and the white races, viewed as a whole, such as to warrant separate classification and discrimination not only for their educational facilities but also for marriage, for access to public places of recreation, amusement or service and as passengers on common carriers and as [sic] the right to buy and own real estate."

"Whether these early judges were right or wrong in their times I do not know," Jackson wrote in his draft. "Certainly in the 1860's and probably throughout the Nineteenth Century the Negro population as a whole was a different people than today." At that time, the draft said, blacks had "little opportunity as yet to show their capacity for education or even self-support and management. There was strong belief in heredity, and the Negro's heritage was then close to primitive. Likewise, his environment from force of circumstances was not conducive to his mental development."

But conditions had completely changed during the present century. "Indeed," the draft asserted, "Negro progress under segregation has been spectacular and, tested by the pace of history, his rise is one of the swiftest and most dramatic advances in the annals of man. It is that, indeed, which has enabled him to outgrow the system and to overcome the presumptions on which it was based."

Thus, in Jackson's view, "The handicap of inheritance and environment has been too widely overcome today to warrant these earlier presumptions based on race alone." Black advances, the draft went on, "require me to say that mere possession of colored blood, in whole or in part, no longer affords a reasonable basis for a classification for education purposes and that each individual must be rated on his own merit." Blacks, like others, must now "be classified as individuals and not as a race for their learning, aptitude and discipline."

Jackson also emphasized the changed place of education in the society. "Nor," he wrote, "can we ignore the fact that the concept of the place of public education has markedly changed. Once a privilege conferred on those fortunate enough to take advantage of it, it is now regarded as a right of a citizen and a duty enforced by compulsory education laws. Any thought of public education as a privilege which may be given or withheld as a matter of grace has long since passed out of American thinking."

The Jackson draft next stressed that changed conditions required a ruling that segregation was invalid. Here, too, changing conditions had its impact on constitutional jurisprudence. "It is neither novel nor radical doctrine," Jackson affirmed, "that statutes once held constitutional may become invalid by reason of changing conditions, and those held to be good in one state of facts may be held to be bad in another. A multitude of cases, going back far into judicial history, attest to this doctrine." In fact, the draft pointed out, "In recent times, the practical result of several of our decisions has been to nullify the racial classification for many of the purposes as to which it was originally held valid."

Now came Jackson's categorical conclusion, already quoted, that segregation was unconstitutional: "I am convinced that present-day conditions require us to strike from our books the doctrine of separate-but-equal facilities and to hold invalid provisions of state constitutions or statutes which classify persons for separate treatment in matter of education based solely on possession of colored blood."

At this point, near the end of his draft, Jackson came back to the enforcement problem. In holding segregation invalid, the draft said, "I have no doubt of the power of a court of equity to condition its remedies to do justice to both parties and I believe that the circumstances under which a large part of the country has grown into the existing system are such that only consideration of that in framing the decree would be just. And, in the long run, I think only a reasonably considerate decree would be an expedient one for the persons it has sought to benefit hereby."

The draft did not deal further with the enforcement issue. Instead, it ended with a reaffirmation of the holding striking down segregation, leaving the question of remedy to be decided the following term: "I favor, at the moment, going no farther than to enter a decree that the state constitutions and statutes relied upon as requiring or authorizing segregation merely on account of race or color, are unconstitutional. I would order a reargument on the contents of our decree and request the Government and each of the parties to submit detailed proposed decrees applicable to each case."

VIII. The Draft Unissued

We do not know whether Justice Jackson was prepared to issue his draft as a *Brown* concurring opinion or whether, as Justice Frankfurter said in his already-quoted comment,[55] "he finally gave

---

[55] Note 46 *supra*.

up" on issuing a concurrence. According to a memo by Justice Jackson's secretary,[56] the draft "was not circulated to members of the Court or used in any way except in conference with C.J. Warren at Doctors Hospital, where Justice Jackson was a patient from March 30 to May 17, 1954." A note in Jackson's *Brown* file indicates that the draft was also read to Justice Frankfurter. There is a handwritten note in the same file which contains a typical Frankfurter reaction: "Bob: When I sometimes tell literary friends of mine that I like a particular piece of theirs, I have been made to feel shabby by their question 'What's the matter with my other writings?' Nevertheless I want to say that this is a particularly good opinion of yours!! F.F."[57]

That Jackson discussed his *Brown* draft with Chief Justice Warren when Warren visited him in the hospital suggests that the Justice took his draft seriously as a potential concurring opinion. There is no doubt that Warren urged Jackson not to issue any concurrence. The last thing the Chief Justice wanted was a separate opinion that would detract from the force of the unanimous opinion that was to be, in Justice Burton's phrase, "a major accomplishment for his leadership."[58] Whether the Warren persuasion would have worked in other circumstances is, of course, unknown. But Jackson had been hospitalized by a serious heart attack and his weakened condition prevented the Justice from doing the work required to convert his draft into a finished opinion.

Chief Justice Warren personally delivered his own *Brown* draft opinions to Jackson's hospital room. At this stage the Justice made his last contribution to the *Brown* decision process. Jackson proposed two additions to Warren's *Brown* draft when it was delivered to him in the hospital. The Chief Justice declined to accept one because he felt it could be interpreted as applicable to segregation in general, and Warren wanted the opinion to be narrowly limited to school segregation. The Chief Justice was, however, willing to add a sentence stressing that "Negroes have achieved outstanding success in the arts and sciences as well as in the business and professional world"[59]—a point tied in to the black progress which Jackson had emphasized in Part IV of his draft.

[56]E.D., SEGREGATION CASES, n.d. Robert H. Jackson Papers, Library of Congress.

[57]F.F.–Bob, n.d. Robert H. Jackson Papers, Library of Congress.

[58]Burton Diary, May 12, 1954. Harold H. Burton Papers, Library of Congress.

[59]Kluger, note 12 *supra*, at 697.

There was still one further service for Justice Jackson to perform in *Brown*. That was on decision day, May 17, 1954. According to his secretary's already-quoted memo, "He came directly to the Court from the hospital that day so that there might be a full bench when these cases were handed down."[60] Early that morning Chief Justice Warren had gone to the hospital to show Jackson a copy of the final opinion. Then, says Warren, the ailing Justice "to my alarm insisted on attending the Court that day in order to demonstrate our solidarity."[61] When the Brown opinion was delivered, all nine Justices were on the bench to underline the unanimity of the Court's decision.

IX. THE "MIGHT HAVE BEEN"[62]

One interested in the "might have been" in Supreme Court jurisprudence can find ample store for reflection in Justice Jackson's draft *Brown* opinion. Had the draft actually been issued as a *Brown* concurrence, it would have been most unfortunate. It would have blunted the effect of Chief Justice Warren's unanimous Court opinion and given support to those who opposed the *Brown* decision itself.

Justice Jackson's law clerk, E. Barrett Prettyman, Jr., told the Justice that he found the draft too negative. "I think," Prettyman asserted in a memo, "that your opinion should *begin*, not with doubts and fears—not with a negative attitude, but with a clear and affirmative statement of your legal position. You have stated this position in only two out of 23 pages, and these two pages are almost at the end of the opinion. They are almost an afterthought."[63]

Prettyman expressed the fear that the doubts expressed by the draft would carry more weight than the statements on the invalidity of segregation. "It is one thing," he wrote, "to have and express many doubts about a difficult decision, as any honest man would in this case; it is another to state them at such length and in such

---

[60]Note 56 *supra*.

[61]Warren, The Memoirs of Earl Warren 286 (1977).

[62]"For of all sad words of tongue or pen, / The saddest are these: 'It might have been'!" Whittier, Maud Muller.

[63]Re Nos. 1–4, n.d. Robert H. Jackson Papers, Library of Congress. See Kluger, note 12 *supra*, at 690–91.

precedence over your affirmative views that the result you reach is swallowed up in them."[64]

One who has read the Jackson draft must agree with Prettyman's conclusion that too much of the draft was negative in tone. At the same time, it must be conceded that at least some of the doubt expressed by Justice Jackson was borne out by the post-*Brown* experience. Certainly, as the draft indicated, the decision that segregation was unconstitutional proved anything but self-executing. The two generations of litigation that the draft foresaw proved, if anything, a conservative prediction. *Brown* was met by what Justice Black had warned during the January 16, 1954, conference would be a "storm over this Court."[65] In the South, Black had asserted, "any man who would come in [in support] would be dead politically forever."

The bitterness of the South's reaction to the *Brown* decision is, of course, now a matter of history. The obloquy directed at the Warren Court had its origins in the desegregation decision. The South resorted to every device, including pressure and intimidation, to block integration. As *The Oxford History of the American People* summarized it a decade after *Brown*, "In the lower South, the Supreme Court's decision was to all intents and purposes nullified and has remained so for ten years; John C. Calhoun would have been delighted!"[66]

The Jackson draft foresaw at least some of the difficulties that would be faced by judicial desegregation efforts. As the draft puts it, "school districts may have to be consolidated or divided, or their boundaries revised, and the teachers and pupils may have to be transferred." This is exactly what had to be done in the post-*Brown* desegregation cases, usually over bitter community opposition.[67] This, too, the draft predicted, saying the courts would have to "require white pupils to shift to the Negro schools, a measure not likely to be accepted without strong local opposition."

But, even if we recognize the Jackson prescience, we must also realize the unfortunate consequences of the issuance of his draft as a *Brown* concurrence. Such an opinion would have given comfort and support to the opponents of *Brown*. The last thing that was needed to detract from the categorical condemnation of segregation

---

[64] This statement is not quoted *ibid.*

[65] Note 41 *supra.*

[66] Morrison, The Oxford History of the American People 1086 (1965).

[67] See, *e.g.*, Schwartz, note 35 *supra, passim.*

in the forthright Warren Court opinion was a separate statement in Jackson's felicitous style stressing the "sincerity and passion" of those who supported segregation, that the law till then did not forbid segregation, and urging the limitations upon the effectiveness of judicial power to remedy the situation.

It is true that, at the end of his draft, Jackson declared unequivocally that laws requiring or authorizing segregation were unconstitutional. But Prettyman was right in asserting that the affirmative statements to that effect were all but "swallowed up" by the doubts expressed in the bulk of the draft.

When Chief Justice Vinson died unexpectedly just before the *Brown* reargument, Justice Frankfurter caustically commented, "This is the first indication that I have ever had that there is a God."[68] One may see the same fortuitous intervention in Justice Jackson's hospitalization soon after he completed the draft of his proposed *Brown* concurrence discussed in this article. If not for his illness, Jackson might well have continued work on the draft and issued it as a separate opinion—with all that that would have meant to *Brown* enforcement.

Hedged in with doubts or not, however, the Jackson draft does show clearly that the Justice held the view that school segregation was unconstitutional. He may, as Justice Frankfurter did,[69] have recognized that, before *Brown* the law had been the other way. He also had no illusions about the difficulties involved in enforcing a desegregation decision. Still, his draft expressed no doubt on the correctness of the *Brown* decision itself. By the time of the case, he was plainly ready to announce the principle that segregation was unconstitutional. And he did so in the draft discussed in this paper.

It is hard to believe that the man who wrote the sentences holding segregation invalid in his draft held the view only a few months earlier attributed to him by Chief Justice Rehnquist— that "*Plessy* v. *Ferguson* was right and should be re-affirmed." So inconsistent, indeed, is this view with the Jackson draft that one may ask a final "might have been": what might have happened had Jackson's unequivocal draft statements on the invalidity of segregation been available when the Senate voted on the Rehnquist nomination to the Supreme Court or his later nomination as Chief Justice?

---

[68]The statement was made to Philip Elman and another former law clerk. The latter confirmed to me that the Justice said this.

[69]Note 53 *supra*.